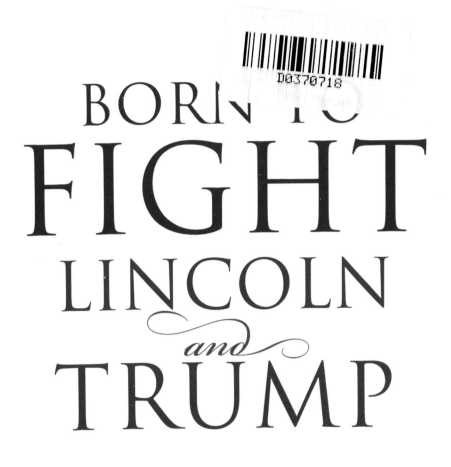

BORN TO
FIGHT
LINCOLN
and
TRUMP

COSTCO
Bestseller
#1534540
$12.49

BORN TO FIGHT

LINCOLN *and* TRUMP

GRETCHEN WOLLERT

PLAIN SIGHT PUBLISHING
An imprint of Cedar Fort, Inc.
Springville, Utah

© 2021 Gretchen Wollert
All rights reserved.

No part of this book may be reproduced in any form whatsoever, whether by graphic, visual, electronic, film, microfilm, tape recording, or any other means, without prior written permission of the publisher, except in the case of brief passages embodied in critical reviews and articles.

The opinions and views expressed herein belong solely to the author and do not necessarily represent the opinions or views of Cedar Fort, Inc. Permission for the use of sources, graphics, and photos is also solely the responsibility of the author.

ISBN 13: 978-1-4621-3941-5

Published by Plain Sight Publishing, an imprint of Cedar Fort, Inc.
2373 W. 700 S., Springville, UT 84663
Distributed by Cedar Fort, Inc., www.cedarfort.com

Library of Congress Control Number: 2020952210

Cover design by Shawnda T. Craig
Cover design © 2021 Cedar Fort, Inc.
Edited and typeset by Heidi Doxey Ford

Printed in the United States of America

10 9 8 7 6 5 4 3 2 1

Printed on acid-free paper

DEDICATION

To Mike, whose strength, forbearance, and faith are all I need.
To my four daughters, a constant joy and encouragement.
And to my Dad, who always knew I would do something bright.

Contents

INTRODUCTION

———————— ⁓⟨⟩⁓ ————————

After graduating high school, I went off to college, taking with me the tenets of my upbringing: work ethic, responsibility, patriotism, charity . . . and freedom. I loved learning, especially about America's founding fathers (and mothers) and the great eras of yesteryear. This fed my independent spirit and proud nature. "We hold these truths," "lives and fortunes," "conceived in liberty," "Ask not what your country can do for you . . . " and "land of the free and home of the brave." I became and remain a very passionate and patriotic student of American history.

Anxious to realize my American dream, I drifted away from the home of my youth and followed Greeley's adventurous mandate of the past and went West. Doggedly persevering through all the ups and downs of this land of opportunity, my opportunity came with a husband and a small farm and ranch that aided the raising of four daughters on lots of chores, wide-open spaces, the Golden Rule, trust in God, and commitments to study hard and treasure freedom. I supplemented an agricultural income with teaching, coaching, and myriad other money-making ventures. My girls learned firsthand the courage and tireless effort required for their own American dream.

While all this was going on, America was taking on a character different than the one I embraced when embarking on my journey westward. She slowly but surely acquired a split-personality—promising freedom one day and taking it back the next. We experienced a school system that disregarded American history in subtle but concerning regularity. "Government of the people, by the people, and for the people," must have been working for some other people. The most helpless and dependent in our nation didn't have a voice. We watched the EPA, the IRS, and the FBI attack ordinary folks. We long ago bid farewell to freedom of religion in public places. Freedom of association was a courtroom away from extinction. Other rights, big and small, were becoming inconvenient to the powers that be. Our cherished nation was looking haggard and conciliatory, and it was sinking fast into mediocrity.

To me Abraham Lincoln was America's greatest president. And I thought I knew a lot about him; after all, I taught schoolchildren for years what a wonderful example of leadership he showed in a very divisive time in our historical past. He was the savior of a nation in turmoil, the epitome of honesty and humility, and an icon of American greatness! Lincoln was the powerful and serious statesman embodied in his memorial statue in Washington, DC, and the masterfully wise and eloquent communicator in the Gettysburg Address. Indeed, he was these things, but he was so much more. I realized that I didn't know Abraham Lincoln after all—not really.

My journey of discovery began in 2016 when a field of talented political stars and presidential wannabes fell like dominoes in the wake of Donald Trump. He was a fighter and seemed to champion the people. He beat the odds (and the polls) and became a brand-new president who wasn't supposed to win. More than half the country voted against him, of which half of them truly hated him! Many in his own party considered him an ill-equipped outlier. These attitudes sprang from a country divided ideologically amidst differences many deemed irreconcilable. Needless to say, a large part of America didn't seem to accept the election and thus began a war of sorts—subversive, constant, and not at all civil. If only they could have seceded. But the nineteenth century was so different than the twenty-first. Or was it?

In fact, 2016 was much like 1860, and the new guy in 2016 is so startlingly similar to the new guy then. The new president was very tall (six-foot-four, give or take an inch,) whose youngest son was ten years old, accompanied by a first lady ostracized by Washington elites and a hostile, biased press. This scenario seemed familiar. Initially, I dismissed the absurdity: Donald Trump like Abraham Lincoln? After four years, forty-six books, endless hours of social media videos and articles, archived interviews, immeasurable news stories and tweets, I concluded and went on to prove the most improbable thing in the world: Trump and Lincoln are more alike than different. And not just in superficial, insignificant ways, such as height or political party, but deep down in character traits such as ambition, faith, ego, humor, tenacity, and the propensity for fighting. The list grew longer and longer as I uncovered more unlikely but true similarities hidden by a historical record sometimes reluctant to fully humanize a martyred president.

Revealing Abraham Lincoln's lesser (and lesser-known) qualities was at times uncomfortable. But he remains my favorite president, for whom I have greater respect now than ever—he became real. And Donald Trump—he became my second-favorite president as I discovered a wealth of lesser-known qualities hidden beneath his well-cultivated façade.

As I reveal to you the man behind the myth, or, rather, the men behind the myths, the experience may be at times uneasy, awkward, and even startling. But the truth promises to betray misconceptions through enlightening if not refreshing discoveries behind these deceptively kindred and very real presidents.

CHAPTER 1

IT'S IN THE GENES

I grew up in Louisville, Kentucky, and from a young age I knew something of Abraham Lincoln's humble beginnings. He was born in a log cabin in what today is Larue County, about an hour south of where I grew up. From Louisville, you take Interstate 65 south and go several miles past Elizabethtown before getting off the interstate. Then you take Highway 61 for a bit before it converges with 31E south. Boom, you're there—Honest Abe's birthplace.

Lincoln's rags to riches story was meant to be inspirational and motivational for us budding American dreamers. Other than that story, all I ever really knew about his ancestry before starting work on this book was that Lincoln was born in a cabin, his dad was a farmer, and Abe, most historians tell us, embodied such character virtues as goodness, kindness, honesty, industry, and obedience. Those, our teachers told us, were commendable aspirations for us all.

Before Donald Trump announced his candidacy for U.S. president, I knew even less about Trump's childhood, his upbringing, and his family. As he emerged onto the Republican primary stage, starting in 2015 after announcing his candidacy, my only impressions of his youth were assumptions—four of them: that he was rich, he was born rich, he grew up rich, and, according to most accounts, he was very rich. By his own account, he was very, very rich.

With such a clear contrast in beginnings, in areas such as geography and wealth (or lack of it), I saw no apparent resemblance between the Lincoln and Trump. Then again, at that point, I had not been looking. I had no reason to. But once I started foraging through all the murky misconceptions and preconceived notions about both men, I discovered a reservoir of startling similarities.

George Washington had his cherry tree, Abe Lincoln his log cabin. If you were a child raised in America and schooled on the rudiments of U.S. history, those two iconic symbols were likely engraved on your mind and have remained there to this day. They rank right up there with the Declaration of Independence, the Liberty Bell, and John Hancock's autograph.

Abraham Lincoln was born February 12, 1809, in a one-room log cabin on the outskirts of Hodgenville, Kentucky, at a spot on the map then known as Sinking Spring Farm. That's where the Abraham Lincoln Birthplace National Historical Park now stands, replete with replica cabins. There's also a large stone edifice that seems a bit out of place nestled in the woods of central Kentucky.

If you visit this historical site, you can't help but notice the neoclassical granite and marble structure, which is fronted by fifty-six steps—one for each year that Lincoln lived—and partially tucked into a frontage of woods, although easily spotted by the grownups and kids stuffed into the vehicles pulling into the nearby parking lot.

The gaudy stone building resembles more a Greek-styled temple than the pathetic (if yet charming in romanticized retrospect) Lincoln birth home described in history books. Once inside, you find a replica of the renowned one-room log cabin, measuring 13 by 17 feet—the original is believed to have been 16 by 18. There's just the one front door with a single window cut out next to it. Inside there is a dirt floor and stone fireplace, the latter a necessity to make life tolerable for occupants on chilly nights or, worse, the occasional bouts of arctic-like cold that threatened a nineteenth-century pioneer family with misery and illness.

Lincoln's parents and sister had moved to Sinking Spring Farm a few months before Abraham was born; his dad having paid two hundred dollars for 348 acres of stony ground situated on the south fork of Nolin Creek. 'Sinking Spring Farm' referred to a spring on their property that bubbled out of a deep cave still visible today, although Abe admittedly could never picture it later in life when asked to recount his childhood. He was only there 'til he was two, and then the family moved just down the road to Knob Creek Farm.

Infant Abraham was the second-born of Thomas Lincoln and Nancy Hanks Lincoln, born into a family that by almost any objective standard, even for early nineteenth-century America, was poor, even if young Abe couldn't yet see it that way. How do you know that you are actually poor if for one thing your mode of living is no different than it is for those who live around you, and for another your upbringing is grounded in work ethic and a familial embrace of virtuous qualities, where success and contentment aren't measured by salary, commissions, and stock options. If nothing else, you don't have time or opportunity to think about what you don't have. What you have is what you've got, and that is enough. As long as Thomas brought in sufficient living to keep clothes on everyone's backs and Nancy could throw together enough food for meals, life was what it was for the Lincolns.

"Poor" is in the eye and ear of the beholder. In "Some New Facts about Abraham Lincoln's Parents," published in the October 16, 1921 edition of *The National Republican*, Kentucky's then–assistant attorney general, Thomas B. McGregor, opines that Abe's parents deserve a "fairer estimate" than what had been assumed by many Lincoln biographers, writing, "In fact, they were well-to-do pioneers of their day; of sturdy, ancestral stock, owned a farm, domestic animals, tools—and a family Bible; (and were) neighborly, sacrificing, and active church-going members."[1] Thomas Lincoln was, in a way, an entrepreneur. Isn't that, after all, what a farmer is? The desire to work for oneself to produce one's own living was a most basic ambition. Lincoln himself, years later, put his own positive spin on growing up on a farm, generously proclaiming, "no other human occupation opens so wide a field for the agreeable combination of labor with cultivated thought . . . an exhaustless source of profitable enjoyment."[2]

Donald Trump wasn't born in a log cabin, but a closer look at his ancestry, when placed next to Lincoln's, offers interesting parallels between the two and their forbears. Put it this way: it's not a huge stretch one way or the other to put them on a similar level.

Generally speaking, the similarities of family ancestries include the fact that both sets of ancestors traveled to new and hopeful places in search of a better life (the Lincolns first from England to Massachusetts, and then a few generations later from Virginia to Kentucky; the Trumps from Germany to America); both sets of ancestors lost assumed inheritances because of the current laws of the land; both paternal grandfathers died young in a sudden manner; neither President Lincoln nor President Donald Trump were ever forthcoming on the subject of ancestry or from where they had come; both imagined or fantasized a different upbringing; and yet both grew up relatively normal, ordinary kids with early happy childhoods.

CB EO

Lincoln's ancestral ties to America date back to 1637, just thirty years after Jamestown was founded as America's first permanent English colony, in what would become known as Virginia. This was just seventeen years after the first Pilgrims had landed at Plymouth in Massachusetts. Samuel Lincoln, the future sixteenth president's great-great-great-great-grandfather, migrated to that famous "rock" along with his two brothers. Their purpose: to save the English Puritan Revolution.[3]

Upon his arrival at the Plymouth Colony, Samuel Lincoln, then fifteen years old, settled in the town of Hingham. That's where he would stay for the rest of his life, his two brothers providing a stabilizing force centered around family, one that grew in number while staying rooted. In 1680—by which time Samuel was in his late fifties—the town of Hingham numbered 280 residents, one-fourth of whom bore the surname Lincoln.[4]

Mordecai Lincoln Jr., Samuel's grandson, was thirty-four years old in 1720 when he moved to Reading, Pennsylvania. From there the son of Mordecai Jr., whose name was John—and who became known as "Virginia John"—eventually headed farther south. At age fifty-two in 1768, John made his way to Rockbridge County in Virginia's Valley, where he would be joined by four of his brothers, all of them settling in next to the magnificent Blue Ridge Mountains.

Virginia John's son, Abraham, had more than a few pinches of Manifest Destiny in his DNA. Near the end of the Revolutionary War, this Abraham—the paternal grandfather to our nation's sixteenth president—set out from Virginia and soon joined up with a distant cousin of his, Daniel Boone (yes, the legendary trailblazer) as well as several other Boones and Lincolns, to make the trek across the Cumberland Gap to Kentucky, which at the time was rumored to be a rich land of plentiful opportunity. This Abraham bought thousands of rich, untilled acres near Louisville, in what he believed to be a wise purchase that would permit his family and their descendants to thrive and prosper. The land would enrich a family legacy with the indomitable spirit of the pioneer, the striving for "riches" beyond the horizon, and culminate in presidential proportions.

CAST

Before there was a Donald Trump, there was a Fred Trump; and before there was a Fred Trump, there was Friedrich Trump: Donald's paternal grandfather—a man Donald never knew or saw.

Friedrich was born and raised in Germany, all the way up to his sixteenth year of life before he bolted in a fit of youthful adventure for a faraway land. He had grown up in the village of Kallstadt in southwestern Germany, in an area known as Pfalz. A century later Pfalz was described as a lush, pleasant, and affluent place,[5] but those many decades earlier it was a disturbing place for a restless lad with lofty ambitions, offering nothing of note for young Friedrich.

No question; he wanted out of Pfalz, a region nestled in the foothills of the Haardt Mountains. Shunning a military service obligation that was to soon kick in for him, sixteen-year-old Friedrich set off, alone, for America in October 1885. In running away from home, he boldly abandoned his family and an inheritance that had become so small as to be almost useless. (Napoleon's mandated apportionment laws meant family lands were divided up equally among offspring.) There was little to tempt Friedrich to stay. Instead, he was determined to seek success and fortune in the United States. He intended to become wealthy with haste by brandishing the grit and determination that had become a Trump trademark.

Friedrich didn't cross the Atlantic, destination New York, without having a trade skill in hand. Back in Germany, he had served an apprenticeship for about two and a half years as a barber, cutting hair. Also, he wasn't entirely alone when he got to America. His older sister, Katharina, had immigrated to New York several years earlier and was now living with her husband, Fred Schuster, on Manhattan's Lower East Side, in a neighborhood of numerous Palatine German immigrants.

Good fortune sometimes comes to the bold. As fate would have it, young Friedrich quickly met a German-speaking barber, who was looking for someone immediately available to take on an assistant's role cutting hair. For the next six years, Friedrich worked as a barber, all the while knowing this wasn't going to be his life's work. It certainly wasn't an occupation that would bring wealth quickly—by the time nine years had passed, he had merely several hundred dollars to his name, accompanied by an itch to get to work for real, and, in his case, to move on to greener pastures.

And what a move it was—completely across the country. Friedrich Trump left Manhattan in 1891 and headed west to Seattle, where he used his modest life savings to buy a restaurant in the city's red-light district, which he furnished with new tables, chairs, and a range. He excelled at serving the public and assured patrons a good meal, a stiff drink, and even more recreational pursuits.

For the next ten years, Friedrich Trump—by now better known as "Frederick" Trump—bounced around the Pacific Northwest, leaving Seattle after only three years. In British Columbia and the Yukon, he

GRETCHEN WOLLERT

rubbed elbows with miners while still making a go of it in the hotel and restaurant business. Eventually, he and a business partner founded the Arctic Restaurant and Hotel in Bennett, British Columbia. Then two years later, in 1900, they launched the Yukon-based White Horse Restaurant and Inn. It proved to be a huge financial success, serving three thousand meals a day, with plenty of space available to feed one's taste for gambling. A year later, Trump sold his share in the business to his partner and headed back to Germany as a somewhat wealthy man.[6]

Back home in Kallstadt, Frederick wasted no time in finding a wife. He married Elisabeth Christ, eleven years his junior, before moving back to New York City in 1902. Elisabeth's homesickness made it a brief stay in America, less than two years. Before leaving the U.S., however, Elisabeth gave birth to their daughter Elizabeth in April 1904. A few months later, they were headed back to Germany. That, too, would be a short stay. Bavarian authorities finally caught up with Friedrich's earlier avoidance of military service, when he had first fled to America. They now labeled him a draft dodger.

A royal decree issued In February 1905 informed Trump that he had eight weeks to get out of the country for not having properly registered his 1886 departure with authorities. He put his wife and baby on a boat and headed back to America for good .That summer of 1905 their first son, Fred, (Donald Trump's dad-to-be) was born.

Having invested in land in the Pacific Northwest about a decade earlier, Frederick wasted little time in buying another chunk of real estate. In 1908, he purchased property on Jamaica Avenue in the Woodhaven area of Queens, New York. Two years later, he moved his family there and rented out rooms in the spacious residence, helping to defray some of the family's living expenses. As he was starting to build his real estate portfolio, Frederick Trump was also working as a hotel manager at a property at 6th Avenue and 23rd Street.

Still in his early forties, Frederick was finally able to enjoy the modest wealth he had accumulated (equivalent to a little over a half million dollars in today's currency), with designs to further expand his investments into land. What he hadn't planned for was an early death. It was on a Wednesday near the end of May 1918 when Frederick Trump and young Fred, twelve at the time, were walking along Jamaica Avenue. They often did this in the afternoon, dropping in to chat with realtors along the way. At some point Frederick suddenly turned to his son, saying he felt sick. They hastened home, where the elder Trump immediately crawled into bed and then died within hours, "just like that," in the words of young Fred, recalling the event years later.[7]

Frederick Trump was forty-nine years old when he died; the cause—Spanish flu. Five days later, his brother-in-law, Fred Shuster, passed away, also a Spanish flu victim, putting them among the tens of millions of people worldwide who eventually died from one of the deadliest epidemics of the twentieth century.[8]

The first Abraham Lincoln, Honest Abe's grandfather, also died at a young age. That Abraham was forty-two, although his death involved different circumstances—he was killed by an Indian in a surprise attack at the family's homestead. This was in 1786, and it occurred in the presence of three of his children; Mordecai was the oldest at fifteen; Josiah, the middle son; and Thomas (Abe's father), age eight.

A few years earlier, Abraham, the elder, had sold his farm in Virginia and moved over the mountains into Kentucky, where, he had been told by others, including his cousin Daniel Boone, that rich lands awaited them, offering golden opportunities for those willing to risk the dangers of a vast, untamed territory. Within several years Abraham had achieved ownership of more than fifty-five hundred acres of land in what was considered to be one of the opportunistic areas of Kentucky. Trouble came while, joined by his three sons, Abraham was planting a cornfield; Indians emerged from the woods and attacked them, killing Abraham. A startled but cool-headed Mordecai sent Josiah running to a nearby settlement for help, while he sprinted to a cabin close by for refuge.

Thomas hadn't followed his big brother to the cabin's sanctuary—the young boy was still at his deceased father's side, in the cornfield, mourning his loss. Once inside the cabin, Mordecai peered out through the cracks between the logs only to see another Indian coming out of the woods, stealthily moving toward an unaware Thomas. Mordecai picked up a rifle, aimed it at a silver ornament hanging from the Shawnee Indian's neck and pulled the trigger, instantly killing the attacker and missing his little brother by inches.

Well into his adult years, Thomas Lincoln would beam with pride each time he related the story, to anyone who would listen, about how quick-acting Mordecai had heroically saved his life. Thomas recounted the story so many times, that it eventually led Honest Abe to describe it as "the legend more strongly than all others imprinted upon my mind and memory."[9]

Because he was the oldest son in the family, Mordecai, according to Virginia law, inherited all his father's rather impressive estate once he came of age. That left young Thomas with none of the family inheritance. On his own, he would have to rely on grit and resolve to determine his future.

As husband to Nancy and father to two children, Thomas was not long in Kentucky, eventually defeated by property laws that rendered the land he had purchased next to worthless. Lands weren't properly surveyed by the state, and between the vaguely defined boundaries and cunning salesmen, who were slick at convincing farmers that their lands were not legally purchased, land ownership was often challenged in court. Expensive litigations were no-win situations for small farmers. Young Abe's dad believed he had no choice but to surrender the legal skirmish and find a new home—in another state.

So, in the fall of 1816, Thomas took leave from his wife and two children to head north and explore Indiana. His intent was to find and claim a plot of land, mark his spot, and then return to Kentucky to gather up his family and make the move. In those days, pioneers could purchase federal land in Indiana, for pennies, that offered plenty of appeal and properly surveyed boundaries. At the time, Indiana was a sparsely populated frontier; it was barely a state, having joined the Union less than a year earlier.[10]

Thomas Lincoln would need plenty of pluck, luck, and tenacity to pull off this move. Traveling alone on the Ohio River on a flatboat he had constructed using his impressive carpentry skills, Thomas came ashore in Troy at the southern tip of Indiana. His trip there had been near-tragic, his boat capsizing at one point, although he was able to recover almost everything that had fallen out of the boat before continuing on the arduous journey.

Once back on land, and now in Indiana, he navigated nine miles along what could generously be called a wagon road, and eventually reached a dense wilderness that was totally unsettled. No more wagon roads, no cleared paths—he would have to hack through seven miles of tall, gnarly underbrush to find a destination he hoped would serve as the family home for the foreseeable future. At first it seemed he would have better luck digging a hole through to China with his bare hands. Undaunted, he eventually slashed his way to a plot of land he could claim as his properly surveyed and U.S.-government-issued corner of heaven. He went about cutting and gathering up brush to pile into each of the lot's four corners, taking the added measure of burning notches into trees to mark his newfound plot with unmistakable certainty. That done, he made his way back to Kentucky— the return trip much easier than the original trek—to retrieve his family and take them to their new Indiana home before winter settled in.

CB BO

As interesting and richly anecdotal as the respective family histories—their ancestry—are, neither Abraham Lincoln nor Donald Trump were ever much for talking about it themselves. It just wasn't a subject that had much appeal for them. It was evident, though, that each man had been greatly shaped by the work ethic and ideals of their ancestors. Both saw themselves as self-made men, but with a reticence to talk about their upbringing or other elements of their ancestries. Their attitudes seemed to be, *Why bother? It doesn't mean anything.*

Lincoln, for instance, simply never saw a purpose in expounding on his family tree. When he was asked in 1859 by supporters for biographical information they could use to tout him for his presidential campaign, Lincoln said only, "My parents were both born in Virginia, of undistinguished families—second families, perhaps I should say." When approached by the *Chicago Tribune*'s John Locke Scripps to write his campaign biography, an apparently unamused, yet unwittingly amusing, Lincoln muttered, "Why Scripps . . . it is a great piece of folly to attempt to make anything out of my early life. It can all be condensed into a single sentence, and that sentence you will find in *Gray's Elegy*: 'The short and simple annals of the poor.' That's my life, and that's all you or any one else can make of it."[11]

In similar manner, Trump doesn't relish questions about himself, his upbringing, or his ancestry. In one account, he writes, "Contrary to what a lot of people think, I don't enjoy doing press. I've been asked the same questions a million times now, and I don't particularly like talking about my personal life. Nonetheless, I understand that getting press can be very helpful in making deals, and I don't mind talking about them. I just try to be very selective."[12] Trump also says that people who watched him on *The Apprentice*, read his books, or attended his Learning Annex seminars, might think they know him, but they know only part of him—his business side. "I usually don't speak much about my personal life or about my personal values or about how I came to be who I am today," he points out.[13]

CS&SO

There has long been a question about Lincoln's true lineage, and it is as much about his father as it is about his mother. It involves a long-held perception that as smart and ambitious as Abe Lincoln was, his father was regarded as neither, at least not in the eyes of some of those who knew both father and son. Some historians have hinted or even concluded that Thomas Lincoln lacked ambition, that he was low on energy and something of a dullard, even shiftless, while Abe would come to be known for his superior intellect—his well-documented love for books fed that assessment—as well as his robust drive and knack for thinking quickly on his feet, even earning a reputation for his occasional, albeit dry, wit (all of which could just as easily describe Donald Trump).

Apparently, it was reasoned, these qualities of Abe's could *not* have been genetic pass-me-downs from his father. That leads to speculation that whatever drove Abraham Lincoln and set him apart from his peers must have been from his mother Nancy's side of the family tree, or, perhaps, Lincoln's biological father was not Thomas. That, in turn, gives rise to speculation that what made Lincoln great could have come from one of the more prominent families in that part of Kentucky, perhaps a Hardin or a Marshall, or one of the other families in that part of the country that held social and intellectual sway.[14]

That sort of scuttlebutt, present in Lincoln's lifetime, displeased Abe to no end. He believed that his mother, Nancy Hanks Lincoln, had been an illegitimate child, a scenario which opened up all kinds of possibilities. During a long buggy ride, an adult Lincoln told his riding companion that his mother Nancy was the illegitimate daughter of Lucy Hanks, the result of Lucy's fling or some other sort of sexual rendezvous with a presumably unknown but well-bred Virginia farmer or planter. Or so the story goes. It was from this mystery man, the future president reasoned, that he had been bestowed his keen analysis, logic, mental acuity, ambition, and whatever other qualities that distinguished him from previous ancestors of the Lincoln family. "God bless my mother; all that I am or ever hope to be I owe to her," Lincoln was quoted as saying, with a strong hint of melancholy.[15]

Fred Trump, Donald's dad, who was forty-one years Donald's senior, had concerns about his own family's heritage, but it had nothing to do with illicit affairs or the like. Fred was described as self-conscious, perhaps even ashamed, of his German lineage, instead telling people that he was Swedish—that his father, Friedrich, had come to the United States from Sweden and not Germany. This is a claim that Donald Trump has repeated in at least one book.[16]

CRSO

Although the two presidential fathers were born and lived separated by more than a hundred years—one a poor backwoods country laborer of southern roots (Thomas Lincoln) and the other something of a city slicker of northern privilege and opportunity (Fred Trump)—both managed to instill, either purposely or unwittingly, similar qualities in their respective president-to-be sons.

Neither Abraham nor Donald were intimidated by their fathers. Even as teenagers and young adults, they were not afraid to stand up to their dads without backing down. Yes, all things considered, Thomas Lincoln, was pleased that his son was determined to improve himself academically by poring over books. (Abraham read as many as he could get his hands on—a point hammered home by the history books.) However, when Thomas perceived that Abe's reading interfered with work around the farm, such as chopping wood or building fences, Thomas would physically punish his son. Impudence was not to be tolerated, and the chores were not to be delayed or ignored. As a young boy, Abraham would occasionally jump into the middle of adult conversations, and Thomas would not tolerate this either, sometimes striking his son to drive the point home. Even as a youngster unable to match his dad physically, Abraham "never balked, but dropt a kind of silent unwelcome tear, as evidence of his sensations."[17]

We know Donald Trump wasn't intimidated by his dad and had no fear of standing up to him because younger Trump said so: "Fortunately for me, I was drawn to business very early, and I was never intimidated by my father, the way most people were. I stood up to him, and he respected that. We had a relationship that was almost businesslike. I sometimes wonder if we'd have gotten along so well if I hadn't been as business-oriented as I am."[18]

It was that Trump nose for business and Fred Trump's business acumen and ambition that set the Trumps apart from the Lincolns's world of modest means. By age twenty-one, Fred Trump was already diving headfirst into New York City real estate, joining forces with his mother, Elisabeth, to do business as E. Trump and Son. Where the Lincolns and Trumps did share a philosophy was in their penchant for playing it safe when it came to business. Thomas Lincoln chose the remote frontier over the conflicts of the settled Kentucky community. In the case of the Trumps, they chose the outer boroughs of Brooklyn and Queens for their business ventures rather than fighting it out with cutthroat developers in the fierce (and expensive!) competitive fires of Manhattan (although Donald would eventually change that).[19]

౭ా

When Abraham was nine, his mother, Nancy, suddenly passed away at age thirty-four, having become violently ill with what was known as milk sickness. It was a malady caused by consuming milk or other dairy products from cows foraging on the poisonous white snakeroot plant, which grew abundantly near the Ohio River during pioneer days. Milk sickness claimed thousands of lives among migrant families in the early nineteenth century.[20]

About a year later, in 1819, Thomas Lincoln remarried, exchanging vows with Sarah Bush Johnston, a widow whose husband had died three years earlier. Sarah's brother, Isaac, had been the one to sell the Kentucky Sinking Spring Farm to Thomas. As a stepmom, Sarah was a blessing to Abraham. She was well-read and highly literate in her own right and enthusiastic about introducing her brainy stepson to a world of literature beyond what he had experienced. This pleased Thomas immensely. As a man of little or no education who could barely write his name (according to his son), Thomas took pride in his son's smarts and in how literary Abe was becoming (as long as he still put work first). When it came to public service, Thomas was active in public affairs and church activities, serving as a militia member, local constable, prison guard, jury member, and road commissioner. Thomas provided a shining example to his son of the importance of performing public service.[21]

Frugality was a hallmark of both the Lincoln and Trump households, each in their own way. For Thomas Lincoln it was a matter of survival, as simple as that. He essentially struggled his whole life, working valiantly to make ends meet between his carpentry and farming vocations, despite being seen by those who knew him as a "tinker—a piddler—always doing but doing nothing great." The financial pressure became more pronounced after he married Sarah; she brought three of her own children from her previous marriage into the house. There they were also joined by Dennis Hanks—a cousin to Nancy Lincoln, who was ten years older than Abraham. This upped the count of household members to eight. It was up to Abraham, now a strapping adolescent, to help out when his father's health started to fail. (He reportedly began losing his sight in both eyes, among other ailments.) This made it necessary for Abraham to spearhead the farming, hoeing, fence-making, and so on to pick up the slack and keep the family afloat. On top of that, Thomas hired his son out to work for other farmers in the area. According to local law, Thomas got to keep all the money Abraham earned until Abraham came of age at twenty-one.[22]

When it came to his version of frugality and being a model caretaker of finances and goods, Fred Trump had few peers. There are many stories about his penny-pinching, such as how he would pick up stray nails at a job site and return them to the workers the next day— simultaneously saving money and setting an example for his son Donald. To cut down on supply costs, Fred had chemists research the formula for the floor disinfectant he was purchasing in large quantities. Then he had workers mix up batches of the disinfectant at significantly lower cost than he had been paying a vendor. If he felt there were any lights that could be turned off without affecting the overall lighting, he would think nothing of getting up on a stepladder and removing the light bulbs.[23] How many Trumps did it take to change a light bulb? One, apparently.

Fred Trump typically worked twelve-hour workdays (also known as "half-days" to the world's most devoted workaholics), sometimes busting it right alongside his construction workers. Fred didn't always click with Donald when it came to business matters, but he respected his son's robust work ethic and his knack for producing great results. At one point Fred told a business magazine, "Everything Donald touches turns to gold!" There were also times when Proud Papa Fred would pull out a photo of Donald in a tuxedo and show it around. Sometimes his audience would already know who the young Trump was, a sure sign of the impact Donald was making in the business world at an early age.

Fred Trump also made it a point to know what was going on in the world around him, especially when it might involve business matters. Following in his own father's business footsteps, Fred discovered something in the mid-1930s that would provide a sustained lifeblood of opportunities in the construction business. At the time Fred was hitting his thirties and Donald was still ten years away from being born. This newfound ticket to business success: the government.

Thanks to a number of New Deal programs pushed into existence by President Franklin D. Roosevelt's administration, new heavily financed opportunities were being offered to help float businesses such as Fred's. He proved skilled at determining how to take full advantage of these programs. In so doing, Fred Trump "joined the ranks of entrepreneurs who constitute one of the oldest fraternities in the Republic: multimillionaires who owe their fortune to subsidies from a grateful government."[24]

Thomas Lincoln never became rich from his government-subsidized Indiana land. He never even approached middle class by nineteenth-century standards, but he managed to exhibit his own means of self-improvement that didn't go unnoticed by his son. The fact that Thomas was able to purchase farmlands in two different states was at least indicative of a commitment to making a better life for his family, despite the critics who had seen him as "piddling." As a carpenter, he was self-taught and came to be respected for his craftsmanship. If nothing else, Thomas Lincoln was a model of self-betterment. Even though Abraham significantly surpassed his father in that regard, there's no disputing that his aspiration to improve himself was something that had been exemplified, to some degree, by his father.[25]

CR ⬩ SO

Fred Trump was described as a man of grit, someone who embodied discipline, consistency, and a determination to get the job done right. If it wasn't right, he would make sure it got fixed, often taking care of it himself. He was not one to give up easily on a matter, even when friends and colleagues suggested that he take another course of action—a quality of stubbornness often associated with Donald. About Fred Trump, attorney Sydney Young once said, "You could never tell Fred Trump what to do. You could tell him how to do it, but not what to do. He was very strong-willed."[26]

Fred ensured that his son was better educated than he. While Trump grew up surrounded by his father's wealth, little was given to Donald during his schooling years. He was put to work, and it was hard work, long hours; there was no coasting for any of the five Trump siblings. Trump's mother, Mary Anne (MacLeod), was part of that hard-work ethic as well, working fulltime in various ways alongside her husband and children.

Many times when Fred went to collect rent from tenants in tough sections of Brooklyn, he would bring young Donald along, as much to learn the business as to be exposed to seedier parts of the city he otherwise would not have cause to visit. At times, Donald watched his dad ring the doorbell at a tenant's residence then stand off to the side of the door, knowing an angry tenant might shoot through the door in lieu of paying rent. "My work ethic came from my father," Donald said. "I don't know anybody who works harder than I do. I'm working all the time. It's not about money—I just don't know a different way of life, and I love it."[27]

Life inside the Trump home on Midland Parkway in Queens was caring but strict, complete with rules and curfews. For Donald's sister, Maryanne, that meant no lipstick. Sweets and snacks between meals were not allowed, and when Fred, the dad (there was also a Fred Jr., Donald's older brother) came home from work at night, Mom would dutifully inform her husband about what the kids had done that day and how they had behaved. Then he would mete out whatever punishments were called for. In that sense, Donald was subject to the same sort of discipline, including physical measures—such as paddling with a wooden spoon—that his presidential predecessor

Abraham had been subject to as a child and an adolescent. "Spare the rod, spoil the child."

All five Trump children—Maryanne, Fred Jr., Elizabeth, Donald, and Robert—were taught to be frugal and respect the value of a dollar. That meant turning out all the lights in rooms not being used, cleaning their plates at every meal, and being aware of and attentive to starving children around the world. Each of them worked summer jobs, which for the three boys included paper routes; their only concession being that when it rained or snowed, they could use a limousine to get to all of their delivery destinations. "The first time I ever realized that my father was successful," Maryanne said, "was when I was fifteen and a friend said to me, 'Your father is rich.' I was stunned. We were privileged, but I didn't know it."[28]

Like Donald Trump, Lincoln, too, worked for his dad into his twenties. In the first half the nineteenth century, young men were more duty-bound to work in ways that probably would be considered akin to slavery by modern standards. Case in point: Lincoln continued working, subservient to his dad, even a year beyond what was required by frontier law or custom. That involved back-breaking work, mostly as a backwoods laborer; Lincoln spent many years wielding that familiar axe in his lean yet strong arms.

During the time Lincoln continued working for his dad, without pay, beyond his twenty-first birthday, he helped his father and the rest of the family make the move from Indiana to their new home in Illinois. This was March 1830. It was a two-week, 225-mile journey. Abe drove one of the two rickety wagons, each pulled by two oxen, fording the Wabash River at Vincennes, Indiana. Then they navigated through swollen streams and water-saturated soil to central Illinois. About a dozen miles west of the small hamlet of Decatur, Illinois, they arrived at a ten-acre plot controlled by the federal government that cousin John Hanks had suggested they try out. Eventually, they decided to purchase it as their new homestead.[29]

Cஃல$

Both Lincoln's stepmother, Sarah, and Trump's mother, Mary Anne, had powerful influences on their sons, the fulfillment of their considerable ambitions and their respective roles as matriarchs of the home. Both women had been adventurous and secure enough in themselves to leave their homes to marry husbands, and both embodied civility, cleanliness, and care. They each nurtured their children, filling their homes with love, but they also prodded their children to follow pursuits of self-betterment, to be all they could be.

It was generally known that Thomas Lincoln had remarried well in choosing Sarah Bush as his second wife. In Sarah, Thomas saw the character and willingness to be a great stepmother to his son. There certainly was a strong mutual respect between Abraham and his stepmother, who took her stepson's embrace of reading and literature to a new level.

In later years, Lincoln expressed ample praise for his stepmother. In fact, he visited her at her home in Coles County, Illinois, right before he went to Washington, DC to be sworn in as U.S. president. In the letters he wrote to her, he referred to her as "Mother," and later he gave her use of a forty-acre tract of land he had acquired following his father's death, allowing Sarah to use it for the remainder of her lifetime.[30]

The strong mother-son connection between Sarah and Abraham had been born almost from the time she moved into the Lincoln home after she and Thomas married. This was in 1818, when Abe was nine. What she brought first into the family was a gift of love. Thomas had been a single parent for a year, and his children were suffering from it. After seeing young Abe and his sister Sarah dirty, not properly clothed, and looking hungry, Sarah took it upon herself to clean the children—soaping and rubbing the layer of filth away.

Next came a makeover of the house itself, a reorganization blueprinted by the stepmom. Thomas Lincoln and Dennis Hanks were convinced to give up hunting long enough to split logs and put down a floor in the cabin, over the dirt. They then finished the roof, constructed a proper door, and cut a hole for a window that was covered with grease paper for added protection against the elements. Other modifications to the log cabin, presumably designed by Sarah Bush and accepted by Tom, were to add a loft accessible by pegs driven into the wall. This loft was where the three boys in the blended family could sleep. Thomas also put his carpentry skills to use by building another table and stools, all done with minimal friction between dad and mom. Sarah's influence transformed a crude cabin into a proverbial castle.

Sarah also pulled off the remarkable feat of blending the two families without tolerating strife or envy, and in the process she grew quite fond of Abraham. "Abe never gave me a cross word or look and never refused in fact, or even in appearance, to do anything I requested of him," she said. "I never gave him a cross word in all my life. . . His mind and my mind—what little I had—seemed to move together—move in the same channel."[31]

There was a similar connection between Trump and his mom, Mary Anne. In Donald's case their relationship involved a shared competitive streak, a virtue when it came to dealing with the vagaries of the competitive real estate business in which they worked alongside Fred. Indeed, Mrs. Mary Anne Trump had a strong bearing and confidence about her, a commanding feminine presence, influenced by the fact that she was fair, tall, and slender with blue eyes and blonde hair, and by her slight Scottish brogue. (She had been born in the Scottish village of Tong, which is closer to Iceland than London.)

Mary Anne MacLeod Trump was a most impressive woman of her era, almost regal in countenance and appearance. She was definitely "queen" of her castle. She made a home as useful and modern as the one Sarah Bush had created in her time, and Mary Anne made sure it was ruled by order, competence, and love—and with as much added splendor as she could muster. "My mother was silently competitive," Donald said, long after she had passed away at age 88, in 2000. "She was a very competitive person, but you wouldn't know that. She had a great fighting spirit, like Braveheart."[32]

Over the years, Donald Trump has been given hundreds of Bibles by admirers who no doubt have hoped and prayed for his faith and his salvation. He says that he has kept all of them safely stowed away in a safe place in Trump Tower. When he took the oath of office as U.S. president in January 2017, he placed his hand on two Bibles—one was given to him by his mother upon his confirmation as a boy, which he counts as the one most special to him—and the other was a Bible that had belonged to a former U.S. president: Abraham Lincoln.

CHAPTER 2

MAN OF FAITH

———————————— ❦ ————————————

I just assumed Abraham Lincoln was a Christian. Brilliant-minded, born and raised in the Bible Belt, and, as reasonable as he was proven to be (to me, being a churchgoer was the most reasonable thing in the world), I took it for granted that a man so committed to truth and unity was in a church pew every Sunday. After all, he was called "Honest Abe," and his most-famous speeches flowed with the language of religion and phrases from the Bible: "Fourscore and seven . . ." and "The judgments of the Lord are true and righteous altogether."

I knew nothing of his turbulent, questioning youth or a rebellious streak in his early years. In fact, I was sure that if he had offered his testimony at a camp-meeting revival, it would have stolen the spotlight as the most humble, sincere declaration of Christian faith from any believer there. But I'd have been wrong.

On the other hand, if you had suggested to me that Donald Trump believed in any power higher than himself, I would have dismissed it as inconceivable. Through the eighties it seemed every other tabloid front-page story about Trump proclaimed yet another outlandish worldly episode in the ongoing saga of his self-serving, lavish, and dissipated lifestyle. How could a person portrayed in the media as such a "bad boy" be a person of faith?

I only knew Donald Trump from what I saw and heard in the news, and what was in the news (until 2015) was never about his "Christian character" or any kind of "redemptive nature." I judged these two men solely by what was apparent on the surface. As I dove into the reality of both and examined the truth beyond the media hype, I realized a depth of faith not readily seen by outsiders.

⋘ ⋙

Abraham Lincoln was no saint. Neither is Donald Trump—we know that practically firsthand. If asked to choose which man more closely depicts the fruits of godliness and a good moral character, you would probably pick Lincoln. Admit it. That's because you don't actually know either man's heart or faith-based convictions.

Some things about Lincoln you probably didn't know: he hardly ever attended church; many who knew him as an adult branded him an atheist or a fatalist; and for a while in his mid-twenties, the young lawyer-to-be spent hours at a time, a Bible in his hands, arguing against the veracity of one verse after another, all the while bitterly cursing God for allowing his first (and maybe only *true*) love, his beautiful fiancée Ann Rutledge, to die from a fever-like illness.

Compare all that to Trump, the pompous billionaire with the jumbo-sized ego, who has been married three times, who has bankrupted at least four businesses (six, if you believe Hillary Clinton), who has had one alleged affair with a porn actress, who has been caught on tape spewing crude locker-room bluster, and who has offended millions of Americans who are unaccustomed to reading a president's unfiltered (yet brutally honest and oftentimes spot-on) tweets that violate the codes of politically correct conduct embraced by the truly enlightened.

Considering all that, it's no wonder that neither of these U.S. presidents has been treated by historians (in Lincoln's case) or contemporary media (in Trump's) as a man of particularly robust religious faith or expression. So they are quite similar in that respect. The remarkable truth is that both were or are men of great faith, even if not in the eyes of their judgmental critics.

Among Christians at least, judgmental churchgoers keep a hopeful eye out for stereotypical demonstrations of a belief in God: prayer, worship, and scripture study. They look for someone with a knack for quoting pet scriptural verses on cue, toting a Bible, and especially emoting during church worship, while perched in a pew every Sunday and other church holidays.

Lincoln wasn't much for checking off any of those boxes, ditto for Trump. However, before we condemn Lincoln or Trump, or both, to an eternity in purgatory, let's remember that the Bible speaks openly of man's sinful nature and the hope for forgiveness available to any man or woman, boy or girl, who seeks a path to God, accompanied by sincere repentance. Lincoln and Trump are afforded that same opportunity.

What exactly does a man or woman have to do to convince family, friends, acquaintances, coworkers, and the general public that they are people of faith submitted to God? Actually, nothing. It's between the person and God; no one else is qualified to make that judgment, despite what they see, hear, or read (or *don't* see, hear, or read). Both Lincoln and Trump have a foundation of faith that dates back to their youth. They grew up in families that honored the Sabbath, the Bible, times of prayer, and church attendance. They both learned about and (hopefully) followed the tenets in their respective flavors of the Christian faith. We know of no evidence that either Lincoln or Trump ever backed off or hid from their faith because a belief about a certain topic was "above their paygrade."

⊂⊃⊂⊃

Historical accounts about Trump's religious upbringing are scattered and relatively scant. One known fact is that his mother, Mary Anne, gave him his first Bible when he was eight years old—a Revised Standard Version (RSV), published by Thomas Nelson & Sons in 1952. The occasion, in June 1955, was Trump's graduation from Sunday Church Primary School at First Presbyterian Church (FPC) in his childhood neighborhood of Jamaica, Queens, New York.[1]

In the years since, hundreds of Trump's admirers—many of whom were presumably concerned about Trump's relationship with God and his eternal destination—have gifted him with Bibles, which he has safely stowed somewhere in Trump Tower.

"There's no way I would ever . . . do anything negative to a Bible . . . I would have a fear of doing something other than very positive," Trump said.[2]

The Bible gifted to him by his mom was one of two Bibles on which Trump placed his left hand in January 2017 when taking the oath of office for the presidency. The other was a Bible that had belonged to Lincoln, an 1853 Oxford University Press edition of the King James Bible. It was given to Lincoln by a United States Supreme Court clerk, moments before his inauguration ceremony in 1861. Lincoln's personal belongings—presumably including his personal Bible—hadn't made it to Washington, DC, in time for the ceremony.

Trump's childhood church is more than 350 years old and is currently tucked among chain stores, Bangladeshi food stands, and halal grocers in

Jamaica, Queens. One ironic thing about the church and its connection to Trump is that it now boasts a congregation predominantly composed of immigrants from a dozen or more countries. On any given Sunday, as described in the July 2016 edition of *The Atlantic*, an attendee might see "women in geles and bright, African-print dresses (sitting) in the pews alongside ladies in floppy church hats."[3]

Although it was believed as of 2016 that Trump had not visited his childhood church in decades, he did send a $10,000 donation to FPC in 2012, according to Pastor Patrick O'Connor. "I attended Sunday school at the church for a number of years," Trump wrote. "Going to church was an important part of our family life, and the memories for me are still vivid— of a vibrant congregation and a lot of activities."[4]

Over the years Trump on numerous occasions has proudly recalled his confirmation into FPC in June 1959, the month in which he turned thirteen, often showing off a photo from the confirmation ceremony. Pictured are seven boys in the back row, most of them wearing dark suits—he's the tallest—with twelve girls in white dresses and holding flowers in the front two rows. Trump kept the photo handy during his 2016 presidential campaign, frequently pulling it out to show people as proof he had indeed been initiated into the folds of the church.

As part of the confirmation process, students were required to sign a document certifying they had "publicly confessed Jesus Christ as Lord and Savior and [been] received into the communicant membership" of the local church. Included in that confirmation process was a service during which the nineteen students publicly confessed, confirmed, and promised to abide by several affirmations. It started with, "Do you confess your faith in God the Father Almighty, Maker of heaven and earth, and in Jesus Christ his only Son our Lord, and do you promise with the aid of the Holy Spirit to be Christ's faithful disciple to your life's end?"[5]

Whether Trump's profession of confirmation of an abiding faith and lifelong discipleship in Jesus Christ could be interpreted as a proclamation of being "born again" is debatable (once saved, always saved?). It seems reasonable to conclude, though, that Trump did successfully complete the confirmation process (perhaps considering it his first exclusive club membership). This process imbued him with a foundation of faith that has been with him his whole life, even if his words and actions haven't always passed muster with other believers—and, of course, nonbelievers.

Most Americans don't see Trump, who identifies as Presbyterian, as religious; half of them don't believe he is a Christian. Those were among the conclusions from a Pew Research Center survey. The survey results were published March 25, 2020, and showed a 63 percent majority of all U.S. adults believed Trump was either "not too" or "not at all" religious. There were 28 percent of respondents who said the forty-fifth president was "somewhat" religious, but only 7 percent said he was "very" religious. Even among survey respondents identifying themselves as Christian, more than half doubted Trump's level of religious faith: 56 percent said he was "not too" or "not at all" religious, and 43 percent chose either "somewhat" or "very" as Trump's level of religiosity.[6]

Even though the Pew Research Center bills itself as "a nonpartisan fact tank that informs the public about the issues, attitudes, and trends shaping the world," its origins suggest otherwise. It was established with its current name in 2004, with roots tracing back to the now-defunct Times Mirror Company. This company published newspapers (e.g., *Los Angeles Times, Newsday, Dallas Times Herald*, etc.) for more than a century, along with other print media.[7]

The Pew Center's survey findings make for interesting reading, especially for anti-Trumpsters craving ammunition with which to launch yet another assault on Trump's character and fitness to lead the country. It's worth pointing out that in its lead paragraph on the story announcing its findings in this survey, the Center acknowledged that Trump's "personal religious beliefs and practices have not been as public as his penchant for surrounding himself with evangelical leaders while also supporting various conservative Christian causes, not to mention his frequent use of religious-oriented jargon while speaking in public."[8]

His detractors might claim that Trump's affinity for Christian language and advisors has essentially been political strategy to endear himself to the Christian and evangelical voting bloc. But such an assumption falls short of properly evaluating Trump's private exercise of his Christian beliefs. While they are at it, his detractors might scrutinize and perhaps adjust their own beliefs and religious practices before ordaining themselves bully pulpit bishops, charged with deducing Trump's personal faith.

CB ⁊D

Abraham Lincoln's personal faith journey parallels Trump's in a number of respects, beginning with his introduction to public worship and church services as a young boy in Kentucky and then Indiana. Where Lincoln's early involvement with religious teachings differed from Trump's is in how they were taught. Trump's introduction to scripture and biblical teachings was carefully structured in a text-book-driven process, leading to a certificate of confirmation, Lincoln's introduction to the Word of God was more organic, less structured, and largely influenced by his parents and stepmother

Nancy Hanks Lincoln was indisputably a Christian woman, who often read to her son from the Bible, even teaching him how to read and write using scripture. Being the bright lad he was, young Abe smartly absorbed many passages and tenets of the Bible.[9] He didn't memorize scripture verses by rote so he could spit them out and impress fawning adults. Rather, he digested the words and their meanings, which would serve him well in later years, such as when giving speeches while running for and then serving as president of the United States.

As detailed in the Register of the Kentucky State Historical Society, Thomas Lincoln and Nancy Hanks were married by a Methodist minister named Jesse Head, although the couple didn't attend a Methodist church. Soon after they were wed, they joined (or "united with," in the parlance of the day) a church affiliated with what was known as—no joke—the "Baptized-Licking-Locust Association of Regular Baptists" in Kentucky. Some years later, after the Lincolns moved to Indiana, Nancy passed away, and Abraham took it upon himself to arrange for Elder David Elkins, their pastor from Kentucky, to come to Indiana to conduct the funeral services at the Lincolns' wilderness home.[10]

After remarrying, Thomas Lincoln requested and obtained his letter of fellowship with his church back in Kentucky. With the letter in hand, he and his second wife united with the Little Pigeon Baptist Church. Its proximity to Little Pigeon Creek meant the church was often referred to simply as "Pigeon Creek church." This church was founded on June 8, 1816, the same year in which Thomas Lincoln had moved to Indiana from Kentucky. Nancy Hanks Lincoln was buried between the Lincoln's home and the church, because the church had not yet started its own graveyard, although Sarah Lincoln Grigsby, Abraham's sister, would be buried in the church's burial ground after she passed away in 1828.[11]

According to the Register of the Kentucky State Historical Society, published in 1921, and citing an article about Lincoln's parents authored by Kentucky Assistant Attorney General Thomas B. McGregor, the Little Pigeon church's first book of records and minutes points out an interesting piece of trivia about the Lincolns and their church involvement. While Thomas, as records show, was quite active in the Little Pigeon church, being described as "one of the pillars of the church, acting as moderator, on committees to investigate the conduct of brethren and sisters, and messenger to associations," young Abraham is nowhere mentioned. While the church's book of records covering the period 1816–1840 shows that Abraham's father, stepmother, and sister Sarah were all acknowledged and active members of what was now "the Hard-Shell Baptist Church of Pigeon Creek," the future president's name was absent.[12]

Whether Abraham was active in the church or not, these records show that Thomas and Sally Lincoln's affiliation to "this little pioneer church of God," is sufficient proof that "Abraham was reared in a home, though rude and humble it was, pregnant with the teaching and the sweet influence of the Lowly Nazarene . . ."[13] So if Abraham Lincoln wasn't making church, worship, or prayer a significant part of his life, what was he doing to follow in his father's—or even his Father's—path of faith?

Lincoln's wife-to-be, Mary Todd Lincoln, would later address her husband's seemingly cool attitude about church attendance. Following his death, she said, "It is true that he never joined a church, but he was a religious man always, I think. He read the Bible a great deal. His maxim and philosophy were, 'What is to be will be, and no cares (prayers) of ours can arrest the decree.'"[14]

Further testimony to Abraham's faithful devotions is apparent in a letter he wrote to his stepbrother John Johnston in 1851, not long before Thomas Lincoln's death. Abraham, by then in his early forties, wrote:

> I sincerely hope Father may yet recover his health; but at all events, tell him to remember to call upon, and confide in, our great and merciful Maker, who will not turn away from him in any extremity. He notes the fall of the sparrow, and numbers the hairs of our heads, and He will not forget the dying man who puts his trust in Him. Say to him, if it is his lot to go now, he will soon have a joyful meeting with loved ones gone before, and where the rest of us, through the mercy of God, hope ere long to join them.[15]

A perception of Lincoln's apparent disinterest, if not disdain, for the repetitive choreography of church services followed him much of his life. There was even talk that Lincoln was an atheist. This sort of thing stayed with him all the way to the White House. The older he got and the more he achieved in practicing law and bouncing around in politics, the more pronounced became the widespread assumption that not only was Lincoln failing in church attendance, he didn't seem to have much at all going in the way of Christianity. That is often viewed as sin in the eyes of devoted churchgoers, who can be as bold in their sense of self-righteousness as in their insincerity with their own faith. Lincoln knew of his misinformed reputation, and he did at times speak out, or at least write, about it. For instance, he penned a "Handbill Replying to Charges of Infidelity," in which he presented his case to the voters of Illinois's 7th congressional district in 1846, while running for a seat in the U.S. House:

> A charge [has] got into circulation in some of the neighborhoods of this District, in substance that I am an open scoffer of Christianity. . . . That I am not a member of any Christian Church, is true; but I have never denied the truth of the scriptures; and I have never spoken with intentional disrespect of religion in general, or of any denomination of Christians in particular. . . .
>
> I do not think I could myself, be brought to support a man for office, whom I knew to be an open enemy of, and scoffer at, religion. Leaving the higher matter of eternal consequences, between him and his Maker, I still do not think any man has the right thus to insult the feelings, and injure the morals, of the community in which he may live.[16]

Then there's the following quote, which is proof, perhaps, that Lincoln did attend enough church services and paid close enough attention to the preaching to know what he liked and didn't like about sermons. If there was entertainment to go along with them, all the better: "The fact is, I don't like to hear cut and dried sermons. No—when I hear a man preach, I like to see him act as if he were fighting bees," Lincoln told sculptor Leonard Wells Volk, sometime around 1860.[17]

If Lincoln wasn't a practicing Christian, at least he was a believer, on some level—his mother Nancy had made sure of that. Her morals and conscience were aligned with the Word of God, something Abraham knew a lot about. He also knew that if he were to run for president, and by the mid-1850s the thought often crossed his mind, he needed to enact a spiritual makeover in his life. Even if he didn't see much value on Sundays in listening to a preacher drone on, if he was ever going to be president, or at least a man continuing to rise in the world, he needed to avoid being labeled an infidel, if not an atheist. The negative feelings he had inside his head and on his heart, if left unresolved, would doom his further ascension to the top of the nation's government.

From about 1854 to 1860 (when Lincoln was elected to his first term as president), the tall, gaunt man became essentially a seeker for all the world to witness—someone in search of a personal relationship with God. He demonstrated such by surrounding himself with church elders, lower and higher members, and ministers.[18] They prayed over him and counseled him in ways of the Bible so that he could carefully yet boldly apply its teachings to his world. This he did in such a way that it would draw notice, or at the very least shoot down any charges of faith infidelity or atheism that might get tossed his way by an opponent or political dirty trickster as the 1860 election drew near. Lincoln wanted to become the man for the time and for the highest job in the land. Little did he, or anyone else, know that he would soon become regarded by most Americans as this nation's savior.

CB ℰ⊃

Membership in the club of presidents not known for their church attendance, and yet open about staking the high ground on matters such as morals, conscience, and biblical principles, has never been limited to Abraham Lincoln. Dwight Eisenhower and Ronald Reagan—both Republicans who regarded their respective eras' fight against Communism as a matter of morality as much as it was political—were not regular church-goers. Ditto for Donald Trump. But it is incorrect to label Trump as apathetic to religion and devoid of an appreciation and love for the teachings of Christ, just because he doesn't speak in tongues or memorize scriptural passages (as far as we know). A perceived lack of piety doesn't make him an atheist or agnostic.

Donald's mother Mary Anne declared her commitment to the spiritual upbringing of her children when she said, "I tried to get it into their heads that they had to believe. Whether it shows or not, it's in there because I put it there."[19]

Other than Mary Anne, Trump's wife Melania, or any of his three adult children, the one person who knows the president's spiritual walk better than anybody else is Rev. Paula White, pastor of New Destiny Christian Center in Apopka, Florida, and chairwoman of Trump's evangelical advisory board. At Trump's presidential inauguration on January 21, 2017, she became the first female clergyperson to speak at such an event. White's detractors point to her belief in the "prosperity gospel" as a sign that she wasn't an authentic Christian. Perhaps, the naysayers say, White was drawn to Trump because of his billions on paper, which in turn might have raised doubt about Trump's own authenticity when it came to religious matters. White is not shy about sticking up for Trump and his embrace of Christianity, the cynics be, well, darned.

As quoted in *The Faith of Donald J. Trump*, by David Brody and Scott Lamb:

"The man that I know is a believer, a Christian, and a man that's hungry for God," White said, even if "he doesn't know our 'Christianese' and perhaps our language that we know in the Christian world." As for the spiritual critics lined up at his door, White asked a very simple question: "If we just want to hold Mr. Trump to saying every day . . . he's going to be just spot on with God, well then I'd say, 'Are you?' No! None of us are. [The Apostle] Paul wasn't. The only one that was, was Jesus Christ."[20]

Like Lincoln about 150 years before him, Trump surrounded himself with Christian and evangelical leaders, although he started doing this years before he announced his presidential run in 2015. Still, without the Christian evangelical voter base behind him, he didn't stand a chance of winning in 2016. Evangelical leaders not already aligned with Trump the man weren't going to hand Trump the candidate their support and endorsements unless he came to them, which he did on September 29, 2016, in a private meeting at Trump Tower. There he gathered with a group of religious leaders that included Christian evangelicals and Catholics. Robert Jeffress, senior pastor of First Baptist Church in Dallas, mediated the meeting. "Many in that group were Never Trumpers, and you could tell they came ready to give him a piece of their mind that they probably couldn't afford to lose," Jeffress said later. "When he walked into the room, and I introduced them, he listened to them, he delayed his departure, and by the end of the meeting he had them eating out of the palm of his hand."[21]

Rev. Paula White, self-professed as having risen out of "trailer trash," wasn't among those Christian evangelical leaders who needed to be won over in 2016. She had already been there for him for more than ten years, since the first time he contacted her by phone after he saw her preach on TV in 2002.[22]

"Way before his run for the presidency, way before involvement in the (Republican) party, way before becoming a politician—he was a man seeking God," White said. "A man who was spiritually hungry, watching Christian television and listening to Southern Gospel music. We are this work in progress that is continually growing, as long as our heart is open to God and as long as we are seeking God."[23]

Another televangelist who has befriended Trump and served as a spiritual counselor for many years is Texas-based James Robison, who has said, "God uses imperfect people to accomplish his perfect will. He always has and always will."[24]

We can all probably agree that Donald Trump is less than perfect.

cs so

As was Lincoln's wont, Trump rarely if ever attends church. And while Trump has been neglectful, if not dismissive, of the public side to his faith, Lincoln openly questioned his own beliefs. Abraham spent years of his life doubting God and biblical authority, while self-banished to his own valleys of the shadows of death. These times were characterized by bouts of deep depression. In 1835, one of the darkest periods descended on him, surrounding the death of his fiancée Ann Rutledge. One of Ann's previous beaus, John McNamar, once described her as

> A gentle, amiable maiden, without any of the airs of your city belles, but winsome and comely withal; a blonde in complexion, with golden hair, cherry-red lips, and a bonny blue eye. As to her literary attainments, she undoubtedly was as classic a scholar as Mr. Lincoln.[25]

Historians who have researched and written about Lincoln's relationship with Rutledge have bounced between calling their courtship and engagement genuine or folklore. William Herndon, a law partner to Lincoln as well as one of the president's closest friends, believed Lincoln truly loved Ann. It has long been speculated that Rutledge, and not Mary Todd, remained locked inside Lincoln's heart as his greatest love—albeit a doomed one—until the day he died in 1865.

Lincoln first met Rutledge in 1833 while he was boarding in her father's tavern in New Salem, Illinois. His fondness for her, and hers for him, gradually blossomed, although she was already engaged to McNamar, a prosperous merchant who had departed from New Salem sometime earlier. Ultimately, McNamar would never see Rutledge alive again. Ann pledged her love to Lincoln and agreed to marry him once she got her release from her earlier promise to McNamar. She even told one of her brothers that she was to marry Abe, who was then twenty-five, once he completed his law studies—and once the poverty-ridden Lincoln could afford it.[26]

No happy ending here. Possibly overstressed by two simultaneous engagements, Rutledge fell ill. Her sickness began with a fever that kept worsening, leaving her bedridden for the rest of her short life. In spite of her doctor forbidding visitors, Ann persisted in asking for Lincoln, finally demanding that her family fetch him. When he arrived, he went in to see her, alone. There is no record of their dialogue or of any promises exchanged between them while she lay on her deathbed, but just days later Ann lost consciousness and passed away on August 25, 1835.[27]

Ann's death sent Lincoln into a tailspin. Mental anguish doesn't begin to describe his state of mind and heart. It would be a level of depression that would revisit him years later, when his and Mary Todd's young son Willie passed away from bilious fever, likely typhoid fever linked to pollution in the White House water system.

"He was very much distressed [over Rutledge's death]" said a friend, who Lincoln visited after Ann's passing. "And I was not surprised when it was rumored subsequently that his reason [sanity] was in danger." One of Rutledge's brothers described the effect on Abe's mind as terrible, saying, "He became plunged in despair . . . [and] his extraordinary emotions were regarded as strong evidence of the existence of the tenderest relations between himself and the deceased." Friends feared that Lincoln was on the brink of taking his own life. Some of them essentially staged an intervention to get him to the house of a kind friend of his, Bowlin Greene, who lived in peaceful seclusion among hills about a mile south of town. Greene watched over Abraham for a number of weeks and was eventually able to bring him back to a world of reason, a favor that Lincoln never forgot. Seven years later, when Greene died in 1842, Lincoln was asked by the local Masonic lodge to deliver the funeral address. Lincoln broke down in the middle of it, his voice choked with deep emotion. At one point he stopped for several minutes, searching for the right words, his lips quivering, before walking away, sobbing uncontrollably and finally being driven away in the widow's carriage.[28]

There is a link between Ann Rutledge's death and Lincoln's occasional wrestling matches with his faith. This link is especially evident in a book—by today's standards, it would be more like a booklet or pamphlet—that Lincoln wrote, entitled *Infidelity*. The kind of infidelity Lincoln wrote of was in those days more closely associated with unfaithfulness in the religious sense, not being unfaithful to a spouse. In this book Lincoln poured out not only the sorrow exploding in his soul, but also his intense anger at God. He wrote it between 1835 and 1836, through the fog of his misery. Likely influenced by a group of New Salem citizens, who were enthusiastically liberal on religious issues, and having read C. F. Volney's *Ruins of Empires and the Law of Nature* and Thomas Paine's *Age of Reason*, Lincoln sat down, grabbed pen and paper, and started composing the essay, formulating an argument against Christianity. He explained that the Bible had not been inspired by God, and that Jesus Christ was not the son of God—the unholy conclusions formulated in his distressed mind.

Once Lincoln finished getting all this off his chest, he took his completed manuscript to the village store. His intent was to discuss it with the locals before getting it published and prepared for wide distribution. But, luckily for Lincoln and his future politcial career, the book never made it onto a press. After it was read at the store a lively discussion broke out, and a gentleman named Samuel Hill snatched the manuscript from Abe's hands and tossed it into a burning stove. If the book had not gone up in flames, Lincoln's political future would have.[29]

There is an interesting difference, though, between Lincoln's depressive reaction to the death of Ann Rutledge and his severe sadness following his son Willie's death more than twenty-five years later. That difference evidenced a 180-degree change in Lincoln's spiritual maturity. Where Ann's death had rendered him almost hopelessly embittered against God and scripture, Willie's death, while leaving Lincoln devastated with grief, ramped up his pursuit of religion for solace. The Good Book was Lincoln's first and apparently only desired source of comfort following Willie's funeral, and his penchant for reading it likely came at the expense of whatever intimacy he had left for his wife.

The burning-book episode in the 1830s didn't pour cold water on Lincoln's bold, albeit borderline certifiable, determination to express his misgivings about God, the deity of Jesus Christ, and the Bible's. A friend of Lincoln's worked in the county clerk's office, where several young men were writing and boarding (a readymade audience). This friend stated that Lincoln would show up at the office toting a Bible, from which he would read a chapter and then immediately start picking it apart, like a prosecuting attorney tearing into a witness's testimony. His small audiences at first were tolerant (if not amused) by Lincoln's abrupt contrariness. As the years passed, Lincoln became more discreet, choosing not to subject strangers to his running commentaries. John T. Stuart (Lincoln's first law partner and occasional audience member at Lincoln's fee-free Bible lessons) said, "He was an avowed and open infidel, and sometimes bordered on atheism."[30]

A better word for Lincoln in terms of his personal nature and faith attitude at the time might be "fatalist." That's how Herndon, his long-time law partner, regarded Lincoln's *Infidelity* book. Herndon qualifies it more definitively as a "burst of despair" and not an admission of or adherence to atheism. Take it one step further, and Lincoln's treatment of biblical principles and God Himself—both within the book and during his chapter-by-chapter critiques—are back-handed acknowledgments that God does indeed exist. Even in his despair, Lincoln was acknowledging that God's inspired Word is worthy of commentary, which falls short of denying God's existence. If anything, Herndon bolsters Lincoln's belief in God's sovereignty by writing:

> [Lincoln was] under the idea that God had cursed and crushed him especially. . . . God rolled Mr. Lincoln through his fiery furnace specially— that he might be His instrument in the future. This purifying process gave Mr. Lincoln charity, liberality, kindness, tenderness, a sublime faith, if you please, in the purposes and ends of his Maker. Mr. Lincoln, as he has often told the world, had faith in the People and God; he has told you, the People, that Providence rules the universe of matter and substance, mind, and spirit.[31]

Perhaps no fuller measure of his charity, kindness, and sublime faith— to choose three of Herndon's apt descriptions of Lincoln—was shown in his deeply moralistic stance regarding slavery and the unfortunate plight of the black man in America.

> Although Lincoln's views of the Negro were not without imperfections, he was far ahead of most of his fellow white Americans of the time. . . . The Negro loved Lincoln first and longest and possesses him like no other American. The Negro's feeling about Lincoln has many roots and takes many forms—hero worship, father figure, messianic deliverer—but whatever its basis it convinced them, for the first time, that they had a stake in America.[32]

With the Civil War still raging in 1864, a prominent group of three black Baltimore pastors and a fourth man presented Lincoln with a Bible with the inscription, "To Abraham Lincoln, President of the United States, the Friend of Universal Freedom, from the Loyal Colored People of Baltimore, as a token of respect and Gratitude, Baltimore, 4th July 1864." In a separate address, the Reverend S. W. Chase said,

> Mr. President: The loyal colored people of Baltimore have entrusted us with authority to present this Bible as a testimonial of their appreciation of your humane conduct towards the people of our race. . . . We come to present to you this copy of the Holy Scriptures, as a token of respect for your active participation in the furtherance of the cause of the emancipation of our race. This great event will be a matter of history.[33]

In his second inaugural address, in 1865, Lincoln spoke of American slavery as "one of those offenses," which God had allowed to happen, but which he now had willed to remove from the American landscape through a terrible war pitting North against South. In his speech the president made reference to "those divine attributes which the believers in a living God always ascribe." Here's more of Lincoln's faith-based inauguration speech, spoken by a man in submission to God in his head and in his heart, if not always in his actions:

> Fondly do we hope—fervently do we pray—that this mighty scourge of war may speedily pass away. Yet, if God wills that it continue until all the wealth piled by the bondsman's two hundred and fifty years of unrequited toil shall be sunk, and until every drop of blood drawn with the lash shall be paid by another drawn with the sword, as was said three thousand years ago, so still it must be said, "The judgments of the Lord are true and righteous altogether."

Soon after giving that address, Lincoln wrote to a friend that he believed this speech would perhaps "wear" better than anything he had ever produced before, even if it wouldn't be popular among citizens until sometime later. "Men are not flattered by being shown that there has been a difference of purpose between the Almighty and them," he continued to his friend. "To deny it, however, in this case, is to deny that there is a God governing the world. It is a truth which needed to be told."[34]

There were other instances when Lincoln openly spoke of how God worked in his life as well as the lives of others. Sometimes he shared these in a generic sense or sometimes he outlined them in the official speeches he gave on numerous occasions. In a letter dated July 4, 1842, Lincoln wrote to his good friend Joshua Speed. Lincoln speaks fondly of Joshua and gently reminds him, not in a bragging manner, of the fact that Lincoln had played a part in bringing together Speed and his wife Fanny, an event that Lincoln says leaves "no doubt He [God] had fore-ordained. Whatever he designs, he will do for me yet. 'Stand still and see the salvation of the Lord' is my text just now."[35]

In another letter, this one written in September 1864 to a woman named Eliza Gurney, Lincoln spoke about how man must trust that God's purposes are perfect, even when we don't perceive them as such in the present. By now well into his fifties, Lincoln was routinely extolling God's perfect virtues and his own submission to His rules, despite his lack of church attendance or lack of devotion to the mannerisms and practices routinely expected of Christians by other Christians. Lincoln wrote to Gurney,

> The purposes of the Almighty are perfect, and must prevail, though we erring mortals may fail to accurately perceive them in advance. We hoped for a happy termination of this terrible war long before this, but God knows best, and he has ruled otherwise. . . . We must work earnestly in

the best light He gives us, trusting that so working still conduces to the great ends He ordains.[36]

Yes, Lincoln faithfully read the Bible (a grand idea, especially during the horrific Civil War), regarding it as a divine source which he interpreted as touting the doctrine of necessity. This religious philosophy aligned with Lincoln's own belief that an individual's actions are predetermined in accordance with the wishes of a Higher Power.[37] In his 1997 abstract entitled "Abraham Lincoln and the Doctrine of Necessity," Allen C. Guelzo of Gettysburg College reinforces the notion that Lincoln was indeed a "fatalist"—that he had been one his entire life—citing a conversation between Lincoln and Isaac Arnold, an Illinois congressional ally, as well as a remembrance by Henry Clay Whitney, one of Lincoln's Springfield, Illinois law clerks. In historical documents Whitney is found to have said that Lincoln "believed . . . that the universe is governed by one uniform, unbroken, primordial law." That, according to Guelzo, was further echoed by Herndon, who stated that the sixteenth president "believed in predestination, foreordination, that all things were fixed, doomed one way or the other, from which there was no appeal." This belief was affirmed by Mary Todd Lincoln, who as quoted previously, observed that her husband was guided by the conviction that "what is to be will be, and no cares of ours can arrest . . . the decree."[38]

"Fatalist" is one word often used to describe Lincoln's faith core. Another is "deist," which Herndon used. He opined that while some cynics believed Lincoln had no religion, Herndon was sure that Lincoln did indeed practice a religion, and that it was his own.

> I have said for more than twenty years that Mr. Lincoln was a thoroughly religious man, a man of exalted notions of right, justice, duty, etc., etc. Lincoln's religion was of the grandest and noblest type, kind. . . . Lincoln was a strong believer in an overruling Providence, no man more so. He had a grand belief here.[39]

As a fatalist, history shows that Lincoln kept fast company. Christopher Columbus (whose first name meant "Christ Bearer"), George Washington, and Martin Luther King Jr. firmly shared Lincoln's belief that their lives had been actively shaped by a higher power so as to serve a higher purpose. (Incidentally these four men are also the only ones with American holidays named in honor of them.) In his book *God's Hand on America: Divine Providence in the Modern Era,* Michael Medved points out:

Washington developed a similar sense of his own predestined role in a grand plan of cosmic significance. As a twenty-three-year-old lieutenant colonel in the Virginia militia, he emerged unscathed from the first major battle of the French and Indian War, in which nearly all his fellow officers had been killed or wounded.

In Lincoln's case, a childhood of mournful, impoverished obscurity unfolded together with an instinctive expectation that he would play a significant part in the development of the young nation. As president, he repeatedly described himself as "an humble instrument in the hands of the Almighty."[40]

That doesn't sound like someone who fancied himself an atheist, but it does sound like a man sold out to God and the destiny God had for him.

ဆၽ

As president, especially one leading a nation at war with itself, Lincoln found comfort in his biblical interpretation of the doctrine of necessity. Much like Lincoln, Donald Trump also discovered that once he became president, he, too, needed to be on the right side of a power much higher than his own. "I've always felt the need to pray," Trump said, "so I would say that the office is so powerful that you need God even more . . . there's almost not a decision that you make when you're sitting in this position that isn't a really life-altering position. So God comes into it even more so."[41]

Mike Huckabee, a two-time presidential candidate and former Southern Baptist pastor, insists he sees sincerity in Trump's proclamation of a prayerful life in a political world where sincerity and authenticity is on life support. Mindful of Trump's occasional bouts with crassness and moral missteps, Huckabee has said that Trump has a "deep, abiding respect, not just for God, but for all people who truly follow God. I think he's intrigued by it. I think it almost is something that he just finds amazing and fascinating. He has real respect for people of faith."[42]

Pope Francis, the worldwide leader of the Catholic Church, wasn't buying it. In 2016, at the same time that Trump was accusing fellow Republican presidential candidate Ted Cruz of telling lies (although without questioning Cruz's Christianity), Pope Francis was disputing Trump's profession of faith: "A person who thinks only about building walls, wherever they may be, and not building bridges, is not a Christian."

Trump's response:

For a religious leader to question a person's faith is disgraceful. I am proud to be a Christian, and as president I will not allow Christianity to be consistently attacked and weakened, unlike what is happening now, with our current president [Barack Obama]. No leader, especially a religious leader, should have the right to question another man's religion or faith.[43]

Long before he announced his candicacy for the presidency in 2015, Trump had already made connections with leaders in the Christian community such as Rev. Paula White, more than a decade earlier. Within several years he was making more new friends in the world of evangelicalism, such as Ralph Reed, who was the first executive director of the Christian Coalition in the early 1990s and a longtime political consultant and lobbyist. With Reed, Trump shared conversations on topics such as the Christian faith worldview and values. Trump then met Huckabee through their frequent interactions at the Fox News studios in New York. And in November 2013, Donald and Melania attended the ninety-fifth birthday celebration for Billy Graham, which was an invitation-only event.

A major part of Trump's political agenda was to, in his words, "protect Christianity. And I can say that. I don't have to be politically correct." Trump caught the attention of evangelicals such as Reed by stating his belief that Christianity is under siege . . . and sticking to it. After Trump secured the Republican nomination for president in 2016, Reed took another look at where Trump stood on the issues most embraced by Christians and liked what he saw, his stamp of approval went a long way in influencing evangelical leaders across America. "He was pro-life," Reed said of Trump. He went on to say,

> [Trump] had just released his list of twenty-one judges for the Supreme Court; he was pro–traditional marriage; he was pro-Israel; he was against the Iran nuclear deal; he was for defunding Planned Parenthood. He was solid on every key issue that we cared about. And Trump was the only candidate who made one of the central promises of his campaign—at least to social conservatives—the repealing of the Johnson Amendment [a provision added to the U.S. tax code in 1954 that disallowed 501(c)(3) nonprofit entities from endorsing or opposing political candidates] and the restoring of First Amendment rights to churches and ministries.[44]

Some viewed this as Trump pandering to Reed and his evangelical teammates, but Reed shot down that idea. By then he had known Trump for more than six years and he shared with the New York billionaire what Reed described as "very heartfelt and transparent conversations that were not in the contest of a candidacy. . . . I didn't flatter him. I gave him the best unvarnished understanding of my views."

Trump didn't begin seeking out Christian leaders and evangelicals right after announcing his candidacy in 2015; he had already established relationships with them, in some cases for more than a decade. To this day he remains committed to his vast network of Christian contacts, often welcoming them into his closer circle. Not all of them are Republicans; Bishop Wayne Jackson, for example, is a lifelong Democrat and Detroit-based, African-American leader of Great Faith Ministries. When Jackson invited both Trump and Democrat nominee Hillary Clinton to speak to his congregation in 2016, Trump accepted immediately; Clinton turned it down. On the day Trump showed up to speak, a bevy of protestors greeted his arrival outside, but "When he got out of the SUV, the Spirit of the Lord told me that's the next president of the United States," Jackson said of Trump.[45]

One of the speakers at the 2016 Republican National Convention was Darrell Scott, an African-American pastor from Cleveland and devoted Trump supporter, even amid rising racial tensions across America, following the shooting of five Dallas policemen by a gunman who had been on the prowl for white people. While much of the media chose to stir up charges of racism against Trump, Scott, accompanied by his wife Belinda, boldly went to the convention in support of Trump, not only as a political figure but also as a brother in Christ. The Scotts knew Trump him well by then; they had already been acquainted with him for five years, since 2011.

"He really is pursuing a deeper spiritual life. I can sense it," Belinda Scott said. "My prayer for Mr. Trump is that he will be more sensitive to God than he ever has before . . . something is going on." Added Darrell Scott: "He's the first one to admit, 'I'm flawed. I'm not perfect. I need to do better. I need to be better.'"[46]

Trump's associations with men and women in Christian ministry are many. They have been years in the making, and they are evidence of his own walk with God and a strong faith that is as much about the company you keep as what you say and do. Others who know him well and attest to his sincerity of faith include Dallas evangelist Lance Wallnau, who claims he heard from the Lord that the forty-fifth president would be an Isaiah 45 president, which he interpreted to mean Donald Trump. Wallnau said that Trump would be a "wrecking ball to the spirit of political correctness," much in the spirit of Cyrus depicted in chapter 45 of Isaiah in the Old Testament.[47] While not openly endorsing Trump for president, Franklin Graham, Billy Graham's evangelistic son, nonetheless said in an interview with the Religion News Service, "I think maybe God has allowed Donald Trump to win this election to protect the nation for the next few years by giving maybe an opportunity to have some good judges."[48]

In the 2016 election, Trump won a decisive Electoral College victory, despite Hillary Clinton's winning the popular vote by a margin of 2.9 million votes. Many Christians saw this as a sign of God's providence. His presidency has done more to advance the Christian Right cause than simply protecting the makeup of federal courts. One of the hallmarks of his presidency has been the White House access he has afforded evangelicals, signaling his commitment to move pro-life efforts forward in spite of an uphill battle. Further, his executive order took the teeth out of the Johnson Amendment. Trump's official direction to the Department of the Treasury was to not take "any adverse action against" clergy members, churches, or other faith-based organizations "on the basis that such individual organization speaks or has spoken about moral or political issues from a religious perspective." At the time of the executive order, though, it was still left to Congress to complete the process by repealing the Johnson Amendment, and with a Democratic-controlled House of Representatives as of 2020, that prospect appeared unlikely.[49]

Election Day 2016 dawned with many Trump supporters seriously concerned about late polls showing Clinton several percentage points ahead of Trump. His election was in doubt. Even Trump, ever confident about his chances of victory (at least publicly), wasn't sure what to expect. "I don't know, Jerry, these exit polls look bad," Trump reportedly said in an election night phone call with Jerry Falwell Jr., president of Liberty University, an evangelical liberal arts institution in Lynchburg, Virginia. Trump had spoken there earlier in the year, showcasing his Christian beliefs with enthusiasm, and now he needed some support in return from Falwell.

"No, no, no, you got it," Falwell told Trump. "I just have a feeling. You're going to win it. I know it. Too much has happened that's been miraculous this year for it not to be of God. You're going to win." Once it became clear several hours later, with one key battleground state after another turning to Trump, that he was headed to victory, Trump again spoke to Falwell, with buoyancy, saying, "Jerry, we're about to win. They're about to announce that we're going to win Pennsylvania."

"That's the game," Falwell responded.

"Yup, that'll be the game," Trump said.[50]

A year later, after being inaugurated in January 2017, Trump returned to Liberty University to give a graduation address to more than fifty thousand in attendance. It was a captive, faith-based audience, of course, that enthusiastically welcomed Trump "home."

It's been a little over a year since I've spoken on your beautiful campus and so much has changed. Right here, the class of 2017, dressed in cap and gown, graduating to a totally brilliant future. And here I am standing before you as president of the United States. So I'm guessing there are some people here today who thought that either one of those things, either one, would really require major help from God. Do we agree? And we got it.[51]

CHAPTER 3

Born to Fight

— ❧ —

He was tough and tall in a gangly, awkward sort of way. Years of axe-wielding and farming had made him strong. And tales of his bounding into wrestling matches and emerging victorious were brought to life in Henry Fonda's starring portrayal in the 1939 film *Young Mr. Lincoln*.

As a teacher, I taught about Abraham Lincoln as a rough and ready pioneer on the still-somewhat-wild Illinois frontier, a man who grew up to be the greatest U.S. president.

Of course, I also knew Lincoln as the commander-in-chief tasked with overseeing the Union side in the War Between the States. That said, I remained quite ignorant of the extent of his early battles, physical and otherwise. It wasn't until much later in my life that I came to realize the horrific toll of the Civil War and Lincoln's part in it.

Abraham Lincoln pushed—undaunted and uncompromising—toward an all-or-none conclusion: No peace without victory, and no victory without a vanquished enemy! His staunch position against compromise (or working across the aisle) deepened the scars and sharpened the pain from which the countryside and her citizens were left reeling. Talk about a fighter!

Then there's Donald Trump. From my youth I knew what had been plastered in the media about his larger-than-life persona, mostly as a New York City-based developer with grandiose plans linked to gorgeous high-rises and spectacular venues. My view of him, however, was more along the lines of "What outrageous fight is he taking on now?" He seemed to have no qualms about saying whatever was in his head about anyone or anything, and at any time.

His NBC TV reality show, *The Apprentice*, must have been the perfect outlet for his over-the-top personality—an aggressive boss in the face of conflict, with his just plain harsh "You're fired!"

During the 2016 presidential campaign, we watched Trump take down "CNN" in a doctored video from his WWE days. The late eighties brought Mike Tyson and Donald Trump together in the form of big promotion, hype, and a lot of controversy. It was in 1988 that Tyson hired Trump to be his chief strategist and adviser, so early in his career Trump had close ties to the fight industry. Some of it probably rubbed off on him.

CB ED

You don't win a four-year, all-expenses-paid stay at the luxurious White House by going at life (and political opponents) wearing white gloves. Campaigning for the office of the U.S. presidency can be a dirt-thrown slog through a gauntlet of assorted enemy troops, among them stop-at-nothing political opponents and a press that is eager to take you down.

Requirements for such a calling include nerves of titanium, the hide of a Little League umpire made thick by parental dissent, the oratorical skills of a Winston Churchill, the courage of a standup comedian performing before a packed house of strangers, the resiliency of a Navy SEAL in training, and the cunning and pugilistic skills of a Muhammad Ali.

Abraham Lincoln and Donald Trump fought the good fight; Trump still does. In their own personally modified ways, they did it better than any of their respective cast of rivals—a worthy comparison, even if separated by 150 years. A hound dog media was hard at work in the Lincoln years, just as it later would be for Trump. And trying to hold together a bitterly divisive nation? Both Lincoln and Trump have been there, although the former had it in spades—the Civil War, remember?

Donald Trump craves a good fight. He's never shy about mixing it up with political, media, or business opponents. He doesn't need a bar (he doesn't even drink), but he savors a good brawl, and battleground states are his forte. Just tell him it's impossible, and he already has a plan to get it done. During a March 2020 presidential campaign appearance at a Fox News town hall in Scranton, Pennsylvania, Trump was asked by an audience member about his controversial rhetoric. He responded with fighting words.

> I wouldn't be sitting here (as president) if I had turned the other cheek. When they hit us, we have to hit back; I feel that. We get hit so hard, and

we have a media that I'd say, to a large extent, is part of the Democratic Party, it really is. It's terrible. It's unfair. I call it "fake news" and people are using that all over the world now. That's the way it is. . . . If we don't fight back, you won't be a fan of mine for very long.[1]

Those who knew Trump when he was a kid might have seen this coming. He was a young boy, a second grader, sometimes known as "Donnie," when he threw a punch at a music teacher, giving the man a black eye. "I punched my music teacher because I didn't think he knew anything about music, and I almost got expelled," Trump later bragged.[2]

The fight goes on decades later. Welcome to Donald Trump's world. "He's a complicated man who is not prone to introspection, nostalgia, or patience," news commentator Bill O'Reilly wrote in his 2019 book *The United States of Trump: How the President Really Sees America*.[3]

Six years after the elementary school episode, Fred Trump moved his thirteen-year-old son out of school and enrolled him at New York Military Academy in Cornwall, New York, an institution founded in 1889 and situated about fifty miles north of the city. What finally pushed Fred to send his son upstate was that Donald, by then a young teen, would sneak away from the family's middle-class home in Jamaica, Queens to accompany buddies to a guys' day out in the Times Square area of Manhattan. Somewhere along the way, Donald got his hands on switchblade knives that he brought home. Eventually his mom and dad discovered the knives. Fred expected better from his five children, but his long hours working at job sites kept him away from home much of the time, hindering his ability to properly discipline the energetic and sometimes unruly and obstinate Donnie. Fred felt he needed to provide that discipline via surrogate. So, military school it was.

Young Donald was in eighth grade at the time, and his dad believed the change to a more disciplined environment would do his son good. It did, putting young Trump in a structured, albeit harsh setting where he could channel his aggression into achievement and eventually graduate in 1964 with the rank of cadet captain. A National Public Radio (NPR) report republished by O'Reilly in *The United States of Trump* sheds more light on the strict experience:

> Back in Trump's day, cadets would wake up near the crack of dawn, hurry into uniforms, and march in formation to breakfast. First-year cadets had to eat their meals squared-off—lifting their forks in a right angle into their mouths. And after breakfast they'd scurry back to clean their rooms for inspection.[4]

Trump's competitive persona had begun with his fascination with brick and mortar. From an early age, he would tag along with his father to construction sites, where the elder Trump was both boss and handyman, getting down and dirty with his men working construction, demonstrating a 1950s version of servant-leadership. Of the five Trump children, Donnie was the only one to show a strong interest in following in his father's footsteps in the construction business. It fueled his competitive fires from an early age with the desire to build things bigger and better than anyone else.

One day when Donald was eight years old—around the same time he was making his music teacher a knuckle sandwich—he grabbed his younger brother Robert's toy blocks and constructed a giant skyscraper out of them, gluing them together and never returning them. This was Donnie's way of constructing a fantasy that would guide his life for the next fifty-plus years—ultimately changing Manhattan's skyline in the process.[5]

To borrow a pet phrase from O'Reilly—one of the few in the media to make a friendly connection to Trump—"bold and fresh" is an accurate depiction of Trump. In his own words, he might say, "I did, and do, things my way." During precious free time away from the rigors of academic studies and military drills at the academy, Trump loved to hang out in his dorm room and "hit the beach." He would insert an ultraviolet light bulb into the ceiling light fixture, then lie down on his bunk and kick back, pretending he was soaking up Florida sunshine. Author Gwenda Blair writes,

> Dropping the usual Trump family reticence about their wealth, [Donald] pegged his father's worth at $30 million and bragged that the number doubled every year. "Donald had a sense of how he wanted to be viewed," (senior-year roommate David Smith) said. "He really wanted to be a success. He was already focused on the future, thinking long-term more than present. He used to talk about his dad's business, how he would use him as a role model but go one step further."[6]

Fred Trump was a mentor as much as a father figure to Donald, and Donald himself was an eager—how else can you say it?—apprentice. There was no noticeable tension or contention between the two, but it was evident that Donald was not reluctant about standing up to his old man. By his late teens, Donald refusing to be intimidated by Fred. All the while, he was cultivating skills that would serve him well in the business world; the world of reality-TV entertainment (*The Apprentice* ran for eleven seasons on NBC); and, finally, the cutthroat, life-on-the-edge world of politics—presidential politics. Note that Trump was the first person ever elected U.S. president without having previously served in any elected office or the military.

Michael D'Antonio, author of *Never Enough*, described Donald Trump's relationship with his dad by saying, "Learning from what he saw, Donald resolved to stand up to anyone who challenged him, including his father. Years later, he would say, 'I used to fight back all the time. My father was one tough son of a gun.' However, he added, 'My father respects me because I stood up to him.'"[7]

It wasn't just Manhattan skyscrapers that rocket-fueled Trump's imagination, pumped helium into his oversized ego, and positioned him in full-fight mode. His bigger and better ethos could manifest itself in other ways, in a manner keeping with what he did best—develop real estate. He wanted to be famous, and we know how that worked out. His name is literally stamped in twenty-foot letters on more than one big-city skyscraper.

Trump undertook his first major construction project, on his own and out from under Fred's wings, in his mid-twenties. It started out in his head as ostentatious plans for a 30,000-unit apartment complex, spread over two properties in Manhattan. If successfully completed, it would be the world's largest such apartment project, containing more units than all of the projects his father's Trump Organization had built over the years. It would be one confident young man's hubris executed to the nth degree.

Trump had procured an option on the old Penn Central railyards, and that's where he would build. Before breaking ground, though, he needed the two sites, one at 60th Street and the other at 34th Street, to be rezoned from industrial to residential. He also needed to persuade banks to help finance the massive construction. Before he could plow his way through either of those obstacles, though, he would need to come up with a design for the complex project that conformed to codes. At times it seemed he would've had better luck building an escalator worthy of replacing Jack's beanstalk.

Trump's pie-in-the-sky plan called for 20,000 units to be built at the 60th Street yards and another 10,000 at 34th Street, with no railroads running beneath them. There were other hurdles to negotiate as well. First, the only way to pay for basic (yet exorbitant) infrastructure items such as streets, sewers, and waterlines would be to build thousands more units than community residents and leaders would be amenable to. Second, without community support, the odds of getting the zoning change were essentially nil. Undeterred, Trump hired one of the city's most prestigious architectural firms to design the companion complexes, even with financing issues threatening to put a halt to his plans. There wasn't much money available to invest in such a gargantuan endeavor, especially one conceived by a relative neophyte, new to how the game was played in Manhattan. In terms of construction costs, the city and the State of New York were close to broke. Plus, federal housing subsidies that had once been the financial lifeblood for Fred Trump's ventures a generation earlier had dried up due to cutbacks from the Nixon administration.[8]

Trump and his entourage of architects, attorneys, and consultants—a publicity manager, too—stayed in formation and continued to march through a phalanx of countless meetings, phone calls, letters, naysayers, and communities in opposition. But there was only so much they could do. Gradually, Trump had to scale down his construction plans in order to keep cracking open doors. His architects' renderings got down to 5,000 units—significantly less than the original 30,000, yet that was still too many for local community approval, and the meetings between Trump and the community board were growing ever more antagonistic.

At times, Fred Trump attended the community meetings, sitting in the back of the auditorium while watching his son give a buoyant presentation complete with colorful slides of parks and trees fronting shadowy groups of yet-to-be-built buildings. Donald's presentation skills became more polished with each occurrence.[9]

Still, Trump's fresh tactics were going nowhere. He needed a viable Plan B for the development of the railyards to get some sort of return on his investment. Almost magically, Plan B materialized in the form of the city's desire to build a new convention center to replace a 1950s facility that now, in the 1970s, was obsolete. City planners, with Mayor Abe (short for Abraham) Beame's approval, had chosen a 44th Street site near Times Square. The city's blueprint showed a modern convention center with a projected $231 million price tag that featured a bold, futuristic design. Once completed, the space-age facility would be supported by a spaceport platform, extending out hundreds of feet over the Hudson River.

Recognizing opportunity, and using the new connections he had made chasing his 30,000-unit dream, Trump made the paradigm shift. His new dream was a convention center, built on a significantly reduced budget. He knew the 34th Street railyards would easily accommodate his team's own design. No longer would there be a need for annoying zoning alterations. This was adaptability at work. Now Donald had a fight he could win. His design associates told him they could design and build a magnificent two-story, bronze-colored-glass structure at about half the cost of the city's 44th Street plan. The structure would all be on land, and it would feature ample space for trucks to load and unload without causing traffic snarls.

Listening closely to his adviser's input, Trump devised a bold marketing and publicity plan for what he called "The Miracle on 34ᵗʰ Street," in honor of the classic Christmas movie. Soon he was giving pitches and presentations to private audiences of influential community leaders. At one point, however, Beame threw a monkey wrench into Trump's construction plans, switching his support from the 44ᵗʰ Street site, which was at that point being labeled untenable, to an alternate site at Battery Park City. Trump stubbornly pushed ahead on his 34ᵗʰ Street proposal, keenly and aggressively drumming up public support to elevate his conception above Beame's. He got word out through the media that Battery Park City (BPC) was a bad choice; one of his newsworthy press releases called BPC a "rip-off." Further support came from a prominent labor negotiator, who told *The New York Times* that a convention center built in Battery Park City would be like "putting a nightclub in a graveyard."[10]

Trump won the fight! He got his convention center at 34ᵗʰ Street, creating thousands of jobs in the process. Blair put it this way:

> The real "Miracle on 34th Street" was not the actual convention center design that was unveiled that day. It was how Donald Trump had managed to combine his father's political connections, his advisers' collective wisdom, and his own budding development acumen to outmaneuver his competitors.[11]

 C3 80

Trump is far from an undefeated champion in the ring of business, media, and politics, but many of his other skirmishes are worth mentioning.

In the wake of his 34ᵗʰ Street "Miracle," Trump jumped at the chance to pull off another major real estate development coup. This one involved the once preeminent Commodore hotel, boasting two thousand guest rooms. Built in 1919 next to New York City's perpetually busy Grand Terminal, this city landmark was named after legendary railroad magnate Commodore Vanderbilt. For Trump, this job wasn't going to be the construction of something new and shiny from the ground up; this time it would be the restoration of a hotel once teeming with affluent visitors but now falling apart from the inside out. Entire floors had been roped off as unusable. Hookers propositioned clients in the lobby, and ownership was in arrears of $6.6 million in real estate taxes on a hotel losing $1 million a year. Trump acknowledged the unseemly grunginess, but he also saw great opportunity. This time, the obstacles included an estimated purchase price of $10 million, a desperate need for a city-authorized tax abatement, and a remodeling proposition that would possibly require a total gutting of the building. Just for starters.[12]

Again, Trump went to work on multiple levels, whacking his way through miles of red tape and minions of doubting Thomases. He called on and met with architects, city officials, bankers. He even spoke with a member of the renowned Chicago-based Pritzker family, who owned the Hyatt chain of upscale hotels. At the time, none of their hotels were based in New York City, so Trump tried to (and succeeded at) convincing them to buy in to his plans. It was a slew of insurmountable tasks, and it took months of showing off and touting impressive-looking and -sounding plans, cajoling, and arranging ever more meetings. Trump ultimately bullied and wheedled his way through the dustup storms and smoke-filled meeting rooms and restaurants to pull together all the disparate pieces and make it happen. He had rescued the Commodore from either a wrecking ball or oblivion by restoring it and repopulating it—much to the delight of his accountants. In the process, he impressed power brokers from one city borough to the next. Fred's kid had his stuff together.

Fast forward to the mid-1980s, where we find Trump, about to turn forty, in a verbal war with New York City Mayor Ed Koch. For the first time, it's business mixed with real politics as The Donald comes out swinging, blasting city government for its lackluster attempt at renovating Wollman Rink in Central Park. This popular venue was designed to allow skaters to bask in their daily reenactments of Currier & Ives-like scenery, especially around Christmastime.

The rink's renovations, which had begun in 1980, were still dragging on into 1986. It was a classic example of governmental agencies not getting the job done, and Trump took notice. This time his punching bag was the embattled Koch, and the verbal war played out in the city's media. The argument—and the inefficiency of the renovations—quickly ended when Trump agreed to finish the job himself, at no expense to the city. He completed the rink's fixes in three months at a cost to himself that was well below what the city had budgeted. Trump claimed victory, revealed more wasteful spending of taxpayer dollars, and gained the kudos of many in the city.[13]

Note that in his 1987 book *The Art of the Deal* (which spent fifty-two weeks on best seller lists, including *The New York Times*), Trump opens by saying, "I don't do it for the money." That might be laughable to his critics and even many of his supporters, but it has a ring of sincerity to David Brody and Scott Lamb, authors of *The Faith of Donald J. Trump.* They write,

> Though we have avoided playing the part of an armchair psychologist with Donald Trump, several people we interviewed who consider themselves to be friends or on friendly terms with Trump stated their opinion that they don't believe Donald Trump's relationship with money flows from a heart of greed. . . . These off-the-record friendly interviewees sense that Trump's ambition stems from a deep-rooted need to command respect—a basic, simple drive to prove that he is the best.[14]

In all the different ways Donald Trump brags—boil it down, reduce it to lowest terms, expose the foundation—that's it: He wants to be the best!

Trump not only relished such tussles, he feasted on them. Longtime business associate Ned Eichler said this about his occasional golfing rival: "The biggest project, the one with the most apartments, that's what was exciting to him. He thrived on conflict, the bigger the better. He loved it. People like him always do."[15]

As you've probably figured out by now, fighting the good fight can involve not only spoken word and deed, but also a pen that is mightier than a sword. After *The New York Times* ran a review of a book that Trump thought included some "juvenile remarks" about him, he wrote a letter to the *Times* that was later chosen "Best Letter of the Year to the New York Times Book Review" by *New York* magazine.

Trump's scathing yet somewhat amusing retort to the *Times* included digs at both the reviewer, Jeff MacGregor, and the author of the book in question, Mark Singer, a *New Yorker* writer who had once interviewed Trump. Trump recalled that interview in his letter to the editor as a meeting in which "this writer (Singer) was drowning in his own misery." Trump's letter also targeted MacGregor, adding "Jeff MacGregor . . . writes poorly. His painterly turn with nasturtiums sounds like a junior high school yearbook entry. Maybe he and Mark Singer belong together. Some people cast shadows, and other people choose to live in those shadows."[16]

Eighteen Republican candidates filed to run for president in the 2016 election, and Donald Trump's entry into the contest was greeted by the usual cavalcade of guffaws and insults from Democrats and many in the media. But by the time of the 2016 Republican National Convention in Cleveland ended on July 21, Trump was the last candidate standing. Written off by most pundits at the beginning, Trump steadily rose through the ranks of GOP candidates to ultimately take down Texas Senator Ted Cruz, whom he vanquished by a final delegate count of more than three to one.

Along the way, Trump broke many of the unwritten rules of campaign and debate performance, generating record crowds at his rallies and turning televised debates into must-see TV. He also did some poking and bomb lobbing of his own, ridiculing Florida Senator Marco Rubio for being vertically challenged ("Little Marco," the 6-foot-3 Trump kept calling him) and former Hewlett Packard CEO Carly Fiorina for her physical appearance ("Look at the face! Would anyone vote for that?" Trump remarked to a *Rolling Stone* magazine reporter when Fiorina's face popped up on a nearby TV screen). Just when you thought Trump's unpresidential posturing would mean a loss of support, his numbers kept going up.

At one point, the debate turned into a war with sexist overtones between Trump and Fox News moderator Megyn Kelly. This was after Kelly posed a question for Trump that he—and many pundits watching—thought was more accusatory than inquisitive, as Bill O'Reilly would later describe in his book *The United States of Trump*. The next day, Trump, speaking on CNN, took a swipe at Kelly, facetiously saying of Kelly, "You could see she had blood coming out of her eyes, blood coming out of . . . wherever." The reaction across America was swift and condemning. Trump later said he had meant to say "nose" in place of "wherever," the latter an apparent reference to a woman's menstrual cycle.[17] Trump was financing most of his campaign, so he wasn't worried about losing donors. When updated polls came out, he was still well ahead in the Republican field. He was, in a sense, politically bulletproof, and when he went through with his pledge to skip the next Fox News–sponsored debate unless the network removed Kelly as one of the moderators, there was no stopping him, at least in the GOP world.

O'Reilly wrote:

That was a turning point for candidate Trump. He began to understand that his in-your-face presentation was actually inoculating him against bad press and pressure groups. The more outrageous his rhetoric, the firmer his supporters stood by him. Modern politics had never seen anything like this.[18]

Marco Rubio tried these same ultra-honest, slap-in-the-face tactics, but they fell flat. Apparently, only Donald Trump could act like Donald Trump and get away with it.

CB ∞

Once Trump was elected president in November 2016, the hits kept coming. Opponents would take a roundhouse swing and miss, and Trump would bob and weave before throwing a haymaker at his latest opponent's kisser. Here are a few highlights:

- When some National Football League players started following San Francisco 49ers quarterback Colin Kaepernick in kneeling in protest during the pre-game playing of the national anthem, Trump shot down the players' actions, saying, "You have to stand proudly for the national anthem, or you shouldn't be playing, you shouldn't be there. Maybe you shouldn't be in the country." Trump even referred to the activist players as "SOBs" during a speech in Alabama.[19]

- When Special Counsel Robert Mueller ended his twenty-two-month investigation into alleged collusion ties between Russia and Trump regarding the 2016 election, Mueller concluded that there was insufficient evidence to charge Trump with a crime. Trump simply said, "The case is closed! Thank you."[20]

- When House Speaker Nancy Pelosi spearheaded impeachment hearings in 2019 against Trump over the contents of a telephone conversation between him and Ukrainian president Volodymyr Zelensky in July of that year, Trump simply referred to his accusers as the "do-nothing Democrats." While he was leaving the country to fly to London to attend a NATO summit, he tweeted, "Heading to Europe to represent our Country and fight hard for the American People while the Do Nothing Democrats purposely scheduled an Impeachment Hoax hearing on the same date as NATO. Not nice!"[21] House Democrats had a healthy majority to rubber stamp articles of impeachment and send them forward to the Senate. But it would take 67 votes in the Senate to oust Trump and Republicans had the upper hand there. Both sides argued in a Senate trial presided over by Supreme Court Chief Justice John Roberts. Then, acting as jurors, senators voted to acquit Trump by a count of 52-48. Again, Trump had fought and survived, even though the odds against his being found guilty in a fervently partisan Senate had been stacked higher than Trump Tower.

Let's end the Trump segment of this chapter by pretending to be a researcher for the TV game show *Family Feud*. If we asked one hundred people to name one word that best describes Donald Trump. I would guess that *arrogant* would be among the top six or seven answers on the board. Let Trump himself explain why that is and why he believes it's a good thing:

Someone asked me if I thought I was a genius. I decided to say yes. Why not? Try it out. Tell yourself that you are a genius. Right away you will probably wonder why and in what way you are a genius. And right away you will have opened your mind up to wonder—and to asking questions. That's a big first step to thinking like a genius, and it might unlock some of your hidden talents.[22]

If we asked the same question about Abraham Lincoln, chances are no one would use the word *arrogant* to describe him, but they would be wrong. *Arrogant* aptly describes Abe Lincoln—the *real* Abe Lincoln. Just like Trump, other words that could accurately describe Lincoln are *ambitious*, *relentless*, and maybe even *ruthless*.

Fighting the good fight is a common link between Trump and Lincoln. Lincoln brought the fight to courtrooms as a lawyer and he brought it to politics, most conspicuously while serving as U.S. president and commander-in-chief from 1861 until his assassination in April 1865. Honest Abe also had his physicality, oddly dramatic in appearance, to bring to bear in various circumstances, such as:

- occasionally stepping into the ring for wrestling matches.
- writing a fictitious account that poked R-rated fun at the Grigsby family (whose son Aaron had been married to Abe's late sister, Sarah) after the Grigsbys had snubbed the Lincolns by not inviting them to the simultaneous weddings of two other sons.
- knocking down another Grigsby son, Billy, in an ensuing scuffle.
- leaving the stage where he was giving a speech to go into the crowd and break up a fight, grabbing the assailant by the neck and the seat of his trousers and throwing him twelve feet through the air, according to a witness's account.

Lincoln was tall and gangly, but he was uncommonly strong. Years of working for his dad and swinging his trusty axe tens of thousands of times had turned the Ichabod Crane-like Lincoln into a most formidable foe—if anyone unwisely chose to make him their foe. One of Lincoln's favorite hustles was challenging any and all comers to see who could hold his seven-pound axe by the tip of the handle, using just three fingers. The goal was to keep the axe perfectly straight out to the side, horizontal to the ground, the longest without wavering. It was no contest. Lincoln's challengers would typically falter within seconds, while he himself could go on for several minutes, keeping the axe as still as a statue. Was it a parlor trick? Or was it a "brag" that fed Abe's ego quietly, but regularly throughout his life, even into his presidency? (More than one young soldier found himself on the losing end of this contest.) Pierce the humble façade, slough off the presidential demeanor, reveal the inner workings of the ambitious "engine that knew no rest,"[23] and that's what Abe wanted—to be the best!

Switching topics from brawn to brains, with some cunning and guile mixed in, Lincoln was much more than just a humble, backwoods country lawyer prior to becoming president. Many superficial historical accounts paint Lincoln as a man of modesty, simple tastes, and a certain sense of almost regal-like gentility, when actually he had other sides to his personality. A description of his true persona merits being fleshed out, as indicated by the following snippets of his history. If some or much of what follows sounds analogous to Trump, it's no accident:

In 1846 Lincoln was elected to represent Illinois's 7th Congressional District in the U.S. House of Representatives as a member of the Whig Party. At that time the Whigs had an established policy whereby each nominee would serve one two-year term before stepping aside to give someone else a chance. Such a rotating system was accompanied by a pledge of united support, but on the flip side it gave each individual Congressman little time to do anything of note or leave a lasting impression. As pointed out by author Doris Kearns Goodwin in her book *Leadership in Turbulent Times*, "Given this single-term system, the Congress of the 1840s seemed an unlikely place to further the fierce aspirations of a man like Abraham Lincoln, thought by one friend to be 'as ambitious of earthly honors as any man of his time' and by another as 'the most ambitious man in the world.'" Indeed, less than a month after making his way to Washington, DC, the newly inducted congressman quickly picked a fight of the highest order by questioning the legitimacy of the just-completed Mexican-American War. Lincoln accused President James K. Polk of purposely provoking Mexico to war.[24]

There were times when Lincoln spoke of aspirations beyond Congress or even the White House, beginning with the supposition that "many great and good men" were content with "nothing beyond a seat in Congress, a gubernatorial or a presidential chair," as stated in David Herbert Donald's *Lincoln*. Donald continues,

> But, he added, in a rare moment of self-revelation, "such belong not to the family of the lion, or the tribe of the eagle." Such honors were not enough for men of ambition and talents. These routine offices would not satisfy "an Alexander, a Caesar, or a Napoleon," from whom the greatest danger to popular government must be expected. "Towering genius disdains a

beaten path," Lincoln reminded his audience. "It seeks regions hitherto unexplored. . . . It thirsts and burns for distinction; and, if possible, it will have it." . . . Few could have realized that he was unconsciously describing himself. His ambition was no secret.[25]

And he was more than ready to unlock his "hidden talents."

Lincoln was not deterred by his failures, and he had plenty of them. "Without question, Abraham Lincoln 'thirsted' and 'burned' for distinction," author Donald T. Phillips reported in his book *Lincoln on Leadership.*

> Yet, even though he often became depressed at failures and setbacks, Lincoln developed the enviable ability to persevere and learn from his failures. Later in life he turned defeat into eventual victory. No endeavor became a hindrance to his overarching goal to achieve. In fact, everything—failures and successes—became stepping-stones to the presidency. In a way, his disappointments in life inoculated him against the coming storm his presidency would bring. After his disappointing defeat for the Senate seat won by Stephen A. Douglas in 1858, Lincoln wrote, "The fight must go on. The cause of civil liberty must not be surrendered at the end of one or even one hundred defeats."[26]

Days after he turned twenty-three, Lincoln announced to the world— or at least to anyone in his parcel of Illinois who happened to be paying attention—that he was entering the political fray. In those days Lincoln was living in New Salem and working as a clerk in a small country store. Following the custom of the times, Lincoln penned a letter to declare his candidacy for public office. To the fine people of Sangamo County, and dated March 23, 1832, Lincoln wrote, "Every man is said to have his peculiar ambition. Whether it be true or not, I can say for one that I have no other so great as that of being truly esteemed of my fellow men by rendering myself worthy of their esteem." It was a bold move by a young man with less than a year of formal schooling under his belt and zero experience with the workings of government. But this was a sign of his supreme self-confidence; Lincoln believed he was at least the equal of any other man in his voting district. On August 6 of that year, Lincoln lost the race for the Illinois House of Representatives, but he was already on his way to greater things. Lincoln confessed once to his best friend Joshua Speed that he wanted to "link his name with something that would redound to the interest of his fellow man."[27] And later in his career, Lincoln envied his long-time nemesis Stephen Douglas's "splendid success," saying, "His [Douglas's] name fills the nation."[28] Lincoln could have no idea that by the end of the century, more than 228 counties, towns, and cities in the nation would bear the name Lincoln! Even in his teens, Lincoln was thinking about leaving his mark on the world. He wrote this little gem of a poem in his boyhood sum book: "Abraham Lincoln is my name, And with my pen I wrote the same. I wrote in both haste and speed, and left it here for fools to read."[29]

Lincoln was a precocious child, with an obstinate streak. In that sense Lincoln was a lot like Trump would be a century and a half later, except Lincoln did not have military school available to shake the obstinance from his system. Instead, the rigors of home life did it for him. "Sometimes Abe was a little rude," his cousin, Dennis Hanks—ten years Abe's senior—would later write to Lincoln's law associate and biographer William Herndon. Hanks lived with the Thomas Lincoln family for a number of years while Abe was growing up, long enough to get to know and become close to his cousin. "When strangers would ride along and up to his father's fence, Abe always, through pride and to tease his father, would be sure to ask the stranger the first question, for which his father would sometimes knock him a rod. Abe was a rude and forward boy."[30] Abe was a farm kid; no military school could compare to the structure and harsh discipline of the dawn-to-dusk taskmaster of hardscrabble frontier farm life. Not a fan of physical work, Abe did it and was exceptional at it, but he never gave it much credit. Lincoln offered little biographical insight into his upbringing when he wrote to newspaperman J. W. Fell in December of 1859: "I was raised to farm work, which I continued til I was twenty-two."[31] Short and sweet. Nothing like a farm to put starch in your jeans!

Mocking Lincoln or otherwise poking fun at him was never a good idea. Such was the case with one Jesse Thomas, a Democrat, whose party affiliation alone was enough to arouse Lincoln's ire—making him fighting mad. The story is that Thomas had "indulged in some fun" at Lincoln's expense, and Lincoln was more than game to offer a counterpunch. Donald Trump would have been proud. In response to Thomas's teasing, Lincoln tapped into his impressive theatrical skills—he was known as a crack mimic—and started impersonating Thomas in gesture and voice, "at times caricaturing his walk and the very motion of his body." Soon a crowd was cheering on Lincoln and laughing, and he then "gave way to intense and scathing ridicule," mocking still further the "ludicrous" way Thomas spoke. Soon Thomas was in tears, disconsolate. Lincoln showed no hesitation in displaying his creative brand of one-upmanship. Soon the "skinning of Thomas" became the talk of the town. Later, realizing he had gone too far, Lincoln went to Thomas and fervently apologized.[32]

Coinciding with his years in the political arena, Lincoln made a name for himself among the elite ranks of lawyers. He was a self-taught one, rumpled suit and all. There was no better place to sharpen his skills as a fighter and polish his oratorical skills than in a nineteenth-century courtroom against opponents who were allegedly savvier, better skilled, and undoubtedly better schooled than an axe-wielding nobody from Nowheresville.

As towering as he was at six-foot-four, Lincoln didn't have a commanding physical presence. Picture him as a tall, gaunt, and thin man, somewhat stoop-shouldered, rising out of his chair to speak to the jury or question a witness. He was an odd-looking man, angular and awkward with somewhat of a shrill voice once described as effeminate.[33] What he had going for him were his superb speaking skills with expert timing and elocution—further sharpened on the political circuit. He also had an epic knowledge of the law, and his omnipresent supreme confidence, call it arrogance, usually hidden behind his simple, unassuming manner. He was without question sage of speech, and sharp as a tack. Lincoln could bring a courtroom to laughter with his wit, and deliver opponents to their knees with his wisdom. His was a commanding presence in its own, unique way.

Over his twenty-plus years as a practicing attorney, or circuit-riding lawyer as they were sometimes known then, Lincoln was involved in more than 3,000 civil and criminal cases, among them more than 25 murder cases. His most prominent of these was a murder trial in 1859 that was the by-then-famous Lincoln's last before he was inaugurated as president in 1861. The defendant was twenty-two-year-old "Peachy" Quinn Harrison, the son of a longtime friend of Lincoln's. Harrison was accused of murdering Greek Crafton, who happened to be a clerk studying law under Lincoln's firm. The murder weapon was a white-handled, four-inch knife wielded by Harrison during a drugstore scuffle with Crafton and Crafton's brother, John. Harrison claimed it had been self-defense against his much-larger antagonist.

Dan Abrams, co-author with David Fisher of the best-selling book *Lincoln's Last Trial*, sets the scene in an excerpt published at history.com:

> Even by today's standards, *The State of Illinois v. "Peachy" Quinn Harrison* would be considered newsworthy. The prerequisite elements for a "high-profile" trial were all there: a well-liked and promising young man stabbed to death by a neighbor with whom he had grown up; a struggle and claim of self-defense; eyewitness testimony, including from the victim's own brother; an alleged deathbed admission; a critical celebrity witness; and a community fiercely divided. That division stemmed, in part, from

the fact that this was one of those close ones where the lawyering could absolutely impact the outcome.

So if Abraham Lincoln had not been retained to represent the accused, the case still would have been closely watched and scrutinized by the community and local media alike. But in 1859, just nine months before the Republican convention that would catapult him to the presidency and eventually schoolbooks of every American child, having Lincoln for the defense made it that much more notable. While hardly a household name yet, political insiders certainly were coming to know of Abe Lincoln, particularly on the heels of the Lincoln-Douglas debates. This trial would serve as an audition for some, a second look for others, but in either case Lincoln had far more to lose than gain. Creating an aura of invincibility is the goal of every person who stands for election, and a loss in the courtroom might easily damage that perception.[34]

The trial lasted four days, during which it appeared that the prosecution had formulated a convincing case against the youthful Harrison, now facing a manslaughter conviction. But the drama wasn't finished, and neither was Lincoln. In what would be described in today's football parlance as throwing a "Hail Mary," Lincoln begged the court for more time. The judge granted the request, giving the resolute attorney an opportunity to return to his office, gather his thoughts, and dig back though his resources to bolster his case. When Lincoln returned to court, he came brandishing an armload of books, which he opened in court, reading from them the legal authorities to support his defense. Eventually, the judge overruled Lincoln's objection, but that only further fired Lincoln with indignation at what he believed to be an absurd ruling against him.

William H. Herndon, Lincoln's law partner at the time was present in the courtroom. (Lincoln's partner for the case was Stephen Trigg Logan, a former judge, also hired by Peyton Harrison, Peachy's father.) Herndon wrote the following account:

> Lincoln kept, in his anger and contempt, just inside the walls of the law, did not do anything, say anything that would be a contempt of court; he was careful and yet the scoring that he gave the Court, through its foolish decision, was terrible, blasting, crushing, withering. I shall never forget the scene. Lincoln had the crowd, the jury, the bar, in perfect sympathy and accord. The Court's decision was ridiculed, scoffed, and kicked out of court. . . . It was a proud day for Lincoln. Lincoln was a grand man, an imposing figure that day, I assure you. The Court was actually badgered by Lincoln into a final decision of the case.[35]

The judge had gotten the message and reversed his ruling on Lincoln's objection—which was believed to involve allowing the testimony of Rev. Peter Cartwright, the defendant's grandfather, who claimed Crafton had given him a deathbed confession (it took Crafton three days to die from the his wounds). This reversal absolved young Harrison of responsibility for the fatal drugstore encounter. It took the jury of eleven men an hour and nine minutes to render a not-guilty verdict for Peachy Harrison.[36]

Lincoln was a man of letters, much in the same way Trump has shown himself to be, such as when Trump (as mentioned earlier in this chapter) wrote a letter to *The New York Times* taking issue with a book reviewer and the author whose book was reviewed. After Lincoln had been assassinated, a search of his papers turned up many letters that Lincoln had written but never mailed. He penned them only as a cathartic exercise to deal with strong emotions, knowing that actually mailing them to his intended recipients might be counterproductive.

One such letter that Lincoln wrote in a heightened state of anger was addressed to General George Meade during the course of the Civil War. This was in July 1863, immediately following the Battle of Gettysburg. The three days of the battle were some of the bloodiest of the War Between the States. Gettysburg had been a Union victory, essentially simultaneous to the fall of Vicksburg and the Union's retaking of the Mississippi River from Cairo to New Orleans. The end of the war was in sight. All that was left was for General Meade, victor of Gettysburg, to go after and destroy Confederate General Robert E. Lee's army, which was pinned in between Meade's advancing Army of the Potomac and the rain-swollen Potomac River. Meade, however, stood still, not pursuing the Gray Fox. Instead he let Lee and his troops escape to Virginia. With the opportunity for a Union victory in July 1863 lost, the Civil War would drag on for nearly two more years, killing many thousands more on both sides of the war.

Lincoln was livid at the time, saying, "If I had gone up there, I could have whipped them myself. . . . Meade and his army had expended their skill and toil and blood up to the ripe harvest, and then allowed it to go to waste." Lincoln took particular offense at a post-Gettysburg message sent by Meade, praising his troops for "driving the invader from our soil." Responded Lincoln, "The whole country is our soil," while also expressing his concern that Meade's true purpose was not to defeat Lee but "to get the enemy across the river again without a further collision."[37]

Lincoln seethed for weeks before sitting down to dash off a rancorous letter to Meade, thanking him for his "magnificent success" at Gettysburg before continuing with a crushing diatribe:

> My dear general, I do not believe you appreciate the magnitude of the misfortune involved in Lee's escape. He was within your easy grasp, and to have closed upon would, in connection with our other late successes, have ended the war. As it is, the war will be prolonged indefinitely. . . . Your golden opportunity is gone, and I am distressed immeasurably because of it.[38]

Lincoln didn't sign or send the letter. Instead he ordered Henry Halleck, his military adviser and general in chief of the armies, to send a wire to Meade, telling the general that his allowing Lee to escape had "created great dissatisfaction in the mind of the president." Meade, upon reading the wire, immediately turned in his resignation, although Halleck, not expecting or wanting the general to resign, followed with a telegram assuring Meade that the wire had not been meant as a rebuke but as motivation for an active pursuit. In Meade's defense, he had been commanding the Army of the Potomac for only four days prior to Gettysburg and had suffered devastating losses there, including some of his "ablest and most aggressive generals."[39]

A little less than two years later, on April 9, 1865, Lincoln would finally get his victory when Lee surrendered to Union General Ulysses S. Grant at Appomattox Court House in Virginia. To Lincoln's great satisfaction, he was able to relish the moment while sitting in Jefferson Davis's chair at the Confederate White House only two days after it had been vacated.[40] Was he there to bask in the victory? Or was this a definitive end mark for the biggest battle Lincoln ever faced? From the few words we have of his lost Bloomington Speech of 1856 (the most moving he ever gave, but undocumented because listeners, including all the newspaper reporters, were too mesmerized to record his words) "Liberty and Union, now and forever. . . . " The Union had won. . . . Period!

Less than a week later, Lincoln was dead, victim to an assassin's bullet. His fight was over.

CHAPTER 4

COMMON MAN

One was a skinny, dark-headed figure with a sallow tan and a chiseled profile, and the other has a more robust, chunky silhouette with a kind of orangish-blonde hue. If compared side by side, the contrast would be stark. But similarities accumulated as I rummaged through their histories.

Abraham Lincoln and Donald Trump were both tall (about six-foot-four), and fairly athletic. They both played baseball (called "town ball" in Abe's day.) Neither smoked nor drank. And I was a little surprised to learn that neither cared for gourmet food, (especially the Donald—what billionaire wouldn't want to live high on the hog?) Instead, simple meals and "fast food," were or are their preference, even during their administrations. For Trump it was burgers and diet soda; Lincoln more likely chose cornbread or a hard-boiled egg with his dipperful of water.

Their common approachability, proven by the incredible access they gave to others in one way or another throughout their lives, and their simple use of language—often verging on the crude and juvenile—demonstrated to me that Lincoln and Trump possessed a very human personality. Both sported a more cringeworthy side (even as president) marked by some graceless, crass and downright nasty episodes, like Trump's now infamous "hot mic" on the *Hollywood Access* tapes and Lincoln's love of scatological humor.

Either one could keep a crowd (the butt of the jokes excepted) hysterical with laughter. But offset that with a shared empathy and heart for the everyday Joe (or Jane) that rivals the most devoted humanitarian, and you have two uncommonly common leaders.

Trump seemed a magnet for blue-collar entertainment. Redneck might be a good description. (Being one myself, the term still seems a bit derogatory.) In February 2020, Trump made a re-election campaign stop in Daytona, Florida, for the Daytona 500. He even took a lap around the track in his presidential limo, known as "The Beast." He made it work, seeming at home in the God and country, flag-waving, gun-loving, hard-working, weekend-warrior, beer-drinking, backyard BBQ crowds. And for Lincoln, Kentucky born and farm-raised, redneck is not a stretch. He made it work, too.

CB80

Half of America will find this difficult to swallow, but Donald Trump is a regular guy—as regular as a billionaire U.S. president can be. He is a working-class kind of man who resonates with blue-collar types, even those who haven't met him. Shortly after Trump won the 2016 presidential election, CNN interviewed such a person, a working-class guy—much like the hordes who turned out by the millions to vote for him—to get his take on Trump's upset victory. No doubt the man made CNN staffers squirm when he said that Trump reminded him of his own father, a family man with an ironclad work ethic. His dad had worked at blue-collar jobs most of his life, the man told CNN, only for his way of life to get scrapped because of politicians and technocrats out for themselves at the expense of the underclass.

"I don't know if Trump will change anything," the man said, fighting his emotions, "and I don't really care if he does. He is the only one who spoke to my dad's broken heart. My dad is now gone, but when I voted for Trump, it was like voting for my dad."[1]

Donald Trump is no ordinary Joe, far from it, but he is a man of the people—and he won't debate or fight back against anyone who describes him as a "populist"—a label that doesn't often get attached to too many billionaires. He is not a man of pretension and is not reticent to let down his guard in public, with or without a microphone in front of him.

One of many examples of Trump's ordinary-man character happened during his 2016 presidential campaign. Trump had finished giving a speech at a small venue somewhere out in America. Following his talk and after leaving the stage, as described by Gene Ho in his book *Trumpography*, Trump walked the halls of the building to retreat to the green room, which offered a sanctuary away from the crowd. "It was a comfortable little room, one with retractable walls to adjust to a suitable size. The room was mostly bare, nothing too fancy, but the tables were draped in cloth, and refreshments were available," writes Ho, who at the time was a photographer tethered to Trump during the campaign.[2]

Just as the door to the room closed behind him, Trump breathed a noticeable sigh of relief. He picked up a bottle of water, removed the top, and poured some of the water on his hands, which he rubbed together to clean them off. He leaned forward a bit, and using his still-wet hands, wiped away the sweat on his face. He then grabbed the loose end of a tablecloth and dried his face with it. This was not the act of a man on guard, afraid to refresh himself in a manner that any ordinary person probably would have done in like circumstances. Miss Manners would not have approved, but he would have received a thumbs up from Bob the Truck Driver.

"I stood in awe," Ho wrote. "The man who I had seen as a seemingly indestructible force for months appeared so raw and human in that moment. . . . In this unedited act, I was reminded immediately who stood before me: a man. He is just a man. He sweats, he bleeds, and he's flawed."[3]

Lincoln's manners were similarly unassuming but still quite his own. He was quick to share a yarn or a joke—he seemingly had an inventory of dozens if not hundreds on the tip of his tongue—in almost any setting. It could be shoulder to shoulder among other national leaders in the capital or decades earlier as a young lawyer. Lincoln was comfortable in his skin in any place on the streets or in a store and regardless of the status of the person with whom he spoke.

In recalling his first meeting with Lincoln, aboard a train that had just left the way-station, fellow Republican and future Union general Carl Schurz described a scene that began with a commotion among other passengers.

> Many of whom jumped from their seats and pressed eagerly around a tall man who had just entered the car. They addressed him in the most familiar style: "Hello, Abe! How are you?" and so on. And he responded in the same manner: "Good evening, Ben! How are you, Joe? Glad to see you, Dick!" and there was much laughter at some things he said, which, in the confusion of voices, I could not understand. "Why," exclaimed my companion, the committee-man, "there's Lincoln, himself!" He pressed through the crowd and introduced me to Abraham Lincoln, whom I then saw for the first time. . . . He received me with an off-hand cordiality, like an old acquaintance . . . and we sat down together. . . . I soon felt like I had known him my whole life, and we had very long been close friends.[4]

Lincoln wasn't just for the people, he was one of them. His upbringing in a backwoods family that had scrapped and scraped to survive had something to do with that. Whatever he did and however he did it, it was done in such a way that people saw him as a peer who embodied humility and earned his way up. He was a Horatio Alger success story around the same time that Alger was starting to write about characters a lot like Lincoln.

Our sixteenth president wasn't just a man without pretense, he was a president without pomp as well. He was not a man of formality, as evidenced in early 1865, when, with the Civil War still raging, he consented to an informal meeting with Alexander Stephens, the vice president of the Confederacy. They met to discuss a possible end to the relentlessly bloody conflict. The North was winning, albeit at a high cost, but the South was not about to abandon its cause.

Stephens and Lincoln met in the saloon of a rover steamboat, each accompanied by two others: Lincoln with General Ulysses Grant and Secretary of State William Seward at his side; Stephens with two men from the Confederacy. The meeting lasted four hours. In a historical sense, it was remarkable for how friendly and without tension it was, almost like a meeting of long-time friends who hadn't seen each other in years. In fact, this was true; Lincoln and Stephens were old friends, and they hadn't seen each other in years. Much of the early talk was about family members. In this meeting there were no secretaries, no one took notes, and an air of respect surrounded the table. It was almost like a handful of former college buddies reminiscing over a few drinks. In other words, it was the type of meeting in which Lincoln was most at ease, lacking fanfare and unwarranted confrontation. In fact, Lincoln had skipped telling his cabinet in advance about the meeting, not wanting to be hampered by advice or direction that might clutter his train of thought.

Lincoln addressed Stephens with the tone of a friend, as did Stephens in return. That isn't surprising considering that some years earlier Lincoln and Stephens had served together in the U.S. House of Representatives. At one point in this almost-social-like gathering, Stephens queried Lincoln about what it would take to avoid the war's continuance, to which Lincoln replied that all the South had to do was end its resistance. His interest apparently piqued, Stephens suggested that settling the main issue of slavery could be delayed; furthermore, he said, Confederate states wanting to secede from the Union should be allowed to do so voluntarily while entering into a new Union. Lincoln rejected that counter, but he did so with casual indifference, presumably not wanting to spark fireworks that might turn the meeting into a skirmish all its own.

As explained by author Emil Ludwig in his work *Abraham Lincoln and the Times that Tried His Soul*, Lincoln continued by explaining the rationale behind his Emancipation Proclamation (an executive order that had become effective January 1, 1863), saying he would not have interfered with slavery had he not felt obligated first, above all else, to keep the Union intact. At the same time, though, Lincoln also acknowledged there were people in the North just as responsible for slavery as southern slave owners, which is why he said he was prepared to offer compensation to the latter (conditional on congressional approval), if the South ceased hostilities.[5]

There was no agreement reached at the meeting in the steamboat saloon. The next day, however, Lincoln submitted to Congress a resolution calling for $400 million to be allotted to the South, with the funds to be distributed to southern slave owners in proportion to what their losses would be once their slaves were set free. Also, all southern property sequestered—not including slaves—would be restored to its owners and pardons would be issued to political offenders. Lincoln argued that such an act would end the bloodshed, saving untold thousands of lives, but this didn't sway Congress; it unanimously voted down Lincoln's resolution. Ultimately, it would be another three months before the Confederacy finally surrendered.

Lincoln enjoyed being around people even while he was at work, inside the White House. Security measures and protocol would prevent such a thing these days, but in the 1860s it was common to see Lincoln personally greeting visitors to the White House. His philosophy was that he would see as many people as he could each day—and not just staffers, members of Congress, and the like. Walk-ins regularly showed up in his office. Instead of shooing them away, Lincoln would exchange greetings with them as well as engage them in conversation, even welcoming their ideas on governance and policy. Lincoln's personal secretaries, John Nicolay and John Hay, estimated that their boss spent about three-quarters of his time meeting with people, regardless of his workload and various duties needing to be performed. Lincoln's liberal accommodation of visitors likely made it difficult to guard him, a factor that might have played into his assassination.

"No matter how busy the president was, he always seemed to find time for those who called on him," Lincoln historian Donald T. Phillips wrote.

> To this extent, he ran the White House much as he had run his law office in Springfield, where the door was always open and anyone who wished to come in and talk was welcome. Often Nicolay or Hay would tell a visitor that the president was busy and they should come back later, whereupon Lincoln would open his office door and welcome the visitor anyway.[6]

Phillips also points out that Lincoln preferred to meet one on one with his cabinet members in their offices. Perhaps he was using any excuse to stretch his long legs and get out of the confines of his executive office. Or perhaps he wanted to make these visits as much a social call as a professional one. "For Lincoln, casual contact with his subordinates was as important as formal gatherings, if not more so, and today's leaders should take note of this style," Phillips wrote.[7]

Phillips wrote this in a book published in 1993, nearly a quarter-century before Donald Trump set up shop in the White House. Trump's own common man approach to the office of the president had its own nuances.

CRSO

Trump brings to mind Howard Cosell, the renowned Brooklyn-raised sports announcer and commentator whose calling card during his forty years behind the mic was "telling it like it is." Cosell was an ego-driven media icon for whom there was no in between. His fame was largely built on his fourteen seasons as part of ABC-TV's vaunted *Monday Night Football* coverage. When sports fans were polled on their favorite sports announcers, Cosell was voted Favorite and Least Favorite—at the same time. Applied to the world of twenty-first century politics, that's Trump—embraced and detested simultaneously.

In Cosell's mode, Trump tells it—and tweets it—like it is. He's all about straight talk, simple language (using few words with more than two syllables), and shooting straight without a filter. He says what he means, and means what he says. Anybody can understand what he's saying—as annoying as the message might be for liberal elitists insulted by such brash language. His supporters listen to him and think, *That's exactly what I was thinking.* Trump knows his audience, and it begins with not speaking down to them but in concert with them. That's how he's made a strong connection with tens of millions of people. He doesn't speak above his audiences, instead he chooses to meet them at their level. Whatever his arrogance factor might be on a given day, it doesn't hurt his ability to communicate with the masses and be easily understood. "I manage to blast through the ridiculous liberal bias of the media and speak right to the hearts of the people—or at least I try," Trump has said. "Even *New York* magazine, hardly a conservative outlet, has given me credit for shaking up the status quo."[8]

Before Trump became president, he was perhaps best known for his starring role in the hit TV reality series *The Apprentice*, which aired for fifteen seasons between 2004 and 2017. Like anything else Trump has been involved in, the show had its enthusiastic followers as well as its detractors, but it did elevate Trump to iconic status in America—and in other parts of the world—mostly because of his brashness and concision. When it was time for a contestant to leave the show, Trump simply said "You're fired!" and that person was gone. That's telling it like it is.

"Those of you who have watched *The Apprentice* will notice that the candidates who can present the facts with the least amount of verbal decoration will have an advantage," Trump wrote in his 2010 book *Think Like a Champion*.

> We don't have the time for loquacious colleagues, and the longwinded diatribes we often have to suffer through will greatly diminish their chances of winning.
>
> Simple as it sounds, there is great wisdom in the short, fast, and direct route. Knowing where you're going in your conversation and demonstrating to others you know where you're going by being concise, is a big step toward leadership and respect. . . . People appreciate brevity in today's world.[9]

Often brief, blunt, and confrontational, Trump is also intolerant of contrarians—many disguised as journalists—who emerge from the woodwork to challenge any of his positions or statements that don't fit the politically correct narrative. Trump came to the White House as an outsider, a businessman without a political pedigree. On one hand he fulfilled the wishes of voters who had long awaited such a paradigm shift in Washington, DC; on the other hand his election peeved capital insiders—many of them manning media outposts—who refused to tolerate anything but politics as usual.

One aspect of Trump's character that often gets lost in the media is his capacity for compassion. In *Think Like a Champion*, Trump recalls a time in 1988 when he received a desperate plea from a Los Angeles rabbi—someone he had never met—asking the New York businessman for help in getting his three-year-old son to New York City. The rabbi hoped that doctors there could find a cure for the boy's severe respiratory condition. The request was a considerable one: Would Trump fly the boy to New York City in his private jet? No commercial airline would allow the boy to fly because of the extensive medical equipment he needed to have with him at all times.

"I had small children at the time, and I immediately said yes to his request. How could I say no?" Trump writes. The future president sent his private jet to Los Angeles to pick up the boy and his parents and bring them to New York City. Although the meeting with health-care experts proved futile, as the young boy soon died, the boy's parents never forgot Trump's generosity. In *Think Like a Champion*, Trump reported that the rabbi had contacted him every year for eighteen years running, on the day before the Jewish holiday Rosh Hashanah, to convey a message of thanks while telling Trump of the blessings they'd had in their lives.[10]

Numerous other instances of Trump's Samaritan ways date back decades before he entered politics. In 1991, his mother, Mary Anne Trump, then seventy-nine years old was assaulted and robbed in Queens—knocked to the ground by a teenager who made off with the cash she had on her. Her fall to the ground broke her ribs, induced hemorrhaging in her brain, and resulted in a permanent disability involving her vision and hearing. A witness to the incident, a truck driver, chased down and apprehended the sixteen-year-old boy. It turned out the truck driver hero's home was about to be foreclosed, and Trump graciously wrote him a check that allowed the man to pay his mortgage.[11] Evangelist James Robison said,

> I've been back behind the curtain with him when he's with people nobody sees, and he keeps noticing the crippled person . . . or the military person, or the person with the police force, or the person that looks like they're poor. Those are the people he goes to when nobody sees him. He notices them. He notices them when he walks out in the crowd. He'll notice the people that nobody else notices.[12]

Empathy and compassion are a core part of Trump's makeup—the part that most of the media never reports. He is at his best in that regard when he is out of the public eye, as was the case in August 2016 when prolonged rains in southern Louisiana produced floods that drove many families from their homes and devastated the area. Tens of thousands of homes and many businesses were submerged, with overall damages estimated at between $10–15 billion. One of the homeowners affected was Tony Perkins, a campaign supporter of Trump's and, at the time, an interim pastor at a large church.

Four days passed, and still there was no governmental assistance. No President Barack Obama onsite to see the damage and console residents. No Hillary Clinton, then the Democratic presidential nominee, either. Seemingly no presidential-level interest, until Trump showed up, accompanied by his vice-presidential candidate Mike Pence and evangelist Franklin Graham, son of Billy.

"Trump was visibly taken aback by how significant the devastation and destruction was," Perkins said. "He told the Secret Service to stop the cars, and he got out and went up and met residents in the neighborhoods. He was so warm and genuine in his concern."

One of the then-homeless Louisiana couples Trump met was Jimmy and Olive Morgan. Trump asked if they were going to rebuild, and the couple said they were "getting up there" in years and didn't know if they had it in them to build another home. At which point, according to Pence, Trump reached over, grabbed Jimmy Morgan by the shoulder, and said, "You're going to rebuild; I know you're that kind of guy. You're going to rebuild." Nine months later, Pence returned to check in on the couple, and found out that they had indeed rebuilt their home.[13]

ಚ ಬಾ

Lincoln's compassion was legendary. He showed it for Civil War soldiers in and around Washington as well as on the battlefield. At times, and as opportunity and access allowed, this extended to soldiers fighting on behalf of the South as well. He shared meals of beans and hard biscuits with the soldiers. He visited their sleeping quarters, typically asking about the families they had left behind. At the Soldiers' Home, he would easily strike up conversations with occupants while ministering to wounded Union and Confederate soldiers. "He cares for us," one soldier said to another, "he makes us fight but he cares."

Almost inconceivably, at least by today's standards, Lincoln had an open-door policy for soldiers. Many took advantage of it, visiting him at the White House when they had the opportunity; once there, they were encouraged to speak their minds and query their commander in chief. Over time, an estimated two thousand fighting men walked through the doors to Lincoln's office, taking advantage of a presidential policy that Lincoln termed the "link or cord which connects the people with the governing power."

Word about Lincoln spread among the troops. They talked about how he was a terrific listener. He assured these young men that he had as much desire as they did for them to be homeward bound as quickly as possible. Many soldiers wrote letters home to their loved ones, often giving accounts of Lincoln's empathy, kindness, and accessibility—speaking of him as one of their own and painting illustrations of him as a fatherly figure. They assigned him respectful honorifics such as "Father Abraham," "Uncle Abe," and "Old Abe." One soldier went so far as to write to his mom, telling her that he would not be coming home when his term of enlistment was up— that he was going to stay and continue taking the fight to the Confederates. In his letter he told her, "A country that is worth living in time of peace is worth fighting for in time of war, so I am yet willing to put up with the hardships of a soldier's life." All because of Lincoln.[14]

As much as Lincoln touched the hearts and minds of his soldiers, he could not escape the brutal reality of the battlefield. Hundreds of thousands of soldiers on both sides were dying, with daily newspaper reports pounding the horrors of war home. Lincoln did peruse the papers, but it wasn't just the newspaper scribes that were describing the nightmare. Letters from soldiers told of the unthinkable suffering of the maimed and wounded.

Lincoln was deeply affected by this news, and it showed in his face and posture. Isaac N. Arnold, a friend of Lincoln's who saw the president often, wrote about how Lincoln was "grave and anxious, and he looked like one who had lost the dearest member of his own family." One night when Lincoln spotted a procession of many ambulances transporting the wounded to a hospital, he looked at Arnold, stark sadness etched in his own face, and remarked, "Look yonder at those poor fellows. I cannot bear it. This suffering, this loss of life, is dreadful."[15]

Another aspect of Lincoln's compassion was his acceptance of other's faults, most notably the shortcomings of soldiers that served under him. Author David Herbert Donald wrote that during the Civil War, Lincoln would spend one morning a week reviewing the court-martial records and sentences of soldiers. He was looking for any rationale to turn the prisoners loose while allowing them to return to their units for duty. Lincoln, to some extent, pinned the blame for the war's "butchering business" on himself. This was his way of shouldering the responsibility for the war and all who suffered because of it.

Lincoln was especially empathetic to the mothers and wives of young soldiers requesting help for their hospitalized sons. These women pledged to nurse their men back to health and return them to the frontlines, provided Lincoln would get them released from the hospital and entrust the wounded to their care. One mother actually visited Lincoln to tell him this:

> My son is wounded badly and in the hospital. I have been trying to get him out, but couldn't, so they said I had better come to see you. If you will let me take him home I will nurse him up, and just as soon as he gets well enough, he shall go right back and help put down the rebellion. He is a good boy and does not shrink from the service.

Upon hearing this, Lincoln teared up and, his lips quivering, penned a note to the woman and handed it to her, telling her she could have her son to take home. He also received hundreds of requests asking for the pardon of young soldiers who had been sentenced to execution for such misdeeds as falling asleep on guard duty or desertion. "It breaks my heart to have these poor boys shot," Lincoln told a friend. "I think [they] can do us more good above ground than underground."[16]

☙

Then there were the stories, metaphors, or illustrations that Lincoln would use to drive home a point. Occasionally he punctuated these accounts with the kind of coarse or crude language you might not expect to hear from America's chief executive, although doing so moved him closer in comportment to the Average Joes and Johns of the world. It was part of Lincoln's charm that he never was too concerned about walking on eggshells—at times he almost seemed to crack the eggs deliberately.

Like his father Thomas Lincoln, young Abe delighted in spinning hilarious tales. His storytelling played well with the poorer citizens and scruffy ruffians who got to know Lincoln when he was in his teens, twenties, and thirties. He began his rise in politics by establishing kinship with the lower class of the American electorate. Do the math: their votes counted just as much in later years when it was time to go to the polls. Call Lincoln just "one of the guys."

As a youth, Lincoln wasn't much of a churchgoer but he did use the opportunities of Sunday church services to gather material for his impromptu "sermons," which were closer in style to being onstage at a comedy club than standing at a pulpit in front of pew-seated worshippers. Once Sunday services were over, young Abraham would gather anyone nearby to see one of his not-to-be-missed shows. Once he had a sufficiently sized audience, Lincoln would jump atop a tree stump to deliver "a perfectly memorized, outrageously taunting rendition of the latest pulpit performance, complete with the right exaggerated gestures at the right sidesplitting moments."[17]

Lincoln was also given to comic humor in which he dialed down sexual material into a more palatable PG presentation, sometimes lacing his performances with off-color content that made mention of flatulence or defecating. When once asked why he hadn't yet published his rather extensive collection of tales and jokes. Lincoln responded, wrinkling his nose as he spoke, "Such a book would stink like a thousand privies."[18]

Even as a president in his fifties, Lincoln kept his bawdy sense of humor. As the Civil War neared its end early in 1865, with the Union armies in the process of taking down the last remaining strongholds of Confederate might, a confident Lincoln was visited at the White House by a delegation. Members of the group were miffed by what they perceived as a lack of progress from Union troops. They were particularly alarmed by General Ulysses Grant's army being bogged down in Virginia.

Lincoln dismissed their concerns, went to a map, and started explaining how Grant was actually close to victory. Lincoln's intent was essentially to stifle the complainants. To seal his point, he told the group about "a wicked and lascivious sinner" in Indiana wanting to be baptized. A preacher took the man to a nearby river and dunked him in. Was the sinner saved? Not yet, apparently. As the man came up for air, "gasping and rubbing his face," he asked the preacher to do it again—to put him under the water once more, and the baffled preacher complied. When the man came up a second time, he proclaimed, "Now I've been baptized twice, and the Devil can kiss my ass." Pausing his story, Lincoln turned back to the map, poked his finger at a specific point and told the delegation that when his army reached that spot, the Union would be victorious. "And then," Lincoln said, "the southern Confederacy can kiss my ass."[19]

CB ⁊D

Donald Trump has been described as "a wrecking ball to the spirit of political correctness."[20] It fits, and it's a description Trump himself would probably agree with and consider a badge of honor. He says what he thinks, so much of which enters airspace as unfiltered soundwaves. Along with that, he also produces moments of self-deprecating humor that progressive media often just don't seem to grasp. When he poked fun at the notion that he might somehow try to wrangle a third four-year term as president (the U.S. Constitution limits a president to two elected terms), many of his political opponents and even some in the media expressed sincere disdain. Ditto in August 2018 when, at a veterans' event in Louisville, Kentucky, Trump was obviously joking when he wanted to award himself the Medal of Honor, saying, "I wanted one, but they [his aides] told me I don't qualify. I said, 'Can I give it to myself anyway?' They said, 'I don't think that's a good idea.'"[21] Again, his comments were taken seriously by many lacking the humor gene.

Here's what Trump is up against. U.S. presidents are generally expected to speak and act with a certain sense of decorum that supposedly suits the office—a well-bred concoction with ingredients that include humility, poise, gravitas, temperance, empathy, and dignity. The common man (or woman) might possess one or two of those qualities on a good day, but the American president is often considered ill-suited for office if he or she is lacking in any of those areas. Aside from his billions, Donald Trump is more common man than he is refined national leader. Again, Trump probably wouldn't argue with that because he doesn't care. He is not part of the enlightened elites that many political enemies embrace. He can be downright uncouth, graceless, and even odd. These are descriptors that many of Lincoln's antagonists (and, probably, even his supporters) would have attached to the man in the stovepipe hat as well.

Self-restraint is not a Trump strong point. In his book *Trump's America*, Newt Gingrich mentions "Trump's ferocity in counterattacking [as] part of his strategy." Gingrich continues:

> As someone who spent his career with blue-collar workers, Trump understands that someone punching you becomes an existential moment. You either fight back or you back down. Trump always chooses to fight. In some ways, President Trump is the first president since Andrew Jackson to understand bar room brawling at a practical level. He applies this brawl model to politics. You have to counterpunch or you will lose.[22]

In his book *Understanding Trump*, published a year before *Trump's America*, Gingrich says that to understand Trump, you have to delve into his psychology as well as his philosophy:

> To really grasp Trump, you must understand his doctrine and his psychology—the collection of attitudes and methods he uses to achieve success. That doctrine is fast, aggressive, disruptive, and confounding to the unwary. . . . He places a greater emphasis on speed than mistake avoidance, sets big goals, and remains flexible. He capitalizes on his opponents' weaknesses and works relentlessly to diminish or avoid their strengths.[23]

Once Trump thinks it, he speaks it. Why is that so hard to understand? Run-on sentences are the bane of Trump's speaking style. Sometimes he'll speak it before he has finished processing the thought. But this is a manner of communication that endears him to the common man and woman. That is how they speak themselves, whether gathered around the dinner table or cozying up to the local bar. It is a healthy mix of shooting from the hip and exercising a sense of humor that begs a thick skin. If you're not comfortable talking straight and find Trump distasteful, then you are probably spending much of your life with a frown on your face.

Then there are the Trump tweets. Among the untold thousands:

- "It used to be cars were made in Flint and you couldn't drink the water in Mexico. Now cars are made in Mexico and you can't drink the water in Flint."

- "I have this thing called Twitter and Facebook, which is amazing actually. It's like owning *The New York Times* without the losses."
- "My biggest opponent was the microphone." (After one of his 2016 debates against Hillary Clinton)

"The sheer volume of people that support him because he's willing to be funny and ballsy and say what he thinks—you cannot underestimate that," an unnamed senior Trump administration official told politico.com in October 2018. Added Brian O. Walsh, president of the pro-Trump group America First Action: "His speaking style is what endears him to his supporters. It's a big part of what fueled him through the [2016] primaries and the general election. The unpolished everyman who says what he thinks."[24]

For years, the most obvious target of ridicule for anti-Trumpsters has been Trump's hair. Is it his or a toupee? Occasionally Trump has played along, such as in those times he has invited people up on stage with him to let them take a good tug. It doesn't come off. It isn't a hairpiece. Audiences love it when he puts out such a challenge, and the hair stays in place.

"Another time he had us laughing until it hurt," author Gene Ho says in *Trumpography*. "He delivered a stand-up-worthy string of one-liners about how he'd contemplated the effects of global warming because he preferred aerosol hairspray to pump action. Then he went on to mimic the *chht, chht, chht* sound of the individual pumps from the squirt bottle. 'We're going to be here all day with pump-action hairspray'!"[25]

"It pays to have a sense of humor about yourself," Trump said, recalling a credit-card commercial he once made, in which a gust of wind atop Trump Tower blew the card out of Trump's hand, sending it down to the street below. The scene ended with Trump climbing out of a dumpster after retrieving his card while a passerby remarked, "And I thought he was doing so well!" Trump said, "If I took myself too seriously, I would have missed out on a lot of fun and a nice paycheck."[26]

Lincoln was also the recipient of barbs over the years. He might still be the comeback king of U.S. presidents—including those who have served since his death. He always had a deep reservoir of rejoinders at the ready. Political slurs were as much a part of nineteenth-century lexicon as they are today. They may even have been more common back then, before our progressive world began considering poking fun at or criticizing another human as the equivalent of committing a crime. In Lincoln's day, the comebackers were a bit more wordy, reflecting a thinking man's level of retorts. Today's listener would have to let them baste for a few seconds before they would register. One time, when dealing with a particularly cruel antagonist,

Lincoln came back, with, "the oratory of the gentleman completely suspends all action of his mind." Lincoln wasn't finished chopping down his opponent, likening the guy to a steamboat. "Back in the days when I performed my part as a keel boatman," Lincoln said, "I made the acquaintance of a trifling little steamboat which used to bustle and puff and wheeze about in the Sangamon River. It had a five-foot boiler and a seven-foot whistle, and every time it whistled the boat stopped."[27]

Lincoln loved telling stories in all settings; when political give and take was at work, he would often use a story as a metaphor—like he did with the steamboat—in place of directly chiding an opponent or, worse yet, driving a verbal knife into his gut. His goal was to avoid unnecessarily wounding an opponent while yet serving the purpose. "No, I am not simply a story-teller, but story-telling as an emollient saves me much friction and distress."[28]

His humor was as much for Lincoln's benefit as it was for anything else, especially during the emotionally draining days of the Civil War. "A funny story, if it has the element of genuine wit, has the same effect on me that I suppose a good square drink of whiskey has on an old toper; it puts new life into me," Lincoln said. "The fact is I have always believed that a good laugh was good for both the mental and the physical digestion." On another occasion, he said, "I laugh because I must not weep—that's all, that's all."[29]

Like any normal person, Lincoln experienced some episodes he would rather were forgotten. One wonders how often presidents wish for "do-overs." One time, disguised in a dark coat and a Scottish tam o'shanter cap, Lincoln dodged possible assassins on his way to Washington as president-elect. It was a comic image reproduced in scathing satire in the tabloids at the time. And Lincoln regretted it.

In an archived Saturday Night Live skit from 2004, Trump dodged the feathered bird costume to settle on a yellow suit instead. It was a comic scene later used by social media to ridicule. Thankfully, he nixed the feathers ahead of time.

Both men supported physical personas unmistakable in a crowd, and personalities beyond unique. They were loved and hated simultaneously, especially by the press and media of the day. Yet Lincoln and Trump commanded the respect and endearment of ordinary folk. It didn't take good looks, or a genius IQ. All it took was that common connection. That's all.

CHAPTER 5

FAMILY MAN

❦

Though Lincoln had only one marriage—to the illustrious Mary Todd—a quick biographical foray into his earlier years revealed not one but two failed love affairs prior to finding his first lady. Ditto Donald Trump. Only his were two failed marriages leading up to his final nuptials with first lady Melania.

Interestingly, both White House women experienced the vitriol from not only the partisan elites of Washington, DC, but also a crazy media that mimicked the tabloid press of the day, concocted drivel and all. Mary and Melania were often targeted by a hateful press for their fashion sense, or rather their fashion offenses toward a press corps that just couldn't accept them for who they were.

Easily apparent in their backstories, Mary Todd, Ivana (Trump's first wife and mother of his first three children), as well as Melania were or are capable mothers and strong, independent women in their own rights. And since fatherhood tended to take second fiddle to climbing their proverbial ladders, Lincoln and Trump were more than happy to leave the child-rearing and homemaking to their wives while they went off to bring home the bacon. (Or in Trump's case, the whole hog!)

Neither man showed any hesitation in beginning a family right away (Robert Todd Lincoln was born only three days short of nine months after his parents wedding, and Donald Jr. was born a whopping six days short of nine months after his parents wed). Abe and Mary had four sons, though two died early in childhood (little Eddie, when he was three, and Willie at age twelve.) Donald Trump's three sons and two daughters arrived over the course of four decades and three marriages.

Differences in familial circumstances aside, Lincoln and Trump remained devoted to their children and first ladies throughout their lives, despite workaholic natures and constant distractions: Lincoln, until he was fifty-six years old when he was struck down by an assassin, and Trump well past seventy.

⋯

Abraham Lincoln as a twentysomething adult male wasn't what a casual observer might describe as a ladies' man. He was more like what young women today would call a mess. He entered mainstream society lacking proper table manners, couldn't dance to save his life (or fetch a wife), and had not been schooled on the finer points of chaste speech when in the company of well-bred women. As to how he dressed . . . well. . . . "He charmed tough frontier matrons," William Freehling writes in *Becoming Lincoln*. "But delicate, upper-class maidens, not so much."[1]

Despite being quick with his wit and adroit in quoting from the countless books he had devoured, Lincoln typically was at a loss for words when around women his own age. "With the wives of old friends, like Mrs. Hannah Armstrong, he could be courtly, even affectionate, but he froze in the presence of eligible girls," David Donald wrote in *Lincoln*. Donald also points out that efforts by New Salem's motherly types to pair Abe with a Miss Short or a Miss Berry ended as misfires.[2] Yet Lincoln's romantic shortcomings were strangely endearing. His social fumbling combined with his intellect and joined by an honest modesty, made Lincoln appealing to women who somehow saw in him the makings of a fine husband. Plenty of young dames craved the companionship of and commitment from a fine, self-made man—if only they could get through to Abe for a nineteenth-century love connection. Adds Donald,

> [The women of New Salem] had matrimonial plans for him. They found his awkward clumsiness touching, and they noted how tender he was with small children and how affectionate he was to kittens and other pets. He needed someone to cook for him and feed him, so as to fill out that hollow frame, someone to clean and repair his clothing, which—except for that expensive legislative suit—seemed never to fit and always to be in tatters. In short he needed a wife.[3]

One young woman in New Salem managed to not only catch Lincoln's eye but also make him comfortable enough to open his mouth and speak without tying his tongue into knots. That was Ann Rutledge, whose father was one of the village's founders and also happened to own the tavern at which Abe boarded. There was plenty about Ann for Lincoln to appreciate. She was pretty with auburn hair, blue eyes, and a fair complexion. She was a little more than a foot shorter than Lincoln, but she compensated for any shortcomings with an engaging, accommodating personality that put Lincoln at ease and drew him in. Actually, he fell for her, head over boots. Separate from Ann, Lincoln steered clear of women who came to the tavern (or inn). He preferred instead to converse with the men and boys, who at the time were best suited to discuss favorite topics of his, such as politics and morality.

Lincoln's usual attire in those days was well below even a poor man's *Gentleman's Quarterly*, consisting of tow-linen pantaloons that were about five inches too short and held up by one suspender; a calico shirt, such as what he had worn in the Black Hawk war; coarse tan brogans (heavy high-top shoes); blue socks of yarn; and an old style straw hat, sans the band.[4] Any woman willing to overlook Abe's non-sense of fashion and shy manner and take the initiative in nudging herself up to him might have made a go of it, except that Lincoln seemed to need a cattle prod more than a nudge. Case in point: one of Lincoln's acquaintances recalled the time that an older woman from Virginia showed up at the tavern to spend two or three weeks there, accompanied by her son and three stylish, attractive daughters—each one presumably single. This presented Lincoln a chance to at least converse with the young lovelies, but "I do not remember Mr. Lincoln's ever appearing at the same table with them," the friend said.[5]

There are two sides to this coin (and we don't mean a Lincoln penny). While young Lincoln was shy toward eligible ladies—confidantes of his knew he had a deep-seated passion for women and could barely keep his hands off them, with only his strong will and honor caging his "animal" instincts. One time when he did release the brakes on a trip out of town in his mid-twenties, he had an intimate fling with a young woman he had just met, an encounter of the most lustful kind that one-time law partner and biographer William Herndon described as "a devilish passion."[6] Of course, Lincoln wanted to keep his reckless rendezvous a secret, although he did reveal it to Herndon. The secret got out when Herndon made note of it in a memorandum he later loaned to U.S. marshal and Lincoln bodyguard Ward Hill Lamon, a move Herndon regretted for years.[7]

Lincoln still had plenty of hound dog in him. Several years later, still single and as passionate and longing for intimacy as ever, he told close friend Joshua Speed that he craved "a little," as Herndon puts it. Knowing that Speed had a pretty lady friend in Springfield, Lincoln asked his buddy, "Where can I get *some*?" In reply Speed said, "If you will wait a moment or so, I'll send you to the place with a note. You can't get *it* without a note or by my appearance." Lincoln grabbed the handwritten note and took off into town with it, where he found the girl and introduced himself, telling her why he was there. At first she objected but eventually she relented. (Lincoln could do smooth talking once he got going.) When Lincoln asked her what the charge would be, she said it would be five dollars. This was too bad because Lincoln informed her he had only three dollars on his person. Even though she told him not to worry—she knew he was good for the rest at a later time, Lincoln told his amour-for-hire he didn't know where his next dollar was coming from, therefore he couldn't accept her offer of credit. He offered the girl the three dollars anyway, but she would not accept it, telling Abe, "Mr. Lincoln, you are the most conscientious man I know."[8]

CRISO

As far as we know, Donald Trump has never been shy about speaking up around anybody, male or female. His lot in life as a ladies' man is a lock, but like Lincoln a century and a half before him, Trump had a higher order of priorities. With Lincoln it had been law and politics; with Trump it was business and success, the latter measured in terms of deals made, properties owned, and dollars in his expanding bank account.

Trump didn't have a matronly brood of community matchmakers, he had parental assistance. As a cadet at New York Military Academy, Trump was often visited on weekends by his dad and mom—Fred and Mary Anne. They would usually be accompanied by a beautiful young woman, a different one each time. These occurrences earned Trump "Ladies' Man" status in the academy's yearbook, even though it was an all-boys school. Sandy McIntosh, a classmate of Donald's and a witness to this parade of beauties said that regardless of whatever nonverbal message Mr. and Mrs. Trump were delivering to their son, "Our biggest advice in our lives came from *Playboy* magazine."[9]

More than anything, this teen beauty of the week ploy was part of Mary Anne's attempt to encourage her son to broaden his horizons, to eventually find a girl and settle down, get married, and have kids. In short, Donnie needed a wife. Perhaps Mary Anne was concerned about what brought Donald to military school in the first place—that wild teenage rebelliousness. She might have pushed the matchmaking in hopes of taming that nature. But Donald's ambitions resided elsewhere—with real estate, success, money, and fame.

Lincoln, by contrast, was ready and willing to settle down—or at least get married—by the time he was in his mid-twenties. Ann Rutledge was the apple of his eye. Not even her being engaged to another man (who had gone away for an extensive period of time) could stop Lincoln in his pursuit of the lovely young woman. The daughter of Lincoln's boss, this rare girl was able to pull Lincoln's attention away from his law books long enough for him to win her heart. For the first time in his life, Lincoln was in love.

Ann was the third child of James Rutledge, who in 1829 had moved to what became New Salem, Illinois from Kentucky or possibly South Carolina. (At least one other source placed James Rutledge in South Carolina prior to his move to Illinois). Rutledge was hospitable and well-liked for his warm spirit, his social graces, and his generosity—qualities which could just as well describe his daughter. Not only was she fair of face and personable in ways that made her widely popular among residents of New Salem, but she was also quite skilled with the needle, her quick and agile fingers elevating her above most other women in the dexterous art of quilt making. It caught Lincoln's attention; he would often escort Ann to and from quilting bees that were as competitive as they were creative. In one instance he even accompanied her inside the house where the bees were held—and where men were generally considered off-limits—sometimes sitting next to her as she worked on the quilt.[10]

Ann Rutledge, four years younger than Abe, was described by a Lincoln acquaintance as "amiable" and with an "intellect [that] was quick, deep, and philosophic as well as brilliant. . . . She had a heart as gentle and kind as an angel, and full of love and sympathy. . . . She was a woman worthy of Lincoln's love."[11] Unlucky at love is what Lincoln was, though, as Ann Rutledge caught typhoid fever and her condition never improved. Her health worsened in the weeks that followed before she passed away at age twenty-two on August 25, 1835. Lincoln fell into a deep depression and later said, when talking about Rutledge's death and her grave, "My heart lies buried there."[12]

Lincoln apparently bounced back within a year because he was involved in another relationship, this time with Mary S. Owens, a Kentucky native who had first caught Lincoln's eye in 1833 while she was visiting her sister, Betsy, the wife of New Salem resident Bennet Able. Mary stayed that first time for about a month before returning home to Kentucky. She returned again three years later—a little more than a year after Ann Rutledge's death. Owens had dark hair and was somewhat taller and portlier than Rutledge, although she had an excellent education. Her father was reputed to be one of the wealthiest and most influential men in the area of Green County, Kentucky. History records the relationship between Lincoln and Owens as a "love affair," although it was more of an arrangement brokered by Owens's sister, Betsy. After her sister had returned to Kentucky in 1833, Betsy prevailed upon Lincoln to promise he would wed Mary if she returned to New Salem. Lincoln accepted the deal, admitting he was well pleased with what he had seen of Mary.

To begin her second visit, in 1836, Mary arrived back in New Salem on presidential Election Day. Her route to her sister's home took her past the polling locale, where there was a gathering of men. One of the gents was impressed enough to write Herndon with the following account, no doubt embellished by the sudden appearance of a presentable young woman of good breeding:

"She . . . had large blue eyes and the finest trimmings I ever saw. She was jovial, social, loved wit and humor, had a liberal English education, and was considered wealthy. None of the poets or romance writers have ever given us a picture of a heroine so beautiful as a good description of Miss Owens in 1835 [sic] would be."[13]

Lincoln was not so enchanted by Mary upon her return, for she had gained a fair amount of weight in the intervening three years. This was enough for Lincoln to start plotting how to wrangle himself out of his handshake deal with Betsy. From that point on, their courtship, if you could call it that, was more an ongoing negotiation and discussion. Lincoln was still attracted to the Kentucky maiden's "lively mind, confident personality, and superb education," but he was mildly repulsed by her change in appearance. Keep in mind, too, that Ann Rutledge's death remained a fresh source of sorrow for Lincoln, and she was a tough act to follow. Lincoln knew he needed to propose to Owens to honor his pledge to Betsy, but at the same time he had to try to convince Mary that she wouldn't be pleased with the new life that awaited her as his bride. Following is part of a letter he sent to Owens, dated May 7, 1837, soon after he had made his initial mention of marriage to Owens and after he had moved from New Salem to Springfield:

I am often thinking about what we said of your coming to live at Springfield. I am afraid you would not be satisfied. There is a great deal of flourishing about in carriages here, which it would be your doom to see without sharing in it. You would have to be poor without the means of hiding your poverty. . . . My opinion is that you had better not do it. You have not been accustomed to hardship, and it may be more severe than you can imagine. I know you are capable of thinking correctly on any subject; and if you deliberate maturely upon this, before you decide, then I am willing to abide your decision.[14]

Owens's decision became evident when she soon returned to Kentucky, accepted a marriage proposal from another suitor, and took off with her new beau to get married in Missouri. Owens had released Lincoln from his pledge, and the future president had to be relieved, as evidenced in a letter he wrote to a long-time friend, Mrs. Orville Browning, selected portions of which follow:

Although I had seen her before, she did not look as my imagination had pictured her. I knew she was over-size, but she now appeared a fair match for Falstaff. I knew she was called an "old maid," and I felt no doubt of the truth of at least half of the appellation; but now, when I beheld her, I could not for my life avoid thinking of my mother; and this, not from withered features, for her skin was too full of fat to permit of its contracting into wrinkles, but from her want of teeth, weather-beaten appearance in general, and from a kind of notion that ran in my head that nothing could have commenced at the size of infancy and reached her present bulk in less than thirty-five or forty years; and, in short, I am not at all pleased with her. . . . In my resolution, I found I was continually repenting the rashness which had led me to make it. . . . Others have been made fools of by girls, but this can never with truth be said of me. I most emphatically, in this instance, made a fool of myself.[15]

The confrontation was avoided, but Lincoln's matrimonial future remained more a product of fate than his own social engineering at this point.

CB EO

It was the summer of 1976, with the Bicentennial celebration at full swing in America and the Summer Olympics about to land in neighboring Montreal, when Donald Trump introduced himself to Ivana Zelnicekova Winklmayr. One night around the time of his thirtieth birthday, Trump was out having drinks with Jerry Goldsmith, a private investment banker. They were perched at a Manhattan restaurant and singles bar known as

87

Maxwell's Plum. The bar was located at 64th and 1st and owned by Warner LeRoy, son of Mervyn LeRoy, a Hollywood producer of *Wizard of Oz* fame. Maxwell's was a popular watering hole frequented by the celebrity set, among them the likes of Barbra Streisand and Warren Beatty. Who could ask for a more appropriate setting for a first encounter between an up-and-coming real estate billionaire and a long-legged blonde bombshell from Czechoslovakia now residing in Montreal? Ivana and several other models had come to New York to model in a fur show, while also promoting the Olympic Games just weeks away.

For a high-profile bachelor like Trump, Maxwell's that night was a target-rich environment for food and frolic, and, from a woman's point a view, it was the place to be to meet good-looking guys loaded with greenbacks and plenty of heavyweight plastic. Abe Lincoln would have felt instantly overwhelmed, but bars like this were as familiar as home to Trump. He frequently mingled and rubbed shoulders with the beautiful people in the city that never sleeps. It wasn't long before Trump got a good look at those long, athletic gams and the hazel eyes of a dolled-up, twenty-seven-year-old Ivana. She wasn't just good sport in a social sense but she was actually quite sporty. A topnotch alpine skier (her specialties were slalom and downhill), she had been vying, several years earlier and ultimately unsuccessfully, for a spot on the Czech national team, with a dream of racing in the Winter Olympic Games.

"There were lots of pretty girls around, but right away Donald latched onto Ivana," Goldsmith said.[16] "The Donald," as Ivana would later call him, went right to work. She had recently divorced her way out of a brief marriage of convenience having to do with passports, and was now living in Montreal with a longtime boyfriend George Syrovatka, a fellow Czech and competitive skier with whom she had been close for a number of years. Trump reserved a table for Ivana and her friends and he picked up their tab at the end of the night. The next day he sent her a dozen roses, followed a few weeks later by a jaunt to Montreal to visit her and take in a fashion show while there. Soon, Ivana was back in New York, spotted around town riding in a silver limo with the license plate "DJT." Trump brought her to Jamaica Estates to meet his parents, Fred and Mary Anne, and soon things became serious between them.

Despite being born on different continents and growing up speaking different tongues, Donald and Ivana were remarkably in sync with one another on a number of levels; both were abundantly self-confident, had been raised by strong fathers, had laser-sharp business acumen, placed great importance on bonds among family members, and enjoyed the sporting life—Donald with his love of and skill for golf, and Ivana with her world-class skiing. Trump soon was referring to Ivana as "his twin as a woman." And wherever he went with her—referring to her often as "Ivaska"—he would proclaim to anyone close enough to hear him, "Isn't she gorgeous? Have you ever seen anyone more beautiful?"[17]

Less than a year later Donald and Ivana were married in Manhattan's Marble Collegiate Church on April 9, the day before Easter 1977. The service was officiated by renowned minister, author, and champion-of-positivity Norman Vincent Peale. Just short of nine months later, Ivana gave birth to their first child, Donald Trump Jr., on New Year's Eve 1977. Donald Jr. was later followed by Ivanka (birth name "Ivana"), born in October 1981, and then Eric, the youngest of Donald and Ivana's three children together, born in early January 1984.

Donald Trump had firmly established himself as his own man and a New York City business icon—well out from under the shadow of his father. He had taken over the family business in 1971 and renamed it the Trump Organization two years later, in 1973. Even with the support of nannies, Ivana dived into motherhood, carving out ample time to be with the three kids. She was the true disciplinarian in the family. But she also devoted her time to frequently being onsite to help her husband in his building of hotels and casinos.

Never content to sit behind a desk, she showed up at job sites, smartly dressed in designer clothes and spike heels and wearing a hard hat, a clipboard in hand. Described as aggressive and inexperienced in her role as a wife and mother, Ivana nonetheless drew praise from her husband. Donald, a stickler for details, was pleased that his wife was an extra set of eyes and ears at worksites ("a natural manager" he once called her). While Trump has an eye for tall, beautiful women (each of his three wives is 5-foot-8 or taller, with modeling or pageant experience), he likes them savvy and independent as well, as also evidenced by his subsequent marriages to Marla Maples and Melania Knauss.

"Mom was tough. She does not put up with nonsense, and I love that about her," younger son Eric Trump said, offering up a description of a mom that could be as fitting for Mary Todd Lincoln. "I think her toughness is her greatest trait. She's also elegant, charming, and funny. Her personality spans a wide spectrum. There are a lot of people who may be charming but may not be as demanding."[18]

Donald has never been a doting dad, but even as a workaholic he has managed to squeeze in time for his kids, even if it meant their best bet to see him was to drop by his office, where he typically allowed them an open door, even during meetings and important telephone calls. But cutting out of work for hours at a time to catch a Little League game, school play, or dance recital rarely happened. As Donald Jr. said:

> If we wanted to see him, we could see him. If we called, he could be in the middle of the most important meeting, he'd take the phone call. If we wanted to show up in his office, we could play trucks while he's dealing with the biggest guys in banking finance. We'd be making noise, and he was totally fine with it.[19]

But tossing a football or baseball around in the backyard, or a driveway game of hoops one-on-one or H-O-R-S-E? That wasn't going to happen. At dinner time, it was usually Mom with the three kids, and two or three times a week Dad would join them at the table. Once the kids were done eating, Dad and Mom would head out to dinner, frequently as part of social functions.

"We'd talk with him (at dinnertime)," Donald Jr. said, "but he'd also be talking with my mother about business. He was good with the kids. He would joke and he'd wrestle with us, but it was for five minutes." In answer to a question if his dad ever yelled at the kids, the younger Donald added, "He got me good once. He was often the instigator. Putting my brother and sister [on the floor] and letting them fight. He'd sit there and laugh, and my mother would have to come in with her Eastern European accent and stop it. He'd get us wound up, then call in my mother to clean up the mess."[20]

When interviewed on late-night television by Conan O'Brien on March 16, 2007, Ivanka, then twenty-five and still single, said of her father,

> He's definitely not a typical father . . . [yet] he was the most accessible dad. He was always there. I would call him in the office . . . he'd have heads of state sitting in the office, and he would put me on speaker phone and tell them how great I was doing in school when I was around nine years old.

All four of Donald Trump's grown children (including Tiffany Trump, the only child Donald and Marla Maples Trump had in their six years of marriage), are highly educated and accomplished in their own right. (Tiffany was a student at Georgetown Law School at the time of this writing.) Yet all have remained close to their dad, even if just emotionally at times, while also working alongside him.

"Truthfully, I was a much better father than I was a husband, always working too much to be the husband my wives wanted me to be," Trump wrote in his 2015 book *Great Again*, right around the time he announced he was seeking the presidency. "I blame myself. I was making my mark in real estate and business, and it was very hard for a relationship to compete with that aspect of my life."[21]

Donald got no argument from Ivana when it was her turn to give her side in her own book, where she wrote about her ex-husband's merits as a father to their three kids. "Donald might not have been the greatest husband to me, but he was a good father to the kids," she said. "Obviously, they adore him and are fiercely loyal to him. If he were a horrible dad, that would not be the case."

Justifiably, Ivana used her published soap box to extol her own skills and virtues as a fulltime working mom. During her fourteen-year marriage to Donald, as she illustrates, she designed the interiors of the Grand Hyatt and Trump Tower, served as president and CEO of the Trump Castle casino (presumably, she opines, the world's only woman in such a role at the time). She was also the president and CEO of the Plaza Hotel, the latter position connected to her being named Hotelier of the Year in 1990. That's in addition to writing three international best sellers and raking in tens of millions of dollars with her own lines of fashion, fragrances, and jewelry. She was ambitious and aggressive as a woman in a man's world.

"No matter how busy I was," Ivana said, "I had breakfast with my children every day. I sat with them at dinner every night and helped them with their homework (I loved algebra), before going out in a Versace gown to a rubber-chicken charity event. Donald and I celebrated, traveled, and grieved together."[22]

Financial problems put a serious fiscal crimp in the Trump Organization in the latter half of the 1980s. The double whammy for the luxury-loving Ivana came when she found out about Donald's not-so-secret affair with the gorgeous Georgia-born Marla Maples. The 1984 Miss Georgia USA runner-up had 37-25-37 measurements that clearly caught Donald Trump's wandering eye. She was also young, seventeen years his junior.

Donald tried his best to keep his relationship with Marla quiet, but he had a hard time avoiding the prying, opportunistic tabloid press. Meanwhile, Donald's hand-built empire was fraying and in danger of toppling. He was living a life of excessive risk and lies accompanied by piles of debts, looming bankruptcies, adulterous actions, and, as Blair puts it, "overcommitted resources." The casinos, most visibly, were coming up snake eyes, not generating even enough revenue to pay for themselves, let alone turn a profit.

"There was one thing he was unable to do—tell his wife (Ivana) it was over," Blair says.

> "I have to confess," he later wrote, "I never sat down calmly with Ivana to 'talk it out' as I probably should have." Nor was his wife able to face squarely the disintegrating situation in which she was living. Meanwhile, Marla Maples was growing tired of being sequestered, of hiding in the back of the limo, of bringing her own escort to public events and standing across the room from her lover, of having a vacation with him mean [having to] travel separately and staying at a different hotel.[23]

Donald, like Abe, was not confrontational when it came to women. His inability or unwillingness to face reality and command the situation (a tact his business side would have relished) allowed fate and others to determine his matrimonial future.

The situation came to a much-publicized head during Christmas 1989. After flying his family out to Aspen, Colorado, where they stayed in a luxury hotel, Donald retrieved Marla in a separate trip to also bring her along to Aspen, where she holed up with a girlfriend in more modest quarters several blocks away from the luxury hotel where Ivana and the kids were staying.

Trump succeeded in keeping his wife and mistress apart for the better part of a week, but Marla and Ivana eventually met up on the same ski slope on New Year's Eve (which was also the birthday of Trump's son, Donald Jr.). No doubt Ivana could have challenged Marla and smoked her in a downhill race to the ski lodge, but instead she chose to stay and confront Maples, warning her younger rival to stay away from Donald. Ivana punctuated her point with a slight shove of Marla—a moment captured by photographers—for added weight in making her point. "Are you happy?" Maples asked Ivana before they went their separate ways.[24]

CB&SO

After two failed love affairs, Lincoln found his future first lady the third time around, and her name was Mary Todd. It was 1839, three years after the inglorious departure of Mary Owens from Lincoln's life. Young, cultured, dashing, and diminutive Mary Todd, age twenty-two, was living with her sister Elizabeth Porter Todd Edwards and Elizabeth's husband Ninian (the son of a former Illinois governor) in upper-crust Springfield. Exuberantly social, Elizabeth and Ninian were known throughout Springfield for their lavish parties, affording eligible young singles the opportunity to meet, enjoy lively conversation, and dance their hearts away. It was a world into which Mary fit comfortably. She was described by Herndon as "cultured, graceful, and dignified." He also noted that she was an excellent conversationalist, albeit prone to brief bouts of unladylike sarcasm, and that "she soon became the belle of the town, leading the young men of the town a merry dance."[25]

By this time, Lincoln, thirty, was a respected lawyer well into his third term in the Illinois House of Representatives. He was welcomed, even expected, at the Edwards's parties. He had learned to distinguish his left foot from his right on the dance floor, giving him the confidence upon first meeting Mary Todd to tell her he wished to dance with her "in the worst way." Mary laughed approvingly, quickly finding herself intrigued by this towering young man, who in turn was "enchanted by this vivacious, intelligent young woman, and soon he was one of her regular attendants at parties, on horseback rides, on jaunts to neighboring towns."

Mary Todd was unlike any other woman close to his age who had drawn his sincere interest. From the beginning, he was at ease chatting with Mary. If he had any shortcomings as a conversationalist, Mary more than made up for them. Abe found Mary's wit alluring, and he was most impressed with her wisdom as well as her will and her nature. But, perhaps most of all, he could talk politics with Mary. She held her own on the hot topics of the day, and Lincoln found this both exhilarating as well as a positive step toward furthering his political career—connections to the Todd family were a definite boon. But he had competition for Mary's attention, including his longtime political rival Stephen Douglas, with whom Mary "flirted outrageously," even though both knew that Stephen was more focused on his career than exchanging rings. Joshua Speed, handsome and charming, was also in the mix, although his attention was focused more on the beautiful and devout Matilda Edwards, a niece to Ninian.[26] One by one, rival candidates were being eliminated.

Time worked in Lincoln's favor with Mary, and the more she got to know the appealingly awkward Lincoln, the more attractive she found him. She was drawn to his honesty, his courtesy, and their commonalities. These ranged from their both being native Kentuckians and lovers of poetry— both had memorized many of the works of Robert Burns—to their shared political affiliations. Like Lincoln, Mary was a professed Whig, in an era where women weren't expected to be actively involved in politics. But she saw something more in Abe. Being ambitious herself and having to temper it as a woman in a man's world, she sensed his ambition, and she determined to be a part of (even the greatest encourager to spur on) his future political career.

It was clear he would be "marrying up" if he were to pursue Mary Todd, and that didn't faze him, at least not at first. He wasn't about to settle for a facsimile of his mother, sister, or stepmother. He was attracted to what Mary could bring to their relationship: a superior education, loads of societal refinement, and financial security. He would be stepping up in society, whether or not his rough manners were ready for the ascent. At times it was clear he still had more work in front of him.[27]

Abraham and Mary became engaged around Christmastime 1840, and almost immediately Lincoln started having second thoughts. His concern: Would he be able to properly support his wife? At the time he was pulling in a thousand dollars a year from his law practice—not a pittance in those days—while also drawing a stipend as a state legislator. Both sources of income were on shaky ground, however. His law partnership with John Todd Stuart—a cousin of Mary's—was about to be dissolved, and for the first time in four elections, he had lost his district when attempting to earn his fourth term in the Illinois House. He and other state legislators were facing angry attacks, with the state looking at bankruptcy amid the failure of its improvements system. Lincoln decided he would not seek another term beyond this one.[28]

Without a home to call his own and no savings, while living on a stretched income, he knew he would be unable to provide Mary with anything close to her accustomed life. He was also rattled by Speed's decision in the spring to move out of their shared abode, which left the notoriously private Lincoln destitute in terms of finances as well as male companionship.

So Lincoln made the rash decision to break off the engagement by telling Mary he didn't love her. He did this in the form of a letter because he was unwilling or unable to confront Mary initially. Speed told him he should burn the letter:

> If you have something to say to her, say it to her face. If you think you have will and manhood enough to go and see her, and speak to her what you have in that letter, you may do that . . . [Spoken] words are forgotten . . . but once [you] put your words in writing . . . they stand as a living and eternal monument against you.[29]

Heeding Speed's counsel, Lincoln tossed the letter and headed straight to the Edwards mansion, where he told Mary he didn't love her. As she burst into tears, she got up from her seat and started wringing her hands in despair, using words from Genesis 29 to exclaim, "The deceiver shall be deceived; woe is me," apparently referring to a time in Kentucky when she had jilted a young man whose affections she had long encouraged. Todd's reaction, what today might be termed as diva-like behavior, greatly affected Lincoln. With tears trickling down his own cheeks, he dropped to his knees and kissed Mary before departing, effectively demonstrating that the engagement was back on. And it was.[30] But they were not out of the woods yet.

Their wedding date was set for January 1, 1841, at the Edwards mansion. As the time approached, meticulous preparations were underway at the large house, with various renovations, rearrangement of furniture, rooms neatly decorated, supper prepared, and guests invited.[31] As the hour drew closer, Mary was adorned in silken gown and veil, adjusting the flowers in her hair in an adjoining room, but still awaiting the arrival of her husband-to-be. Guests, abuzz with excitement, started arriving. Word soon circulated, that something indeterminate was delaying Lincoln, but the expectation was still that he would come strolling through the door any moment.

It was a moment that never arrived. There was no explanation and no Lincoln; not even his closest friends knew where he was. After about an hour, guests departed and a disconsolate Mary retreated to her room. Where was he and what had happened?

A persistent search ended around daybreak when friends found Lincoln in a state of emotional chaos—restless, miserable, and desperate. In the weeks that followed, his acquaintances kept a close eye on Lincoln and made sure to keep sharp objects away from his reach. Three weeks later he wrote a letter to Stuart, saying, "I am now the most miserable man living. If what I feel were equally distributed to the whole human family, there would not be one cheerful face on earth. . . . To remain as I am is impossible."[32]

For some time after the canceled wedding ceremony, Abraham and Mary avoided each other, although each managed to keep tabs on the other through mutual friends. Finally, a Mrs. Simeon Francis, wife of the *Sangamo Journal* editor (a good friend of Lincoln's), invited both Lincoln and Todd to a social event. There she arranged a face-to-face meeting and insisted they "be friends again." Abe and Mary complied and commenced spending time together, but did so in secrecy—usually at the Francis residence. This was mainly to keep their reunion from the attention of the Edwardses, who, after the failed wedding at their home, had made it clear to Mary that she and Abraham "had better not ever marry—that their natures, mind—education—raising, etc., were so different they could not live happily as husband and wife."[33]

Later that year Lincoln renewed his offer of marriage, and the wedding finally took place on November 4, 1842. It was a last-minute event that was actually held at the Edwards's house but this time it was a much simpler ceremony. Mary's sister Elizabeth had only a few hours to prepare, and Lincoln waited until that afternoon to ask close friend James H. Matheny, who had worked with him in the circuit court office, to be his best man. When Joshua Speed spotted Lincoln getting dressed and blacking his boots, he asked his old friend where he was going, to which Lincoln responded, "To hell, I suppose."[34]

C3 80

There's little question Abraham and Mary Todd Lincoln were about as different from one another as any couple could be, beyond the fact that Lincoln was more than a foot taller than his spouse. Where she was perky, outgoing, talkative, and sociable, the future president moved slowly and was moody, prone to melancholy and extended periods of silence.

> Indifferent to what other people thought, he was not troubled when visitors found him in his favorite position for reading, stretched out at full length on the floor. She, who had grown up in houses with liveried black servants, was embarrassed when he answered the doorbell in his shirtsleeves.[35]

But both were aspiring and determined, a common thread that bound them together through all other differences.

There was often an underlying tension in the Lincoln household, mostly because of finances. In marrying Abraham, Mary wasn't just taking a step down. She was jumping off a steep precipice, going from a wealthy lifestyle complete with servants to survival mode, where stretching the family budget meant living in a small house that lacked a dining room; instead meals had to be consumed in the kitchen. Even though Mary had had a good idea what she was getting into by accepting Abraham's marriage proposal, she was mentally and emotionally unprepared for the cold reality of how her life had suddenly changed. She now had to cook, clean, scrub, and go outside behind the house to pump water, which she then had to haul back inside. When a fire was needed in the fireplace to warm the house, it was up to her to keep the fire going. Her willingness to take this downward plunge relied heavily on her vision of a future payoff: She might have already suggested to friends that Abe was destined for the White House.

Lincoln, his mind stuck in politics and law when home, was practically oblivious to the load his wife was shouldering. If there was any domestic help, it was around only for brief periods, such as when Lincoln's cousin, Harriet Hanks, showed up while attending a Springfield seminary to help out in the house. One problem with that: Harriet and Mary didn't get along. They often quarreled, as did Mary with an Irish-born maid, whom she found unreliable and lazy.[36]

Life as a wife and mother took its toll on Mary, giving rise to a reputation around Springfield that she was ill-tempered, chewing out maids or workmen around the house. Lincoln didn't escape her occasional wrath, either. Mary's moodiness was only exacerbated when the newborns started arriving, beginning with Robert Todd in 1843 and followed three years later by Edward "Eddie" Baker. Adding to the strain on their marriage, Lincoln would be gone three months a year; his various lawyerly and political duties had him away from home, "riding the circuit," leaving Mary essentially alone at home to deal with most of the housework as well as two attention-seeking young boys. She did her best to keep them well-tended, happy, and healthy in the absence of Dad.

Even when Abe was home, his inattentiveness to family matters could be a source of severe annoyance for Mary. Once such instance found Abe quietly sitting in his rocking chair in front of the fireplace, his nose in a book, unaware the fire was about to go out. His big mistake: paying no heed when Mary called to him from the kitchen where she was cooking dinner to tell him to do something about it. Twice more Mary called out; each time Lincoln just sat there, reading. Enraged at being ignored, Mary walked to the fireplace, grabbed a piece of firewood, and smacked her husband in the nose with it. It presumably wasn't hard enough to break his nose or draw blood, but it was enough to make her point.[37] Lincoln, as with Trump, often neglected the household workings, leaving them pretty much exclusively to the capable hands of his wife while he remained committed to and busy with climbing that proverbial ladder.

Lincoln had his own moments, such as one witnessed by a neighbor—a Mr. Whitehurst—whose backyard was as visible to the Lincolns as theirs was to him. What Whitehurst saw was some sort of confrontation in which Abe grabbed Mary's shoulder with one hand and her "heavy end" (her hips) with the other, forcing her in through the back door while giving her a push that was more like a spank. Lincoln said to her, "There, damn it, now stay in the house and don't disgrace us before the eyes of the world." There's no mention of what precipitated the backyard incident as related by

Herndon in *The Hidden Lincoln* (apparently not hidden from view in this circumstance).[38]

There were times, though, when Mary would show abundant kindness to her neighbors. Shortly after Mary gave birth to her fourth son Tad (Thomas) in 1853 (third son Willie had been born in 1850), she learned that Mrs. Charles Dallman was ill and thus unable to nurse her newborn infant. Upon hearing this, Mary offered her wet nurse services to the Dallman baby, while also breastfeeding Tad. Other times, her quick temper would get the best of her, such as when she chased Abraham out of the house and down the street, for reasons unknown, with gossipers claiming she had a butcher knife in hand, although others insisted it was a broomstick.[39]

Years later, in describing her husband in a letter to Herndon not long after Lincoln's assassination, Mary spoke of Abe in glowing terms, referencing both his role as a husband and as a father to his boys, all of whom, except Robert, tragically died of illness before reaching adulthood. If anything, Mr. and Mrs. Lincoln might have been too lenient with their boys, spoiling them even, perhaps choosing to cherish their existence and to forego strictness, especially after Eddie's death in 1850, five weeks shy of his fourth birthday. It was presumed that Eddie died from tuberculosis, although a form of cancer also was speculated. Willie, born ten months after Eddie's passing, would die a premature death as well, succumbing in the White House to a fever at age eleven in 1862.

Mary wrote of Abraham in her letter to Herndon:

As to his nature, he was the kindest man, most tender husband, and loving father in the world. He gave us all unbounded liberty, saying to me always when I asked for anything, "You know what you want, go and get it." And never asking if it were necessary. He was very indulgent to his children. He never neglected to praise them for any of their good acts. He often said, "It is my pleasure that my children are free and happy, and unrestrained by parental tyranny. Love is the chain whereby to bind a child to its parents."[40]

Among the issues Mary and Abraham agreed on was their belief that their children were exceptional. When they had friends over to the house on social occasions, they would dress the boys up and have them perform acts such as reciting poetry and dancing. Equally entertaining, in an odd sort of way, was Abe, the dutiful dad, hauling wee Willie and Tad around outdoors in a wagon, pulling it down and back on the street in front of the house, one hand grasping the handle and the other holding a book. One time Abe was so engrossed he didn't notice when one of them had spilled out of the wagon some distance back.

Lincoln as a father was much like Trump would be years later, allowing his children to join him in his law office to play on the floor, while he toiled away writing declarations, pleas, and assorted legal documents. Meanwhile, the boys would make a mess of things—Lincoln apparently not minding when they spilled ink, broke pens, grabbed books, and even peed on the floor. Herndon, at the time his law partner, would later reveal his thoughts about what he had seen,

> I have felt many and many a time that I wanted to wring their little necks, and yet out of respect for Lincoln I kept my mouth shut. Lincoln did not note what his children were doing or had done. When Lincoln finished his business, he would haul his children back home and meet the same old scolding or a new and intensified one. He bore all quite philosophically. . . . What a home Lincoln's was! What a wife![41]

After Willie passed away in 1862, Lincoln compensated by taking a more active role in helping Tad raise his kitten and train his dog, and withholding most if not all forms of discipline from his parental inventory.

Even at the age of nine, Tad still was not able to dress himself; nor could he read or write despite the assistance of tutors. On top of that, the young lad had a speech impediment, noticeable in such times as when he burst into one of his dad's cabinet meetings, calling out "Papa-day" to him, interpreted by those accustomed to Tad's speech patterns as "Papa dear."

One father-son relationship with which Lincoln struggled was the one with his oldest boy, Robert, the only one of the four Lincoln boys who would make it past eighteen years of age. Lincoln biographer David Donald speculated that Abe regarded his son as competition, at least in an academic sense, although he bragged on Robert to others, claiming his son was receiving "the best of educations" while also praising his intelligence. As the biographer points out, though, the two never seemed to have much to say to each other, with Robert awkward around his dad, while those who knew Robert well found him well-humored in private conversation.[42]

Robert was several months shy of his eighteenth birthday when the Civil War broke out in April 1861. By then, he was enrolled at Harvard College (now University). Followed his undergraduate studies, he matriculated at Harvard Law School, only to return home at Christmastime and announce his intent to take up arms in defense of the Union, saying it was his duty to "see something of the war before it ends." His father supported Robert in his intentions, while Mary was of mixed sentiments. In one respect she accepted her oldest son's desire to do the "manly and noble thing," but she was also hysterical at the prospect of losing a third son. In January 1865, Lincoln wrote to General Ulysses Grant, asking the Union's top military commander to give Robert "some nominal rank" and permit him to join the general's entourage. Grant complied with haste, commissioning Robert a captain and assigning him the relatively safe assignment of escorting Army of the Potomac visitors around. It didn't last long; the war was over three months later when Confederate Commander Robert E. Lee surrendered to Grant at Appomattox.

CS SO

Once she got to the White House, Mary Lincoln flourished. In time she was considered by some historians one of the most memorable first ladies (up to that point in history), on par with Dolley Madison. By the 1850s, her husband's law practice had been prospering, and the financial stress of the early years of their marriage had given way to success, comfort, and prestige. This freed Mary from what had been a persistent state of anxiety. Once in the White House, she was determined to become the "First Lady of the Land." She proved herself an excellent hostess at the Executive Mansion, a role she enjoyed as she probably knew she would, having been raised with a keen interest in public affairs and politics.[43]

It was a two-edged sword, however. What came with the territory was some scorn as well as suspicion, such as when the U.S. House Judiciary Committee began an investigation searching out possible Confederate sympathizers in the employ or service of the federal government. During this time the *New York Herald* managed to publish Lincoln's State of the Union address before the president had had a chance to present it to Congress. It turned out the newspaper had placed a shady character named Henry Wikoff into Washington society to mingle among the politically powerful and see what he could come up with for newsworthy fodder. He hit the jackpot with Lincoln's speech. With his cosmopolitan worldly charm and slick manner, Wikoff had gained the confidence of Mary Lincoln, earning him ready access to the White House and the written speech, which he turned over to the *Herald* to run in its pages.[44]

The House committee decided to investigate the White House, and fingers pointed to Mary, who had never been well-liked among DC insiders. She was a native Kentuckian (as was her husband), which in the suspicious minds of insiders made her sympathetic to the Southern cause, a sentiment further abetted by the fact that some of her brothers had joined the

Confederate army. The attacks on her character started to pile up, with the *Cincinnati Commercial*'s Murat Halstead calling her "a fool—the laughing-stock of the town, her vulgarity only the more conspicuous in consequence of her fine carriage and horses and servants in livery and fine dresses and her damnable airs." Her claim of being able to speak French was lampooned by a prominent New Yorker, and local scuttlebutt started linking Mary and Wikoff, the latter eventually testifying that it was not Mrs. Lincoln but White House head groundskeeper John Watt who had delivered the Lincoln speech to him.[45]

Critics of Mary Lincoln skipped no opportunity to disparage the first lady, even post-tragedy. Following the second death of a son, (Willie, from typhoid fever in 1862), Mary prohibited the Marine band from performing its weekly concerts at the White House, explaining, "When we are in sorrow, quiet is very necessary to us." Out came the boobirds, including a local merchant who sarcastically wrote, "I suppose Mrs. Lincoln will be providentially deterred from giving any more parties which scandalized so many good persons who did not get invitations."[46] Another member of the Hate Mary Lincoln Club was Herndon, who was perhaps still stung by his first meeting with Mary back in 1837, when she rejected his request for a dance. He had tried to compliment her dancing skill during a waltz, stating she glided "with the ease of a serpent. To which she said, 'Mr. Herndon, comparison to a serpent is rather severe irony, especially to a newcomer.'"[47]

CR ℘

It was just after midnight, early morning on November 9, 2016, and the scene inside New York City's Javits Center was a mixture of tension, anger, and dejection, as if something—or someone (Hillary Clinton maybe?)—was about to explode. The Clinton campaign had rented the Javits Center for what they were confident was going to be Hillary's victory party on Election Night. Yet it was 12:30 a.m. and the presidential race between her and Donald Trump had not yet been called. And that was bad—no, shock-ing—news for Hillary, her campaign people, the Democratic Party, and much of the media that had been poised to celebrate a Hillary election as America's first female president.

In the media room, however. word came that Trump had won yet another key battleground state. He was edging closer to the 270 electoral votes he needed to beat Clinton and claim a prize that she believed was rightfully hers. When the announcement came of another state victory for Trump, some reporters in Javits angrily slammed their tables—as reported by a *Hollywood Reporter* correspondent onsite. Stunned victory party guests quietly filed out of the venue, with Hillary supporters muttering "heartbroken," "disappointed," "confused," and "in shock" to describe their feelings as they headed out the door.[48]

This much was clear: In winning the U.S. presidency, Trump had assured himself that his next four years and two months—including the gap between his election victory and Washington, DC, inauguration—would see a steady stream of criticism, second-guessing, and mocking from a left-leaning media. The trickle-down was that his family members would also be caught in a frenzy of guilt by association (and party affiliation). That, of course, included Trump's third wife, Melania, whom he had married in January 2005 and who was now set to become America's First Lady. It also included their son, Barron, ten years old at the time his father moved into the White House—the same age that Willie Lincoln was when Abraham Lincoln was inaugurated.

Not only was Melania (Knauss) Trump just the second First Lady to have been born outside the USA (Louisa Adams was the first), she was the first who had been an immigrant to the U.S. and the first for whom English was not her first language. It was, in fact, the fifth language in which she is reportedly fluent; she also speaks French, Italian, and German, in addition to her native Slovenian.[49] The fact that she was also a former supermodel with enviable fashion tastes—indisputably one of the most beautiful women in the world—and married to the much-hated Donald Trump gave the media its journalistic license to take aim at Melania. Unlike her predecessor, Michelle Obama, who had been practically worshipped by much of the media, Melania gave the press two public figures (herself and Donald) for the price of one. In the media world some of the most prominent public figures get preferential treatment, and some, like the Trumps, don't. Melania, like Mary Lincoln, has often been the subject of controversy, and some of that controversy was engineered by the media.

Media disrespect toward Melania ramped up a notch or two after her husband declared his presidential candidacy, even before her husband had won the election. One media organization that climbed aboard the anti-Melania train early on was the *Daily Mail*, a British tabloid newspaper that in August 2016 published an article that claimed Melania had worked for an escort service during her days as a model. Mrs. Trump filed suit against the *Daily Mail* and settled with the newspaper for a judgment of $2.9 million, with the newspaper retracting the story and admitting its falsehood.[50]

Her modeling past also became a source of controversy when it was found she had been part of a sexually explicit photo shoot in the January 1996 issue of a French men's magazine[51] as well as a cover photo for the January 2000 edition of *GQ* magazine. For the latter, she had posed nude, except for diamond jewelry, in a reclining position on fur—in Trump's custom-fitted Boeing. Of course, both photo shoots took place more than fifteen years before Trump won the 2016 election and more than five years before they were even married. Donald Trump defended his wife's professional past, saying, "Melania was one of the most successful models, and she did many photo shoots, including for covers and major magazines. . . . In Europe, pictures like this are very fashionable and common."[52]

Around the same time as the appearance of the *Daily Mail* story, Melania was accused of plagiarism when the speech she gave at the 2016 Republican National Convention reportedly included a paragraph similar in wording to a segment of Michelle Obama's speech at the 2008 Democratic Convention. A Trump speechwriter later took responsibility for the "confusion." Another charge of plagiarism made against Melania, concerning a booklet that accompanied her Be Best public awareness campaign, was found by fact-checking web site Snopes to be "mostly false."[53]

Other digs against the First Lady have been groundless, a distortion of facts, or simply taking her to task for meaningless "indiscretions," such as discussing certain topics and not others during an interview in which someone else was asking the questions.

Case in point: CNN contributor Kate Anderson Brower opined in a December 2018 commentary that Melania "doesn't understand what it means to be First Lady." Brower's objections to Melania concerned an interview with Fox News's Sean Hannity in which Melania stated that "opportunists who are using my name" was one of the most difficult parts of being First Lady. Brower griped that Trump should have talked about the struggles of Americans she had met in her role as First Lady, such as women and babies dealing with opioid addiction.[54]

Welcome to *All in the First Family*.

CHAPTER 6

KEEPING IT REAL

I always believed "Honest Abe" was a legitimately earned nickname. To me Abraham Lincoln was an irreproachable American hero who not only led an exemplary life but directed a truly exceptional presidential term. But the reality of the 1850s and 1860s in our nation revealed an embattled and turbulent administration not entirely as sure-footed as I once believed. Through it all, though, one thing is certain, Lincoln always kept it real.

As candidates, both Lincoln and Trump had a knack for telling it like it is. To say what you mean in the political arena is not exactly customary of public office seekers. Measured and sanitized responses always beat impulsive slips of the tongue—at least they used to. The year 2015 brought a promising field of presidential hopefuls to challenge the new normal. Round after round of rock'em, sock'em political roughhousing dominated the most unusual nine months I have ever witnessed. And the last man standing was the most unlikely champion of the Republican Party. He was a fighter who would charge fearlessly at even the most absurd questions meant to take him down. It gave me pause to wonder what made people place so much trust in this bull dozer of a candidate.

An anxious American public took sides and watched as freedom of speech made a comeback at the same time censorship seemed to spike. This election cycle took a page straight out of the 1850's playbook. Trump began punching the politically correct culture the same way Lincoln waylaid the hypocrisies of his day. Both men spoke their minds in the political fray with a transparency cheered by masses ready for a little more honesty and a lot less doubletalk. The stubborn way Lincoln and Trump held to the mantra "A promise made must be kept" endeared them to an American people worn out by disappointment and desperate for a different kind of hope and change.

CB ഇ

The old adage "The truth hurts" does not seem to apply to Donald Trump. It doesn't seem to hurt him, at least. He tells it like it is, shooting straight, which is a bold concept most politicians shy away from. That's why a populist such as Trump has so many people drawn to him. His appeal is grounded in straight-shooting truth, telling people what they need to hear even if it's not always what they want to hear.

Trump refuses to be stifled by political correctness. That sets him apart from career politicians who are skilled in expressing themselves through carefully selected speech that sounds good but doesn't say anything. The truth hurts? Much of what Trump says is painful to those who don't like him, or at least to those who still resent him for winning an election he wasn't supposed to win. The truth according to Trump has several interpretations, or versions, than can't be neatly rolled up into one tidy statement. If he offends anyone, that's their problem, not his.

Another way of looking at the conundrum we call Donald Trump is that he believes he is telling the truth even when, technically, he isn't—such as when he's exaggerating or expressing opinions, assessments, achievements, etc. through the art of hyperbole. To his detractors—and they are many—all those types of statements get categorized as lies. To his supporters—and there are many, too—they are not to be taken literally; they only represent the kind of big talk commonly spoken by common people. With Trump, we get the point.

For example, in giving an inventory of his accomplishments in the first couple of years of his presidency, Trump said that he had "enacted the biggest tax cuts and reforms in American history." He lobbed another log onto the fire when he said that "our economy is the strongest it's ever been in the history of our country."[1] A fact check shows that the first of those two Trump brags was statistically incorrect—the tax cuts and reforms were actually the eighth-largest. The bit about the economy wasn't yet true at the time it was spoken in 2018, although it might have been true or close to true a little over a year later, by early 2020, just before the COVID-19 pandemic hit U.S. shores.

But was any of that really lying—being untruthful by its very definition? It depends. Like anything else going on in America that could be construed as political, it's in the ear of the beholder. If you belonged to the half of the American populace that detested Trump, then what he said was a nasty lie. If you were in the other half of the nation that remained loyal to Trump, you would call it speaking the truth in the sense that the gist of what he's saying *feels* true. Such tax cuts and reforms had been a long time coming; even if the indicators didn't exactly match up with certain unprecedented thresholds. The economy sure felt like it was the best it had been in a very long time. That's what Trump was implying, using words that were already on the minds of many Americans. At worst, the economy was doing just fine—a whole lot better than it had been during the recession of 2008–2009, barely ten years earlier.

In his bestselling book *The Art of the Deal*, written decades before his election, Trump gave an honest preview of what America would see with him as president.

> The final key to the way I promote is bravado. I play to people's fantasies. People may not always think big themselves, but they can still get very excited by those who do. That's why a little hyperbole never hurts. People want to believe that something is the biggest and the greatest and the most spectacular. I call it truthful hyperbole. It's an innocent form of exaggeration—and a very effective form of promotion.[2]

This is Trump's way of keeping it real, even if what he says isn't the factual truth. Trump isn't your run-of-the-mill politician speaking a politician's version of shooting straight. He is quite clearly a nonpolitician speaking a nonpolitical brand of straight talk.

Trump is an outsider who broke into the inner circle of Washington, DC's politically powerful elite. Most of them—even some of his fellow Republicans—clearly don't want him there. He is an outlier, which *Merriam-Webster* defines as "a person or thing that is atypical within a particular group, class, or category." Even among the politically incorrect, Trump is politically incorrect—and he knows it. He says what he means, and it doesn't come out filtered. He'll say it to crowds at rallies, and he'll say it to media members, knowing that in many cases those reporters will cherry pick his statements out of context or twist the meaning of his words to make them fit into a liberal narrative. Often what results sounds nothing like what Trump actually said or wrote. Yet, Trump soldiers on, being who he is. A fly in the ointment of the Washington elite.

Somewhere, in another place, Abraham Lincoln has to be applauding this fellow president who is all about going against the grain and speaking the truth—keeping it real.

"The fact is I give people what they need and deserve to hear—exactly what they don't get from politicians—and that is The Truth," Trump said in his 2016 book *Great Again*. (Incidentally this publishing was the paperback version of a hardcover he originally put out a year earlier, in late 2015, with the politically incorrect title *Crippled America*.)

> Our country is a mess right now, and we don't have time to pretend otherwise. We don't have time to waste on being politically correct. . . . I think the big problem this country has is being politically correct. I've been challenged by so many people, and I don't frankly have the time for total political correctness. . . . What I say is what I say, and everyone that knows me really appreciates it.[3]

One of the most telling portrayals of Trump as a truth merchant was related by *Washington Post* columnist Marc A. Thiessen. In 2018, a little more than a year and a half into Trump's first term, Thiessen wrote that Trump might be remembered as the most honest U.S. president in American history, while conceding that "Trump lies all the time." It is a total contradiction, and yet it isn't, which deserves an explanation from Thiessen, who has often appeared as a guest on Fox News:

"In part, it's a New York thing—everything is the biggest and the best," Thiessen wrote in a *Post* column entitled "Trump Could Be the Most Honest President in Modern History."

"But when it comes to the real barometer of presidential truthfulness—keeping his promises—Trump is a paragon of honesty. For better or worse, since taking office Trump has done exactly what he promised he would."[4]

Thiessen backs up this seeming stumper of analysis by rattling off numerous examples of how Trump had fulfilled promises he made while campaigning for office. Thiessen cites Trump's fulfillment of a pledge to move the U.S. embassy in Israel from Tel Aviv to Jerusalem, something all three of his immediate predecessors had been unable to do. He also points out that Trump established and enforced bans on travel to the United States from countries deemed as havens for international terrorists, as promised. Further, Trump nominated and won appointments for Supreme Court justices who would fit the Constitutional mold of Justice Antonin Scalia (those turned out to be Neil M. Gorsuch and Brett M. Kavanaugh), just as he had promised. And finally, Trump followed through on introducing and securing Congressional passage of historic tax reforms that included the first significant revamping of the U.S. tax code in decades.[5]

"Whether one agrees or disagrees is not the point," Thiessen says.

When Trump says he will do something, you can take it to the bank. Yes, he takes liberties with the truth. But unlike his predecessor [Barack Obama], he did not pass his signature legislative achievement on the basis of a lie ("If you like your health-care plan, you can keep it.")—which is clearly worse than falsely bragging that your tax cut is the biggest ever.

The fact is, in his first two years, Trump has compiled a remarkable record of presidential promise-keeping. He'd probably say it's the best in history—which may or may not end up being true. It's too soon to tell.[6]

Trump has admitted he is a man that the media loves to hate. In part, that's because he fights back. Go after him with criticisms and accusations, and if he believes these are false charges or incorrect reporting—what he calls "fake news," a term that Trump has cemented in the American lexicon—if he believes you're adding to the lies, you'll get another dose of Trump counterpoint delivered, usually via Twitter or a direct callout in his next news conference. Trump never seems to tire of this incessant volleying between himself and members of the media, not for the sport of it, but for the purpose of pointing out where the news has steered itself wrong.

Trump also refuses to accept any poll that paints him, his policies, or his promises in a negative or false light. If nothing else, he has motivated, even forced, the media in general to take heightened responsibility for its conduct and accuracy of reporting. If you're looking for Trump to follow unwritten rules about what a president's decorum ought to be or to limit his brash talk because of his office, you can forget it. Not with him. Again, he refuses to use filters to appease anyone, especially those who are looking for him to engage the traditional doublespeak or follow carefully crafted talking points. He will never be like those traditional politicians (and there are many) who would rather camouflage their commentary than speak the unvarnished truth of whatever convictions they might have.

Trump has said,

> It hasn't taken me long to learn how truly dishonest the political media can be. . . . I'm perhaps a controversial person; I say what's on my mind. I don't wait to hear what a pollster has to say because I don't use pollsters. The media loves my candor. They know I'm not going to dodge or ignore their questions. I have no problems telling it like it is.[7]

Telling it like it is—that's Trump's forte. If he says he's going to do something, he forges ahead on it. "Trump promised to cancel President Barack Obama's Clean Power plan, withdraw from the Paris climate accord, approve the Keystone XL and Dakota Access pipelines, and open the Arctic

National Wildlife Refuge to exploration," Thiessen writes. "He fulfilled all of those pledges."[8]

Critics have castigated Trump for having the gall to cancel programs or undo policies and executive orders put in place by his predecessor, Barack Obama. It is not the content or agenda of these programs and policies themselves that have stuck in the craw of Trump's political enemies—it is the fact they consider his presidency an illegitimate one because he lost the national popular vote, even though he won the electoral vote, which by constitutional law determines the outcome. Anti-Trumpsters have been taking it out on him ever since, persistently calling him a "liar," a "racist," and a "misogynist," and attempting to discredit and twist his words at every opportunity.

Trump stays firm against these attacks:

> The most important lesson in this—*stand behind your word, and make sure your word stands up.* People who have done business with me will tell you that I never say something unless I mean it.
>
> I don't make promises I can't keep. I don't make threats without following through. Don't ever make the mistake of thinking you can bully me.[9]

Even when the media steps in to assist the anti-Trumpsters, Trump circumvents the process like no other prominent public official before him. If the media—like CNN reporter Jim Acosta, a master at baiting and bashing Trump—goes on the offensive, Trump often resorts to Twitter to get his words out, unvarnished and untwisted, straight to the American people, love him or hate him.

"He is able to communicate directly to the people over the heads of the media, to make sure the people know what's going on, the work that he's doing," political pundit Tammy Bruce said, during a January 2020 interview with Stuart Varney of Fox News.

> This is a man that, for the first time ever, we've seen a president who is so transparent and consistent in who he is, what his attitude has been. You don't see this man changing; you don't have to wonder if he is telling you the truth. You might not like it necessarily, all the time, but you know that you can trust him . . . that he's telling you *honestly* what the situation is.[10]

It has been interesting to watch and read how the media reacts to the answers Trump gives, whether those answers are honest or evasive. For example, Trump gave a sit-down interview outside the White House with Fox News's Chris Wallace on a steamy day in July 2020. Truth in reporting is as important as what comes out of the mouth of the American president, and, in dealing with Trump, this is where the media often falls short. Some post-interview accounts described Trump as drenched in sweat ("flop sweat"). In fact, you could watch the interview and see some sweat on Trump's face, mostly limited to the small area between his nose and upper lip, and dabs of it high on his cheeks, but nothing that resembled true flop sweat. (Think of Albert Brooks's news reporter character in the movie *Broadcast News*, getting his disastrous shot as a nightly news anchor.)

Late in the interview, Wallace asked Trump if he would be a good loser if he were to lose the 2020 election. Trump admitted he isn't a good loser, and that he rarely loses, but that his concern for 2020 was that widespread mail-in voting would be rigged. Many conservative-leaning voters believed mail-in voting—which was expected to be higher than normal because of the lingering effects of the coronavirus pandemic—would leave voting vulnerable to corrupt practices. Wallace then asked Trump, "Are you saying you might not accept the results of the election? . . . I asked you the same question at [one of Trump's three 2016 debates against Democrat challenger Hillary Clinton]."

"I will tell you at the time; I will keep you in suspense," Trump said. "You know, she [Clinton] is the one who never accepted (her loss in 2016). She never accepted her loss, and she looks like a fool."[11]

In being noncommittal on the issue of accepting the election result, Trump drew the wrath of many in the news media and many more on social media, who interpreted him to mean that he would refuse to leave the White House. They speculated that he would need to be taken out of office by some show of force. This is the world that we were living in, in 2020—with words being twisted at every turn.

Trump was being forthright, expressing his honest, reasonable feelings—that indeed he might have something to say if evidence showed there were irregularities in voting. Why wouldn't he? Presumably, his Democratic opponent would do the same thing; after all, we saw what happened after the 2016 election: Robert Mueller was appointed a special counsel to investigate whether there had been collusion between the Russians and Trump's campaign. Further, Clinton bashed the Electoral College (mandated by the U.S. Constitution) and hopped from one election-related accusation to another, blaming a variety of factors for her loss (unexpected to her, the Democratic National Committee, and much of the media). She even wrote a book about it.

One important thing about Trump—and the same could be said about Abraham Lincoln—is how Trump deals in honesty. He's not a politician; he's a businessman, and he speaks and acts without a filter. For decades Washington, DC, needed an outsider to come in and speak plainly without a concern for appeasing people or acting presidential. They needed someone who would appeal to, and make his appeals to, the common man and woman—people he could connect with by speaking to them about what was on his mind. He's not a polished politician spouting talking points, but instead he makes credible points with a refreshing air about him, being a bit rough around the edges.

Trump photographer Gene Ho writes in *Trumpography*:

> Donald Trump might not have been the perfect candidate, but he was ours. He took to the podium, with a mic and the gumption, to give us the gross, honest truth. It was raw and unpolished. And in those glorious flaws came a truth that unraveled while we were watching: "A flawed man fighting for what's right is any man fighting for what's right."[12]

Trump doesn't weigh or mince his words before speaking them; he says what's on his mind and he's loaded with opinions, most of them better supported than what his detractors give him credit for. If you don't like what he says, that is 100 percent your problem. And he reacts like we do to things that we see and hear. When National Football League football players started taking a knee during the national anthem, Trump said if he were in charge, he would fire them. It was a statement for which he got blistered by a left-leaning media, sympathetic toward players disrespecting the flag and their fans, especially those who had served their country. Trump's critics take unrelenting potshots at him, devising every trick in the book to try and get him out of office. Like when a Democrat-led House of Representatives passed articles of impeachment against him, even though at least half of America knew the impeachment premise was a political and procedural sham.

When Trump gets ready to open his mouth or grab his mobile device to tweet, the media is poised to pounce. On a good day, they will also report.

About a month after his election in 2016, Trump took a phone call from the Taiwanese president, sending the federal intelligence and foreign affairs sectors into a tizzy. They were horrified, believing that the new president-elect was, in effect, thumbing his nose at China. For many years Chinese officials had demanded that America not recognize Taiwan as a sovereign entity. By taking the phone call, the media reported, Trump was violating a diplomatic tradition with China, not a superpower we want to cross swords with, not even in a diplomatic sense.

Amid the angry, overwrought protests that came Trump's way, he tweeted out, "Interesting how the U.S. sells Taiwan billions of dollars of military equipment, but I should not accept a congratulatory call."

In fact, it had been a call that had been scheduled months earlier. One of the agenda items turned out to be the offer of congratulations to Trump for his election victory, surely not a sentiment worthy of setting off World War III. And yet, in accepting the call and engaging in conversation with his Taiwanese counterpart, Trump was demonstrating that a new era had arrived in U.S.–China relations, one that would not necessarily adhere to past policies.

To much of the world beyond the city limits of Washington, DC, Trump's pragmatism was quite reasonable; it made sense. It was a real world action, not another dose of abstract appeasement typically accompanied by a dangerous dance around the core issues.[13] The hard part was explaining all this to the media. The media is at its best when it exercises healthy cynicism, but that's not the tact most members of the press take with Trump. Even before he came up with the phrase "fake news" to describe how news outlets reported on himself and the nation in general, the media hound dogs were already in a left-leaning, combative mode. They were looking for whatever gotcha material they could dig up—or make up. This type of cynicism is not a matter of poking through the talking points to find out the truth behind them; it's taking pokes at a president that was unwilling to acquiesce to the politically correct narrative.

"The other thing I do when I talk with reporters is to be straight," Trump said. "I try not to deceive them or to be defensive, because those are precisely the ways most people get themselves into trouble with the press."[14] Trouble, it turned out, was the media's goal—trouble for Trump. Their maniacal desire was to hound and badger him into awkward or damning positions. Without missing a beat, Donald Trump would verbally veer off the trail and decisively deflect their intended blows.

As such, and perhaps unwittingly, Trump was following a blueprint that had been laid out by Lincoln some 150 years earlier.

CB ◊ SO

Calling a public figure "Honest Abe" in this day and age would be met with laughter and mocking, if not a few tossed rotten tomatoes. Trying to define *honesty* today is a tough endeavor, open to interpretation, as any such definition would be subject to debate and subjectivity. Lincoln historian and author Donald T. Phillips took it a step further, suggesting that the nickname Honest Abe could very well be considered pretentious, even contrived, which is to say it could be readily tagged on its intended bearer even if it wasn't deserved or warranted, perhaps as an attempt to win favor where none was deserved.

"But the fact is that leaders who tell their subordinates the truth, even when the news is bad, gain greater respect and support for ideas than their less virtuous counterparts," *Lincoln on Leadership* author Donald T. Phillips writes.

> Even though he had some detractors, Lincoln attained success, admiration, and a positive image by maintaining his honesty and integrity. Those who questioned his upbringing and education, or even his political affiliations, tended not to doubt his integrity.
>
> Lincoln showed the same degree of fairness and decency whether disciplining or congratulating a subordinate. Emulating his style will earn leaders the trust and respect that ultimately foster passionate commitment. This approach shows that the truth is a common denominator for all interactions, among any group, and with people of varying personalities.[15]

Honesty isn't just about truth—whether spoken or borne out through one's actions—it's about integrity. It's about being a person of conviction, doing the right thing when no one is watching, and following through on a promise. It has to be developed and nurtured faithfully over the years, long before reaching the public eye. That's how Trump described it, speaking of his own life long before he entered politics. "When I went into business for myself, I made it a point to establish a reputation that bankers and other professionals would be comfortable with, and I knew that eventually my integrity as a businessman would be intact," Trump said. "People are more apt to want to work with you if they feel they can trust you."[16]

In order for Lincoln to rise to the level of Honest Abe, he had to live through the long-held maxim about "not being able to go home again," or, more pointedly, what it says in Proverbs 25 about "familiarity breeding contempt." Although he wasn't born in Springfield—or even Illinois for that matter—Lincoln was a son of Springfield. Arguably, he was not its favorite son, at least not in the eyes of Lincoln's law partner and biographer William Herndon.In Herndon's view, Lincoln's stubborn commitment to honesty and the courage of his convictions drew the scorn of some, if not many, of the city's residents, or at least those with higher levels of influence. (It sounds like Trump isn't the only one who had to deal with naysayers.)

"Mr. Lincoln was not appreciated in this city, nor was he at all times the most popular man among us," Herndon writes.

> The cause of his unpopularity, rather the want of popularity, here arose out of two grounds. First, he did his own thinking, and, second, he had the courage of his convictions and boldly and fearlessly expressed them [as would Trump more than a century later]. I speak generally, and especially of his political life. Mr. Lincoln was a cool, cautious, conservative and long-headed man. Mr. Lincoln could be trusted by the people; they did trust him and they were never deceived. He was a pure man, a great man and a patriot [again, as Trump would be decades later, in a similar vein].
>
> In the practice of the law, he was simple, honest, fair, and broad-minded; he was courteous to the bar and to the Court; he was open, candid, and square in his profession, never practicing on the sharp nor the low. Mr. Lincoln met all questions fairly, squarely, and openly, making no concealments of his ideas, nor intentions, in any case; he took no snap judgments, nor used any tricks in his business.[17]

Lincoln, like Trump later, was occasionally given to proclamations of hyperbole, or exaggeration, or what detractors would choose to call "lying," even if it was simply an innocent bending of the facts and not an outright lie. In fact, Lincoln mastered the art of blasting a rival's exaggeration in one breath while coming back with a whopper of his own in the next breath. In one instance, writing in an 1858 letter, Lincoln referenced his most renowned political rival Stephen Douglas, poking fun at Douglas in the aftermath of the latter's endorsement of the Dred Scott decision. Lincoln wrote, "His tactics just now, in part, is to make it appear that he is having a triumphal entry into; and march through the country; but it is all as bombastic and hollow as Napoleon's bulletins sent back from his campaign in Russia."[18]

Continuing, Lincoln goes on to say that he once was present at a reception for Douglas in Chicago, which was very well attended and imposing. However Lincoln was certain, based on the opinions he solicited from those gathered, that there was enough opposition there to actually vote down Douglas. Lincoln was buoyed by the fact that those in attendance urged him to speak. The future president then added, "Our meeting, twenty-four hours later, called only twelve hours before it came together and got up without trumpery, was nearly as large, and five times as enthusiastic [as the Douglas event]."[19]

Though history books have trumpeted Lincoln's modesty alongside his other admirable qualities, he could bluster with the best of them. He and

Trump together probably would have made a great team on the speaking circuit, perhaps even a duo on par with the likes of Lewis and Martin, Rowan and Martin, or, dare we say, Hope and Benny. The two presidents would have exchanged comedic quips, tall tales, and illustrative metaphors, one trying to outdo the other. They both would have kept it real, of course, but they also would have mixed in just enough humor, braggadocio, banter, and bloviation to keep things moving and stay on point. The truth would always have been there for the taking, even if both sides did a little fudging at times to keep things interesting.

As for Lincoln's purported modesty and self-deprecation, Lincoln has had few peers in American history, outside of comedian Rodney Dangerfield. Humble Abe was best at dishing it when greeted by overly boisterous crowds giving him a rousing welcome when he stood at the podium. He always made it a point to downplay the rock-star-level adulation from his fans.

Writing in his book *Lincoln*, author David Herbert Donald paints the picture:

> He had been elected president, he said, with what was surely excessive modesty, "by a mere accident, and not through any merit of mine," he was "a mere instrument, an accidental instrument, perhaps I should say," of the great cause of Union. He called himself "the humblest of all individuals that have ever been elected to the presidency," a man "without a name, perhaps without a reason why I should have a name."
>
> The journey was punctuated by constant calls on Lincoln to speak— to welcoming committees, at receptions, to state legislatures in Indiana, Ohio, New York, New Jersey, and Pennsylvania. The demands were so numerous that he became hoarse, and at times he lost his voice.[20]

In the twenty-first century, Trump has shown the same kind of drawing power at speeches and rallies, even when conniving political opponents are hoarding event passes so that when they purposely don't come, the empty seats will be used against Trump. Over the years campaigning and serving as president, Trump's crowds have easily dwarfed those of opponents such as Hillary Clinton and Joe Biden. People love to hear Trump speak, just as throngs loved hearing Lincoln in his day.

Lincoln built his trustworthiness through his consistency of character and by how he conducted business affairs and the affairs of office— whether it was the office of a frontier-bred lawyer, a politician and public servant, or eventually the U.S. president. "He was consistent in how he treated people, and how he made assignments and promotions; consistent in his interaction with his cabinet members and generals; and consistent in how he administered and managed the government and its war machine." That is how author Donald T. Phillips sums up Lincoln's mastery at gaining public trust.[21]

Lincoln was also adept at, even sly about, telling stories, such as borrowing from Aesop's Fables to get a point across or deflect attention. He was not a master of deception but certainly he was among the greatest at deflection—an art as well as a craft that every politician must eventually grasp to stay in the game—Lincoln and Trump were both skilled at it. Lincoln could read people well, and he always had a story, fable, metaphor, or joke ready to pull out as needed. Storytelling is a means to an end, a way to deflect criticism so as to avoid answering a tough question or to shoo away a dogged reporter or any other inquisitor prone to stick around as a pesky annoyance.

One time a former Kentucky governor Charles S. Morehead started pushing Lincoln to make concessions to the secessionists. This was Lincoln's cue to tell Morehead of the Aesop's fable about a lion-like creature in love with a beautiful woman,

> whose parents were opposed to her marrying the beast but were afraid of his long claws and sharp teeth. Claiming that their daughter was frail and delicate, they asked the lion to have his claws cut off and his tusks drawn lest he do serious injury to her. Desperately in love, the lion consented, and as soon as his claws were clipped and his tusks removed, the parents took clubs and knocked him on the head.[22]

After listening to Lincoln's account of the fable, a miffed Morehead acknowledged that while it was an interesting tale, it failed to provide a sufficient answer. But that was all he was going to get out of the president. "Lincoln used this technique throughout his presidency, to the bafflement of those who had no sense of humor and the rage of those who failed to get a straight answer from him," Donald writes.[23]

Speaking untruthfully to Lincoln was an unpardonable sin, even though that's probably not how he would have put it, being a man whose interest in religion was less than keen. Instead, he might have just reached deeper into the corridors of his mind to retrieve another story. At one point during the Civil War, it was brought to Lincoln's attention that a number of so-called Union patriots were actually spies relaying confidential information to the Confederacy. The revelation shocked the president, perhaps revealing in him a degree of naivete. It wasn't just the security aspect of the news that grieved Lincoln, it was also knowing that people he had believed in were devoid of loyalty and honesty—trademarks of his own persona.

After Lincoln was informed, Secretary of War Edwin Stanton asked his commander-in-chief if he had instructions. Until that point, Lincoln had been silent but his distress showed in his countenance, Lincoln told the story of the conundrum faced by an elderly farmer whose house rested underneath a huge, towering shade tree. The tree threatened devastating consequences were it ever to fall. Lincoln said:

> It was a majestic-looking tree, and apparently perfect in every part—tall, straight, and of immense size—the grand old sentinel of his forest home. One morning, while at work in his garden, he saw a squirrel [run up the tree into a hole] and thought the tree might be hollow. He proceeded to examine it carefully and, much to his surprise, he found that the stately [tree] that he had [valued] for its beauty and grandeur to be the pride and protection of his little farm was hollow from top to bottom. Only a rim of sound wood remained, barely sufficient to support its weight. What was he to do? If he cut it down, it would [do great damage] with its great length and spreading branches. If he let it remain, his family was in constant danger. In a storm it might fall, or the wind might blow it down, and his house and children be crushed by it. What should he do? As he turned away, he said sadly, "'I wish I had never seen that squirrel."[24]

Part-deflection, part-denial, Lincoln's metaphorical account acknowledged that there were truths you could wish not to know about—such as there being traitors in your midst. This story is heartbreaking evidence of the travails of war, especially a war that pitted brother against brother. But deflection is also a politician's survival tactic, something to provide an opening for an escape or at least a reprieve from a particular line of questioning. As a lawyer, Lincoln was well familiar with "the lawyer's dodge," a ploy he practiced well during his tumultuous decades as an attorney. He knew how to take a detour around the truth when it served his needs or the needs of his client.

Lincoln's most memorable use of the lawyer's dodge—speaking a truth which becomes a truth only because of some behind-the-scenes machinations—came in the last few months of the Civil War. This was at a time when he was as determined to outlaw slavery as he was to find a peaceful end to the war. It was in January 1865. Union forces were starting to forcefully exert their superiority along battle lines when Lincoln learned that a Confederate peace delegation was making its way through Virginia and headed toward Washington, DC. Its mission was to broker a peace with Lincoln and the Union. As part of this, the South would lay down its weapons in return for permission to continue slavery without legal interference, a proposition that Lincoln had no intention of accepting.

His committment to opposing slavery was unassailable, and it was a position he had firmly held for years. His convictions in this matter literally transformed him. During one impassioned speech referenced by Phillips in *Lincoln on Leadership*, Lincoln was first described by a news reporter as being

> so angular and awkward that I had for an instant a feeling of pity for so ungainly a man. . . . His clothes were black and ill-fitting, badly wrinkled—as if they had been jammed carelessly into a small trunk. His bushy head, with the stiff black hair thrown back, was balanced on a long and lean head-stalk, and when he raised his hands in an opening gesture, I noticed that they were very large. He began in a low tone of voice—as if he were used to speaking out-doors and was afraid of speaking too loud.[25]

Soon, though, Lincoln changed.

> He straightened up, made regular and graceful gestures; his face lighted as with an inward fire; the whole man was transfigured. . . . I forgot the clothing, his personal appearance, and his individual peculiarities. Presently, forgetting myself, I was on my feet with the rest, yelling like a wild Indian, cheering the wonderful man. In the closing parts of his argument, you could hear the gentle sizzling of the gas burners.[26]

What was Lincoln talking so ardently about that he was able to turn a jaded newspaper reporter into part of an exuberantly cheering crowd? Slavery, and his adamant aversion to it. "When he finished, the audience approved the glorious triumph of truth by loud and continued huzzas," as reported by the *Springfield Journal*.[27]

One part of the speech that particularly fired up Lincoln was his political arch-rival Stephen A. Douglas's proslavery stance. Douglas believed that America's Founding Fathers had endorsed slavery. Just the thought of Douglas promoting this view inspired Lincoln to give a speech that historian and author Doris Kearns Goodwin, referencing contemporary accounts, termed as

> the most accessible, persuasive, and profound argument ever made against the extension of slavery. He penetrated his subject with deep insight and carried his listeners along to his way of thinking. What persuaded and changed minds was the sincerity, clarity, conviction, and passion of the story he told.

Kearns Goodwin drives the point deeper, quoting a young reporter present at the speech. (It's not known if this was the same exuberantly cheering reporter referenced earlier.) The reporter said,

> His speaking went to the heart because it came from the heart. I have heard celebrated orators who could start thunders of applause without changing any man's opinion. Mr. Lincoln's eloquence was of the higher type, which produced conviction in others because of the conviction of the speaker himself.[28]

Lincoln biographer William Herndon described his one-time law partner's pursuit of abolishing slavery as a "war." Lincoln's mission was to wage such a battle "until its destruction was effected, but he always indicated a preference for getting rid of slavery by purchase rather than the war power. He was an artful man, and yet his art had all the appearance of simple-mindedness."[29]

Lincoln wasn't just an artful man; he was an artful dodger, which bring us back to January 1865, and the Confederate contingent on its way to Washington, DC, to hammer out a peace agreement. As much as Lincoln wanted an end to the war, he wouldn't accept it without resolving the issue of slavery—and he was determined that that resolution would be the proposed Thirteenth Amendment to the U.S. Constitution that would abolish slavery. But it was going to be tricky, and it would take some maneuvering to make it happen. His strategy was a lawyer's dodge that only someone as skilled as Lincoln would be able to pull off at such a high level and in such a treacherous time, in order for Congress to buy it.

Foremost in Lincoln's plan was the passage of the Thirteenth Amendment. Only once that was done would he pursue a peace settlement. Again, the trick for Lincoln was to get the amendment passed before a peaceful settlement to the war was reached, and he didn't want debate and a vote on the amendment shelved until the re-assembly of Congress in the fall. Lincoln needed to get it done now.

By this time, with Savannah in the South about to fall and Sherman's March to the Sea soon to be underway, the Confederacy was crippled militarily and spiritually and ready to make a peace deal. Lincoln knew he was in a strong position. The U.S. House of Representatives had taken up debate on the amendment bill, and Congress actually had the votes needed, including those from lame-duck Democrats, to push the amendment forward. Lincoln's ploy came into play. He knew that if peace were on the table, the Democrats would not vote to pass the bill to abolish slavery.

Word soon spread in the halls of Congress and across DC that the Confederacy had sent peace-seeking agents to Washington. Rumors circulated that they might already be there. (They weren't; Lincoln had secretly seen to that). He had wired his commanding general Ulysses Grant and told Grant to block the three Confederate commissioners from coming any farther north, essentially holding them as prisoners in City Point, Virginia, until such time that they could be "safely" released.

The key evidence of this Lincoln tactic was an exchange of notes he had with U.S. Representative James M. Ashley, who had sponsored the bill calling for the Thirteenth Amendment. Ashley wrote: "The report is in circulation in the House that Peace Commissioners are on their way or are in the city and is being used against us. If it is true, I fear we shall lose the bill. Please authorize me to contradict it, if not true." Lincoln's brief response, dated January 31, 1865, was: "So far as I know, there are no peace commissioners in the city, or likely to be in it." Classic.[30]

With Grant holding the three peace seekers in Virginia, Lincoln, in good faith—if not the highest of scruples—told Congress that, contrary to reports, there were no members of a Confederate peace contingent in the city, nor were any headed their way. (Grant was seeing to that.) Soon, Congress passed the Thirteenth Amendment, and Lincoln signed off on it. Officially, slavery was now illegal.[31]

CB EO

Lincoln had his detractors, yet he embodied integrity and honesty, and he did so consistently. In assessing Lincoln's character traits, Herndon singled out truth and candor as the two that were strongest in Lincoln's repertoire. "He was utterly incapable of insincerity or professing views on this or any other subject he did not entertain," Herndon writes in *Herndon's Lincoln*.

> Knowing such to be his true character, that insincerity, much more duplicity, were traits wholly foreign to his nature, many of his old friends were not a little surprised at finding in some of the biographies of this great man statements concerning his religious opinions so utterly at variance with his known sentiments.[32]

It is true that Lincoln never actually belonged to a church, and apparently didn't believe in any church or align himself with a particular denomination, but he still managed to be "intensely sincere and honest," Herndon adds.[33] "He was brave without being rash and never refrained from giving utterance to his views because they were unpopular or likely to bring him in to danger; at the same time he abstained from needlessly giving offense."[34]

Another factor that made Lincoln so effective in gaining the respect of acquaintances and audiences was his simplicity of character, which in large part ties into his strength of humility. He was blunt but he was plainspoken, easily understood with few, if any, airs about him. Another way of putting it: he wasn't a phony. Indeed, he endeared himself to others quite readily, which made him entirely credible in the eyes and ears of those who either knew him or knew of him from his public appearances.

"He had no affectation in anything," Leonard Swett, a civil and criminal lawyer who sometimes advised Lincoln on political matters, wrote in a letter to Herndon.

> True to nature, true to himself, he was true to everybody and everything around him. When he was ignorant on any subject, no matter how simple it might make him appear, he was always willing to acknowledge it. His whole aim in life was to be true to himself, and being true to himself he could be false to no one.[35]

Much of the same could be said about Trump, whose detractors and obsessive second-guessers let their hate and disdain toward him color how they interpret his speeches, interviews, and so on. When Trump exaggerated the size of the crowd at his January 2017 inauguration, they proclaimed him a liar. Just as they did with myriad other things he said or wrote.

What Trump actually has is a no-nonsense approach to life and the presidency. This approach sounds perfectly reasonable and sensible to anyone living outside of or not brainwashed by the politicalspeak that permeates life and corrupts the thinking of those along the Potomac. This policicital posturing produced an environment of pandering that masquerades as statesmanship. But that is not how Trump operates, and it wasn't how Lincoln did either. As former House Speaker Newt Gingrich puts it in *Understanding Trump*,

> Trump wants to set aside the abstract establishment theories and get to what makes up the real world. In a way, I would argue that Trump's way of thinking is a reversion to Tocqueville, Lincoln, and Washington. If you look at the original American system, it was extraordinarily fact-based.[36]

Robert Kiyosaki, best-selling author of *Rich Dad, Poor Dad*, and a friend of Trump's, sees the forty-fifth president as consistently straight to the point and truthful, even when it hurts.

In most instances, his thoughts, words, and actions are the same. Maybe this is why he is direct and blunt. He can be blunt because his thoughts, words, and actions are integrated, congruent, acting as one. Many of us know people who are, actually, three people. They think one thing, say something else, and do not do what they say or think.[37]

Kiyosaki could just as easily have been describing Lincoln, who, like Trump after him, didn't let a crowd's occasional negative reactions to something dissuade him from saying it. Herndon bears that out in quoting Judge David Davis who said of Lincoln, "When he was convinced on any question, when he believed he was right, he acted, and the terrors of mob opinion had no terrors for him."[38]

Ditto for Trump, who campaigned on a number of pledges he would bring to the presidency, some of them entailing reversals of policies and executive orders issued by his predecessor, Barack Obama. He sticks to his guns despite an opposition that impeached him in a failed attempt to remove him from office. When he's wrong—in his judgment, not someone else's— he will backtrack, just as he did when he ultimately abandoned a plan to completely pull U.S. forces out of Afghanistan. While Trump has bent the truth at times, it's nothing compared to the outright fibs of Obama, whose signature legislative victory—one that gave us Obamacare—was based on a blatant lie: ("If you like your health care plan, you can keep it.") Obama also lied in his explanation for what caused the terrorist attack on the U.S. embassy in Benghazi, resulting in the deaths of four Americans.

When he first ran for president in 2016, Trump needed the backing of Christian evangelicals. It was an endorsement he quickly won, despite his personal baggage that included two failed marriages, one known illicit affair (Marla Maples), and accusations, albeit unproven, of at least one affair with a porn actress—Stephanie "Stormy Daniels" Clifford. What ultimately sold Trump to the Christian base was his authenticity, a quality long admired by evangelicals who fully understood the concepts of forgiveness and redemption. "President Trump represented to the evangelical community a warrior to fight the encroachment of the federal government in their lives and in their institutions," the *Washington Post*'s Robert Costa wrote. "In a sense they forgave him for all his personal misdeeds because they believed he could be a strong man in taking away regulations or different federal guidelines that they saw as a burden for their church, or for their religious institutions."[39]

Texas-based evangelist James Robison, a friend of Trump's, is among millions who cherish his "give it to me straight" philosophy on life, business, and politics. One of the things Robison told Trump during the latter's presidential campaign in 2016 was to avoid using religious terminology in public discourse. Robison knew such language might come across as phony and hurt Trump's election chances. "It'll backfire," Robison said he told Trump. And "he did it. He never tried to prove to you or anybody else he's a great spiritual giant. I made it clear that he was growing in his faith. But here's what he knew. 'I can't win without evangelicals and professing Christians.' "[40]

In his commitment to authenticity, Trump reveals a pet peeve: hypocrisy. He has a sincere aversion to it, and that includes the treatment of Christians in America. "I don't understand why the same people who demand respect for their beliefs often don't show respect for the beliefs of others," Trump has said. "It seems like every week there is a negative ruling on some issue having to do with Christianity. I think it's outrageous, totally outrageous."[41]

And that's the truth.

CHAPTER 7

SELF-MADE MAN

What exactly does it mean to be a self-made man? Horatio Alger defined the idea in his nineteenth-century novels as a person who comes up from nothing. His parade of poor, humble characters who rose from the bottom rung of the ladder to become successful in life portrayed true rags-to-riches tales. Titles such as *Ragged Dick, Fame and Fortune,* and *Bound to Rise* were devoured by young adults craving the hopeful storylines and happy endings.

Abe Lincoln could definitely have played the part of one of Horatio's boys. (He even gave it a title: *Annals of the Poor.*) But Donald Trump? How absurd is it to ponder a millionaire's son rising up the ladder—wasn't he already at the top? Maybe that's the question: Must one rise from nothing? I think the beginning level of poverty or lack thereof may be less significant than how far one rises above that first step.

Perhaps "self-invented" or "self-determined" are better labels for climbers who rise above their initial circumstances by their own stubborn will. Lincoln told young men that "will" was the most important quality for success. Trump wrote a book on it titled *Never Give Up.* And, let's be honest, Alger strategically placed wealthy benefactors along the trail of his poor boys. Perhaps to prove that it takes a village after all.

Just as in Alger's stories, Lincoln and Trump both had helpers along their way to success. Unearthing those influential helpers perched on the Lincoln and Trump ladders revealed some things: Success doesn't happen by chance, and rarely entirely on one's own. Dogged determination and having a village of supporters are certainly steps along the way. But what about energy and ambition, and just plain good fortune? (In Trump's case—really big fortune!) In truth, many ingredients have to converge for one human being to make something of himself or herself.

After all my digging into Lincoln's and Trump's histories, the metaphor of a man climbing a ladder just didn't seem to fit anymore. A ship at sea was more like it. And these two men had ones that were well-fitted and with expert crews. When clouds formed on the horizon and roiling seas tossed them about (waves that would have swamped anyone else's boat) these elements aroused in each man the right stuff to navigate the storm.

CB ED

Calling Abraham Lincoln a self-made man makes perfect sense, considering the poor conditions into which he was born and the dire lack of educational opportunities afforded someone growing up in the desolate backwoods of Kentucky, and then Indiana.

Compare that to the privilege and opportunity that awaited Donald Trump more than a century later: born into wealth, his father a highly successful developer who was eventually worth more than a quarter billion dollars. Appearances and circumstances reveal little, if anything, in common between Lincoln and Trump, yet both men made their way in the world by creating their own opportunities. Each in their own distinct manner overcame steep odds to become president of the United States.

After all, no one would have thought a thrice-married prima donna, billionaire businessman who was once embroiled in bankruptcy while publicly flogged by a henpecking media—a man without a shred of political experience—would bounce back to be elected to the highest office in the land. And this was after naysaying pundits nationwide had predicted with near certainty, even just twenty-four hours prior to his win, that he would be defeated at the ballot box.

Look at it this way: Trump was a different kind of self-made man. Although the elder Trump was already a wealthy man by the time his fourth child—Donald John—was born in 1946, Fred and Mary Trump had gone to great lengths to shield their five children from the domestic trappings of a wealthy existence. One of the only exceptions was the occasional indulgence of Donnie being allowed to use a limo on his newspaper route when the weather was especially disagreeable.

"We had a very traditional family," Trump wrote in his best-selling book *The Art of the Deal*.

My father was the power and the breadwinner, and my mother was the perfect housewife. That didn't mean she sat around playing bridge and talking on the phone. There were five children in all and besides taking care of us, she cooked and cleaned and darned socks and did charity work at the local hospital. We lived in a large house, but we never thought of ourselves as rich kids. We were brought up to know the value of a dollar and to appreciate the importance of hard work.[1]

As a teen and later while in college and immediately after, Donald learned the ropes of the construction business at his father's side. He was still in his twenties when his dad kicked himself upstairs to become chairman of the board, leaving the briefly vacant president's chair to become Donald's. Yet, the younger Trump harbored other ideas. He wanted to be on his own. Not long after consolidating his dad's corporate holdings under one umbrella, now known as the Trump Organization, Donald struck out on his own, moving from the world of Brooklyn and Queens to an almost entirely separate orbit in Manhattan. There, for all practical purposes, Donald was starting over. In Manhattan, he would have to deal—and scrap and scrape—among an entirely new cast of movers and shakers.

"He had upscaled his own life as well, with a move to Manhattan's Upper East Side," Gwenda Blair writes in *The Trumps*.

> Settling into a small, dark studio on the seventeenth floor of a twenty-one-floor building, he blithely referred to his new living quarters as a penthouse and began carving out a new life as a debonair bachelor. "Moving into that apartment was probably more exciting for me than moving, fifteen years later, into the top three floors of Trump Tower," he wrote later.[2]

The move—both in terms of greater New York City geography and career orientation—was a bit of a mystery to Fred Trump. Apparently he had assumed Donnie would inherit the family business—as the only Trump child deemed capable of or otherwise willing to take on such a handed-down responsibility—and stay there for decades to come. Young Trump's itch for the brighter lights and bigger city was too much for him not to chase Manhattan. "He thought I was crazy," Trump would say years later of his dad. "Nevertheless, he had a confidence in me. I'll never forget when he told my incredible mother, 'Look, I don't know if he is right or wrong, but I've got to let him do it. He has great ability and talent.'"[3]

Trump also said, "I want to be in mid-Manhattan, where all the top stuff is going on. I'll never be involved with the old man's property except when he needs me."[4]

In a coincidental twist, Trump's uptown move was remarkably similar to the story line of a popular 1970s television sitcom spun off from another show. The year that Trump moved out of Queens was the same year that the classic-to-be sitcom *All in the Family* (with politically incorrect Archie Bunker as head of the household) debuted on TV. One set of recurring supporting characters on the show were the Jeffersons, a couple who came into some money and started a cleaning business that quickly became very successful and made them wealthy, inspiring them to leave Queens and make the big move up ("movin' on up") to the East Side of Manhattan—roughly around the same time that Donald Trump was settling into his new digs in the same part of the city.

Author Gene Ho extolled Trump's self-made-man virtues in his book *Trumpography*:

> Man is made or unmade by himself. The pursuit of knowledge, experience, understanding, common sense, and insight map the path to wisdom. Still, having a map doesn't guarantee one will arrive at his or her destination. It takes conscious effort and a focused objective to work relentlessly toward personal improvement. Wisdom is not a set destination but found in the journey. Through that journey, the truth boils down to one human philosophy—Wisdom comes from living well.[5]

CBEO

Lincoln never lived really well—until he made it to the White House. He never made it to Manhattan, at least not to live there or to build skyscrapers there; he had Kentucky and then Indiana and Illinois to deal with. His lot in life was much more spartan than anything in Queens, let alone Manhattan. Lincoln didn't just rise above his circumstances; he rose from nothing—nothing but a small cabin with a dirt floor in the middle of backwoods Kentucky. There were no limos to help him make his rounds (whatever those might have been in his small parcel of the world).

What young Abe Lincoln did embrace at an early age was the belief that he was meant for something far better. It was an inner drive that he ambitiously nourished before anyone else arrived in his life to contribute to that effort. Other than a stepmom who fed into Abe's growing fascination with books and reading, and the occasional kick in his butt from a dad more concerned with cutting down trees and clearing bush than feeding Abe's intellect and daydreams, Lincoln the boy and then Lincoln the adolescent was mostly on his own with his own devices (curiosity, work ethic, and so on), and he wasted little time exploiting those. There was a tension, a strain, between youthful Abe Lincoln and his father, Thomas, but Abe chose to let that friction feed his yearning rather than stifle it. It was a sign of resiliency that would serve him well in overcoming obstacles and bouncing back from political defeats.

Historian Doris Kearns Goodwin observes:

> Year after year, as he persevered in defiance of his father's wishes, managing his negative emotions and exercising his will to slowly master one subject after another, he developed an increasing belief in his own strengths and powers, He came to trust "that he was going to be something," his cousin Sophie Hanks related, slowly creating what one leadership scholar calls "a vision of an alternative future." He told a neighbor he did not "intend to delve, grub, shuck corn, split rails, and the like. I'll study and get ready, and then the chance will come."[6]

Goodwin adds, "From the beginning, young Lincoln aspired to nothing less than to inscribe his name into the book of community memory."[7]

At any given moment, the world in which Lincoln lived and the people and settings around him didn't define who he was. From the time he was a young boy, Lincoln demonstrated a gifted mind that was exceptionally well-ordered and intelligent, with a knack for inquisitiveness that would be relentless in his pursuit of knowledge and retention of it. He learned how to read and write at the age of seven while attending ABC school in rural Kentucky. While he was there, others observed how Abe was able to learn more quickly and grasp the material more deeply than his peers. He was at or near the top of his class, despite being frequently pulled away from school by Thomas Lincoln, who needed his strong, reliable son to help work on the family's scrimpy farm. "He was the learned boy among us unlearned folks," is how one of his classmates would put it later. Lincoln biographer David Hebert Donald admired Lincoln's maturity: "He carried away from his brief schooling the self-confidence of a man who has never met his intellectual equal." Added Goodwin: "A dream that he might someday be in a situation to make the most of his talents began to take hold."[8]

When Lincoln did make it to school, he was usually an early arrival and he focused intently on his studies and the classwork. Interestingly, though, he wasn't considered a fast learner, but a diligent one. He would immerse himself into his lessons and reading material with gusto, repeatedly going over material until it stuck to his brain like glue. All this despite the fact that his father saw any type of formal education and reading as a distraction— and annoyance likely—from the important work at hand, which was whatever manual labor his father needed help with at the time. Essentially, until he reached the age of twenty-one, Lincoln was an indentured servant to his dad. Despite the limitations placed on him, Abe almost always had a book in hand, even while working. At such times as plowing or clearing land, he often appeared with a farm implement in one hand and a book in the other.

"Abe's love for books, and his determined effort to obtain an education in spite of so many obstacles, induced the belief in his father's mind that book-learning was absorbing a greater proportion of his energy and industry than the demands of the farm," William Herndon writes.

> The old gentleman had but little faith in the value of books or papers, and hence the frequent drafts he made on his son to aid in the drudgery of daily toil. He undertook to teach him his own trade—he was a carpenter and joiner—but Abe manifested such a striking want of interest that the effort to make a carpenter of him was soon abandoned.[9]

One of Abe's cousins, Dennis Hanks, took credit for teaching young Lincoln how to write by putting a buzzard's quill pen into his hand—Dennis reportedly took credit for shooting the bird that begat the pen, too. Then Dennis put Abe's writing hand in his, moving his fingers to let him become familiar with the exercise of penmanship. Another cousin, John Hanks, described Abe as "somewhat dull . . . not a brilliant boy . . . (who) worked slowly but surely," although Abraham's stepmother was more generous with her assessment of his academic skills and knack for learning, saying, "He must understand everything—even to the smallest thing—minutely and exactly. He would then repeat it over to himself again and again—some times in one form and then in an other and when it was fixed in his mind to suit him, he . . . never lost that fact or his understanding of it."[10]

Piecing together various historical accounts of Lincoln's schooling as a youth, it is believed he attended three different schools between the ages of seven and fifteen, although these schools were nothing like the public education facilities of today. Lincoln's schools—the ones his sister Sarah also attended—were conducted in what apparently were one-room cabins with a single adult in charge. One of those adults was Andrew Crawford, a justice of the peace who ran a subscription school, for which parents of students paid tuition in cash or by exchanging some other commodities. Crawford's school didn't give out grades. It was what was called a "blab school" because students recited their lessons out loud, with Crawford listening carefully for errors that he could point out to the students, correcting them in the process. According to Lincoln biographer David Herbert Donald, Lincoln's formal education came to an end when he was fifteen years old, when "the aggregate of all his schooling did not amount to one year."[11]

Lincoln's lack of formal schooling didn't prevent him from becoming an exceptionally learned man. But he was almost entirely a self-taught one. All he needed were books, including the *Bible* and *Aesop's Fables*. He was a voracious reader, and his powers of retention were remarkable. To his friends, classmates, and others who knew him, Lincoln had a gift. This was a perception that he disputed, claiming that, in fact, he was slow to learn, yet slow to forget what he had learned once he had absorbed it. "My mind is like a piece of steel," he said, "very hard to scratch anything on it, and almost impossible once you got it there to rub it out." There was also a method to the arduous process involved in his self-teaching and engraving things into his memory, as his stepmother pointed out: "When he came upon a passage that struck him, he would write it down on boards if he had no paper and keep it there until he did get paper, and then he would rewrite it." He would then insert it in a scrapbook for his easy reference any time he needed to take another look at what he had copied multiple times already.[12]

Paper to write on was usually scarce, so Lincoln would often resort to writing on boards, and when they became too black for him to write legibly, he would shave off the old writings with a drawing knife and continue on with his work, a newly blank "slate" at his disposal—the resourceful mark of a self-made man. He was also drawn to mathematics, for which he gathered a few sheets of paper that he sewed together to create a small notebook. In this book he recorded lengthy calculations such as 34,567,834 times 23,423 or 4,375,702 divided by 2,432. "He also solved problems concerning weights and measures, and figured discounts and simple interest"— skills that would come in handy years later when he was working behind the counter at a store in New Salem, Illinois. He even worked his way through a geometry textbook, anything to work his brain and round out his practical knowledge beyond just history and, later, law.[13]

It wasn't just that Lincoln read relentlessly and sought out ways to expand his acquisition of knowledge, it was how he read books that caught the attention of others, a certain peculiarity in how he kept his nose in his books—often lying on his back, his feet sometimes propped up against a wall. Maybe it was a way to take the strain off his back, a distinct possibility considering how fast he grew and how lean he was. His cousin John Hanks recalled how, at around age fourteen, Abe and he would return to the house after a day's work, at which time Lincoln typically would go straight to the cupboard, grab a piece of cornbread, sit down, take a book into his hands, lift his legs as high as his head, and settle into reading for a long time.

To some observers, Lincoln looked lazy—with a book in hand almost constantly, whether he was lying down or performing manual labor upright at half speed It wasn't just that he was reading, but he was doing so as if in deep meditation, practically oblivious to the world around him. One of those skeptics concerning Lincoln's work ethic was a neighbor, John Romine, who employed Lincoln from time to time. "(He) was always reading and thinking," Romine said. "I used to get mad at him for it. I say he was awfully lazy. He would laugh and talk—crack his jokes and tell stories all the time; didn't love work half as much as his pay. He said to me one day that his father taught him to work, but he never taught him to love it."[14]

If the work didn't get Lincoln's full attention, some of the books he read did, such as *The Life of George Washington*, authored by Parson Mason Weems. It was a book that influenced young Lincoln greatly and stayed with him the rest of his life, no doubt having a part in his eventual journey to the White House. Decades later, when Lincoln was on his way to his first inauguration as president, he told the New Jersey senate of how Weems had portrayed Washington's struggles at Trenton, describing them in his talk as "the crossing of the river; the contest with the Hessians; the great hardships endured at that time." Clearly the book had left a lasting impression on Abe. "I recollect thinking then, boy even though I was, that there must have been something more than common that those men struggled for," Lincoln told the state senators.[15]

Yet another self-teaching tool that Lincoln used was a preference to read aloud from his books while in the presence of others. It wasn't so much an act to get other people's attention as it was a manner in which he was better able to focus, and to remember the material going forward. "When I read aloud," Lincoln would later say, "two senses catch the idea: first, I see what I read; second, I hear it, and therefore I remember it better." His finely tuned memory also helped him early on to develop his sensibility "for the music and rhythm of poetry and drama," as Goodwin puts it. "He recited long stanzas and passages from memory,"[16] just as he would often relate stories from *Aesop's Fables* to make a particular point, drawing on analogies that made it easy for listeners to grasp whatever he might be illustrating. Again, his recall for such stories and skill in retelling them, combined with the lessons of elocution he gleaned from other books, all worked together to make Lincoln one of the great public speakers in American history, a master at the art who could inform and entertain with unbounded aplomb.

CB EO

Donald Trump's schooling was completely different from Lincoln's. He had great schooling and educational opportunities, although there was still a sense that he was doing things his own way and seeking or creating opportunities for himself outside the norm of the privileged school child. At the age of three he started attending Carousel Pre-School, which at the time wasva new nursery program located in Jamaica Estates, not far from home. Carousel's director was Shirley Greene, who had been trained in early childhood education at two prestigious programs, including one at Columbia University. Greene had established what was regarded as a model nursery school in an old house. Described as avant-garde for its time (this was the late 1940s), Carousel's focus was on "individual development and hands-on learning experiences from gardening and outdoor play to collecting snowflakes [the kind falling from the sky on wintry days, not persons of an especially lightweight form of liberal political persuasion], and especially building with blocks." Said Greene, "Donald was a beautiful little boy, very blond and buttery. He was a nice size for his age, very attractive, social, and outgoing. He wasn't fat, but he was really sturdy, and really quite jolly."[17]

At age five Trump was enrolled in Kew Forest, a private school with a more structured environment than Carousel. Students wore mandated school uniforms and sang hymns every morning at assembly. The dress for boys was a navy blazer with the school crest on the pocket, accompanied by a school tie and charcoal-colored pants. Girls wore a white blouse to go with navy blue jumpers. This was Donnie's introduction to discipline and regimentation outside of the home. Over the years it would become evident that with his suave yet competitive nature, he enjoyed living outside the rules when possible.

It was at Kew Forest that Trump met Peter Brant, who likewise came from a wealthy family and who would end up being Donald's best friend for many years. Together, they were more than a handful for most teachers and school officials. Though similar in terms of comportment (or lack of it), they were physical opposites—Peter was shorter and chunkier with a darker complexion, while Donnie was tall for his age, with the fair-haired look of a choir boy. Both Peter and Donnie were of above-average intelligence but with below-average grades, apparently saving their energies for outside the classroom, where they excelled as athletes, competing on several teams and winning more than their share of medals and trophies. "Sports was our whole life then," Brant said years later. "We were in our own world."[18]

They were in their own world in more ways than one; the two boys were frequently committing mischief, seeing what they could get away with,

shooting spitballs and cracking jokes—no doubt attempts to garner attention and get a rise out of teachers. "They were extremely competitive and
had to be on top whichever way they could," classmate Fina Farhi Geiger
said.

> They really pushed the limits in terms of authority and what they could
> get away with. . . . We grew up at a time when everyone basically went by
> the rules, which means being respectful. Peter and Donald didn't do that.
> They weren't respectful. They did their own thing. Donald was very sharp
> and knew just what he could get away with.[19]

The tipping point for young Trump came after he and Brant sneaked
off for an excursion into New York City. As mentioned in a previous chapter, Trump returned home with a switchblade that his parents soon discovered. Fred Trump decided it was time to crack down and send his son,
now thirteen, off to military school. He enrolled Donald in New York
Military Academy about fifty-five miles north of the city in the small
town of Cornwall-on-Hudson, near West Point (the United States Military
Academy). Donald's life at the military school was about to smooth off some
of his rough edges. No more goofing around.

From the day they arrived, new cadets quickly found themselves drilled
and ordered around by higher-ranking upperclassmen. They learned how
to march, how to salute, how to perform basic military maneuvers. Often
and at random times, they were told to stand at attention and recite academy traditions and rules that they were supposed to memorize. They ran
errands at an upperclassman's whim, dropped and knocked out push-ups,
ate square meals, and basically did whatever they were told to do, no matter
how troublesome or vexing. "It's not an easy task for a boy away from home,
having people bark at you, do this, do that, get in step, keep your mouth
closed, take a shower, do your homework, go to bed, get up," said Col. Ted
"Doby" Dobias, an NYMA graduate and World War II veteran who was a
tactical training officer and athletic coach at the school. "Kids would burst
into tears and beg to go home."[20]

Not Donald Trump; he was no washout. In fact, he seemed to take
everything in stride; doing what he was told, keeping his nose clean, and
tolerating academy life better than most boys there. His character was being
built. He was learning to be organized. And he seemed to know what he was
doing all the time, even when a more-senior cadet was screaming things in
his ear that would have made many of his peers cringe. Although he wasn't
one of the top overall students in his class, he did okay competing for grades

and at one point managed to get the highest grades in geometry, a subject that Lincoln, too, had liked and learned well.

Trump was drawn to Dobias and sought instruction from the military veteran. This is an important key to understanding why Trump indeed is a self-made man, and not one who had everything handed to him on a silver platter, like a spoiled, entitled real-life version of comic book icon Richie Rich. According to Dobias,

> (Trump) caught my eye right away because he was so aggressive but so coachable. Lots of kids you can talk to until you're blue in the face and nothing happens, but Donald would react to instructions. If you told him he wasn't throwing the baseball correctly, he'd do it right the next time. If you said he wasn't blocking a tackle high enough, he'd correct it. He was very sure of himself, but he also listened.[21]

That made Trump an avid learner, willing to put ego aside to accept guidance and correction. He listened and learned, and he adjusted accordingly. These are traits that would serve him well in the business world, where listening is often more important than talking during a negotiation.

New York Military Academy was all about hierarchy, respect for authority, handling physical and mental duress, and performing under pressure, complete with spit-shined shoes and brilliantly polished brass buckles. Trump didn't just survive those five years there, he thrived. Over time, as Fred and Mary Trump visited him, they could see that their son had been transformed.

Something had taken hold of Donald Trump at New York Military Academy and it served him well when he got to college. He spent his first two years at Fordham and his last two at Wharton (the University of Pennsylvania), where he was one of a handful of students who majored in real estate. In majoring in business, he meant business. This was a key component to prepare him for life not only beyond college, but several years later after he had broken away from the family business to stake his own claim in Manhattan. Military school had shaped him up and sharpened his focus on who he was and what he wanted to do with his life. He could have taken the easy route, simply working fulltime for his dad if he so chose. He didn't.

By the time he got to Fordham—a Roman Catholic school run by the Jesuits (Trump was not Catholic)—he had matured and had a suave personality liked by both boys and girls. He was someone who didn't let things bother him. The older cadets at Cornwall-on-Hudson had driven that out of him, apparently. But why did he choose Fordham? "I'd been away at school

(NYMA) for five years, and I wanted to see my parents," Trump said. When asked the same question, though, his sister Mary Anne simply said, "It's where he got in."[22]

At Fordham Trump stood out, and it wasn't just for the signs of his family's wealth evidenced in his well-tailored clothes or the expensive red sports car he drove around in. Although the sixties were a time when cigarette smoking was chic and sophisticated, Trump was having none of that. He didn't smoke and he avoided alcohol. When it came to sports, he kept his cool, even in defeat, never smashing his squash racquet after a loss, as did some of his teammates. "He had a certain aura," teammate Rich Marrin said. "He didn't have tantrums, and he was never late. If anything, he was more of a gentleman than we were, more refined, as if brought up in a stricter family, with more emphasis on manners."[23] Well, there was one exception when, on a team trip to Washington DC, he pulled a new set of golf clubs out of the back of his car and hit about a half-dozen new balls into the Potomac River, an impulsive yet extravagant exhibition that teammates watching never forgot.

When his sophomore year at Fordham was over, Trump decided it was time to move on to more serious matters—in this case his education, or, more specifically, his business education. His destination was Wharton, the University of Pennsylvania's prestigious business school. Because he was a transfer student, Trump wasn't eligible to join any varsity athletics teams at Penn, not that it mattered to him. His top priority was learning, and Wharton had one of the few real estate departments among American colleges and universities.

"For the next two years, Donald and his [five] classmates [all taught by one departmental professor] studied finance, mortgages, accounting, and money and banking," Blair writes.

> Working together in teams, they learned how to analyze neighborhoods and make appraisals by walking around and going into bars to see what ethnic groups were there. . . . For Donald it was familiar and welcome territory. For the first time in his life, what he was studying seemed relevant. Finally there was a classroom competition he wanted to win.[24]

Real estate was a language Trump could speak with professional fluency, making him the expert in the class . . . certainly in the eyes of the professor. In Trump, he had a student with whom he could commiserate on real estate matters beyond what was taught and discussed in the classroom. "I remember the professor talking to Donald like one insider to another," said fellow real estate major Peter Gelb. "We were the students, and they were the pros."[25]

CB SO

By the time Lincoln was seventeen, he was a full-grown man, and his aspirations reflected that. He was keen on taking on more worldly responsibilities, beyond what his father could offer him on their farm. By law, however, he was still tethered to his dad until his twenty-first birthday. The axe was his primary work tool but Abe also found work assisting in the management of a ferry-boat operation on the Ohio River. For this, he was paid the unprincely sum of thirty-seven cents a day. While working on the ferry, Abe still managed to squeeze in time between the river-crossing excursions to continue writing. His primary composition called attention to the "necessity of preserving the Constitution and perpetuating the Union,"[26] a theme remarkable in the fact that it would define his presidency some thirty-five years later.

It was in their twenties that Lincoln and Trump both made their boldest moves to take control of their lives and careers. Lincoln packed all his belongings into two saddle bags draped over a borrowed horse to make the move to Springfield at age twenty-eight (in 1837); Trump at a similar age broke away from his father's company to make his mark on Manhattan.

This was a gutsy move for Lincoln, leaving little New Salem for the bright lights of Springfield, the future state capital of Illinois. Lincoln—given his propensity for mood swings and bouts of depression—made the move with trepidation, for what awaited was an iffy proposition of professional and political success for the backwoods lawyer.

Upon his arrival in Springfield, Lincoln made the acquaintance of one Joshua F. Speed, who would soon become one of his best friends and confidantes. Lincoln arrived in in mid-April, and quickly made his way to the A. Y. Ellis & Company general store on the western edge of the city square. There he asked how much it would cost for a mattress, sheets, and pillow. Speed, one of the store's proprietors, did some quick math and came up with a price tag of seventeen dollars. Hearing this, Lincoln acknowledged the fairness of the price only to admit he couldn't cover it, explaining to Speed that he had come to Springfield to "experiment" with being a lawyer. The sheepish Lincoln then asked if he could be extended credit until Christmas—eight months away—in a sad voice adding, "If I fail in this, I do not know that I can ever pay you."[27]

This sort of thing was another of Lincoln's gifts—he could evoke pity or empathy in others who would then take stock of his plight and jump in with both feet to come to his rescue. Speed took the bait. No doubt his decision was influenced by Lincoln's reputation as well as the fact Speed had once heard Lincoln give a speech. "I have a large room with a double bed upstairs, which you are very welcome to share with me," Speed told Lincoln. This sleeping arrangement would raise a few eyebrows today, but it was fairly common at the time. Back then practicality trumped what we would construe as "modern behavior" or "alternative lifestyles." After accepting the offer, Lincoln moved his bags upstairs to Speed's place and soon returned newly energized and in a positive frame of mind, proclaiming, "Well, Speed, I am moved!"[28]

"Such a quick alternation from deep despair to blithe confidence was characteristic of Lincoln's early years in the new state capital," biographer David Donald explains.

> He was trying to put together the fragmented pieces of his personality into a coherent pattern. Sometimes he felt he was the prisoner of his passions, but at other times he thought that he could master his world through reason. Often he was profoundly discouraged, and during these years he experienced his deepest bouts of depression. But these moods alternated with periods of exuberant self-confidence and almost annoying optimism. In short, he was still a very young man.[29]

Even at a young age, Lincoln had remarkable willpower and self-motivation, even if he was temporarily derailed at times by the dark clouds of depression. His drive to push ahead, persevere, and accomplish was uncommon. He had multiple talents inside him waiting to be cultivated and nurtured, and he was determined to exploit all of them as best he could. "The ambition of the man soared above us," childhood friend Nathaniel Grigsby said. "He read and thoroughly read his books whilst we played."[30] This wasn't just a phase Abe was passing through. He never quit building on to who and what he was.

Goodwin points out that when Lincoln returned to Illinois at age forty to resume his law practice following his first extended foray into politics, he realized he had lost ground in the ever-evolving practice of law, saying, "I am not an accomplished lawyer."[31] Even with twelve years of practicing law under his belt, he realized that much of what he had known about the law was, if not obsolete, at least in serious need of fine-tuning. "He felt that his legal prowess had atrophied while the profession had grown more complex and sophisticated in his absence, requiring greater powers of reasoning and 'a broad knowledge of the principles' beneath the statutory law."[32] Upon Lincoln's return to his practice, Herndon could see a marked change in his partner's demeanor, one that was more serious and focused in place of the occasional lack of discipline he had been known for years earlier. "No man had greater power of application," Herndon observed. "Once fixing his mind on any subject, nothing could interfere with or disturb him."[33]

As president and commander in chief, Lincoln wasn't content to sit back and let his generals and admirals run things; he was determined to master the intricacies of military tactics and strategy. This was similar to how Lincoln had tried to join adult conversations as a child and young man. He was always eager to learn things beyond just what he read in books. Lincoln's private secretary, John Hay, lived in the White House, and he could often overhear Lincoln walking around in his bedroom around midnight. Lincoln was soaking in military strategy from books, no doubt reading and thinking aloud much of the time, perhaps even having question and answer sessions with himself. "He gave himself, night and day, to the study of the military situation," Hay would later write.

> He read a large number of strategical works. He pored over the reports from the various departments and districts of the field of war. He held long conferences with eminent generals and admirals, and astonished them by the extent of his special knowledge and the keen intelligence of his questions.[34]

Until he became president, Lincoln's only military experience had been thirty years earlier in 1832, when he served as a volunteer in the Illinois Militia for three months during the Black Hawk War. He never saw combat during his short stint—history records that he never even fired a shot—but at age twenty-three he was elected captain of his first company and helped to bury the dead after two of the war's battles. Once he assumed the office of the presidency, however, Lincoln checked out a number of military-themed books from the Library of Congress to educate himself—pragmatic learning, as it might have been described. He later used that knowledge to replace generals when they failed and promote them when they achieved successes (with some help from their troops, of course).[35]

This pragmatic approach to self-education on unfamiliar subjects is something Trump has also undertaken, such as when he accepted the challenge to rebuild Wollman Rink in New York City's Central Park. It was a formidable, hot-potato type of task, which no one in the city—Mayor Ed Koch included—had been able to figure out. Along came Trump. As a practical businessman, familiar with the concept of learning by doing, and having already gone public in criticizing Koch's efforts to rebuild the rink, Trump accepted the exasperated Koch's challenge: six months to build the rink and restrict the cost to $3 million or less. Trump would need to rebuild the rink within a strict budget and tight deadline, even though he had no idea what it took to build a major ice rink.

To get up to speed, Trump didn't check out books from a library. He had a better idea, and that meant aiming north—where the official national pastime was ice hockey. "So Trump decided he needed to talk with someone who was an expert at building skating rinks, which naturally made him think of Canada," Newt Gingrich writes in *Understanding Trump*.

> Ultimately, he got in touch with a Toronto-based company that had built the rink for the Montreal Canadiens hockey team. Trump got a crash course in what it takes to build a quality skating rink, then he had some people from the company fly down to look at Wollman Rink with him. . . . Within three months, at a cost of $2.25 million, the rink was open for business. It's still there and still making ice—and it is now called the Trump Wollman Rink in Central Park. I love this story because it shows that Trump is a pragmatic, sensible conservative who knows how to finish difficult projects under immense pressure.[36]

Trump, like Lincoln, is a natural learner; someone who chooses to learn on their own and to learn by doing—by not being shy about asking the right questions of the right people. Roger Schank, of the Institute for the Learning Sciences at Northwestern University, says that people learn by doing the things that they want to do. On his website he says, "Learning occurs when someone wants to learn, not when someone wants to teach." Schank is the author of a study titled "What We Learn When We Learn by Doing," which is referenced by Newt Gingrich in his book *Understanding Trump*:

> To consider learning by doing from a psychological point of view, we must think more about learning in real life, which is, of course, the natural venue of learning by doing. There is, after all, something inherently artificial about school. Natural learning means learning on an "as needed" basis. In such a learning situation, motivation is never a problem; we learn because something has caused us to want to know. But school has no natural motivation associated with it. Students go there because they have no choice. The same is true of most training situations.[37]

Lincoln likely would have been a fan of Schank's reasoning, meaning he was not a big fan of the schools he attended. He called them "so-called" schools. "No qualification was ever required of a teacher, beyond 'readin', writin', and cipherin'." Lincoln wrote. "If a straggler supposed to understand latin [*sic*], happened to sojourn in the neighborhood, he was looked upon as a wizard [*sic*]."[38] While Lincoln's putdown of his schools was largely merited, these schools had, in fact, given him the basic tools he needed to educate himself in the future.

Another angle to Lincoln's self-making abilities was his knack for getting other people to help him. He was a magnet to friends and acquaintances who couldn't resist his rustic charm—like when Speed offered Lincoln the chance to share a bed and save seventeen dollars. These folks admired his chutzpah, work ethic, and ability to figure out academic subjects on his own, but still saw him as endearingly hopeless at times. Maybe it was his poorly hidden moodiness and bouts of depression that drew Samaritans to his side. Whatever it was, there's no question that Lincoln in his natural state made friends, and friends help friends. Lincoln also returned the favors, not because he was keeping score, but because that's just what friends do. And Lincoln had his share of friends. There is a certain genius to that.

Herndon described how William Butler, a businessman who provided room and board for Lincoln from 1837–1842, never charging Abe:

> Butler saw in Lincoln a gloom, a sadness, melancholy, etc., and deeply sympathized with him, wanted to help him. Lincoln is painted by men who did not know him as having a hard time of it in his struggles for existence, success, fame. That is all *bosh*, nonsense. No man ever had an easier time of it in his early days, in his boyish, in his young struggles than Lincoln; he had always had influential and financial friends to help him; they almost fought each other for the privilege of assisting Lincoln. . . . Lincoln was a pet, a faithful and honest pet in this city; he deserved it.[39]

One such Samaritan was a friend of Lincoln's, James Short, who bailed out the future president from a pickle. At this point young Lincoln was serving as both a surveyor and a mailman, with his headquarters in Samuel Hill's store. Between the money he was making from his work in the post office and as a surveyor, Lincoln was starting to get along fairly well financially and was now able to pay for necessities and have a little bit left over. But the good life came to a screeching halt when Lincoln was hit with a lawsuit concerning a bad note that had been paid on the store debt. The lawsuit was the result of an incompetent business partner, but the judgment was levied against Lincoln, forcing him to relinquish all his personal effects, his horse, and his surveying equipment. This would have put Lincoln back at square one. However, Short stepped in, bought the property, and restored it to Lincoln, giving evidence of the sort of friends Lincoln was making and the respect he had earned. "His case never became so desperate but a friend came out of the darkness to relieve him."[40] Lincoln's life bore out the truth that even for self-made men it does indeed take a village to make them whole in life.

Another of Lincoln's many benefactors was Stephen A. Logan, a circuit court judge who had originally certified Lincoln for the bar and would later become his second senior law partner. Logan was eager to impart useful legal wisdom upon Abe. He saw in Lincoln a junior partner who needed more general knowledge of the law, an area in which Logan regarded Lincoln as "never very formidable." Lincoln's school-ingrained "blabbing" method of studying made him proficient in mastering legal details, but Logan could see that the practice did not encourage legal philosophizing. This was something Lincoln would have to master if he had any hope of fulfilling his destiny as a capable lawyer. Subsequently, under Logan's mentorship Lincoln "mastered complicated tactics for his several hundred Illinois Supreme Court cases." Lincoln listened to his sage senior partner well, taking in philosophical subtleties of the law so that he could look upon his younger law-practicing self and see his own weaknesses. Logan helped Lincoln learn how to prepare his cases while also bolstering the younger lawyer's confidence. "In his 1850 'Notes for a Law Lecture,' Lincoln implicitly scored his pre-Logan self. 'Young lawyers,' he warned, commit no 'more fatal error . . . than relying too much on speech-making.' Exceptional 'powers of speaking' provide no ''exemption from' legal 'drudgery.' Lawyers' 'leading rule' must be 'diligence,' whereas 'negligence' assures 'failure in advance.'"[41] In other words, neither give in, nor give up.

CB SO

Trump was old school in his own way while coming up in the world. Before setting off on his own to build grand hotels and casinos, he was at his father's knee, so to speak, often performing mundane tasks and running errands. These were the sort of "gofer" things that a no-name apprentice—no pun intended—would start out doing at the ground floor in hopes of working his or her way up the ladder.

While still a teenager, Trump worked on the maintenance crew at a foreclosed FHA project—an apartment complex—in Maryland that his father had bought. It was there that Donnie Trump got his hands dirty. "I wore a T-shirt and worked in the machine shop," he would say years later. "I loved it, working with my hands, and I saw a different world, the world of the guys who cleaned and fixed things." Other beginning-level grunt work young Trump performed included collecting coins from the washer and dryer machines in laundry rooms of buildings his father owned, hosing down dust at the Trump Village construction site, and chauffeuring his father around from one job site or appointment to another. "He was a real eager beaver, a go-getter," Trump Village architect Morris Lapidus said. "Whenever his father gave him something to do, he would be off and running. You could tell that he was going to get somewhere."[42]

It's all about being teachable, as well as paying it forward. Visualization is also an ingredient to being a successful man or woman, at least in Trump's eyes. You need to have a purpose in what you are doing and see it through to the end, picturing the project before you get to work on it. "So I want you to ask yourself: What is it that you are aiming for?" Trump writes in *Think Like a Champion*.

> What precisely is your motivation? What's the point of building a bridge if you're not sure you want to get to the other side, or if you don't know what you'll do once you get there? A bridge must serve a specific purpose, and your goals have to be just that specific. Visualization is a powerful tool for bringing your intentions into focus.[43]

Both Lincoln and Trump, through their writing, advised success seekers to study something other than basic business—Lincoln said to study history, and Trump points to English literature, more specifically the works of William Shakespeare:

> I was having a conversation a few years ago with a few people when one guy mentioned that the Trump name had become a famous brand around the world and then added, "What's in a name?" he then sort of laughed and said to me, "In your case, a lot!" I noticed that one guy seemed out of the loop about the quip. So I said, "That's Shakespeare. 'What's in a name' is a famous line from Shakespeare." So he still looked perplexed and asked, "From what?" And although I knew it was from *Romeo and Juliet*, I said, "Look it up. You might learn some interesting things along the way." . . . Don't be left out! Take a few hours a week to review the classics in literature or history or something outside of your usual range of interests. Limiting yourself is not the best choice.[44]

Trump also calls on Shakespeare in giving some of his best career advice.

> Shakespeare put it this way, in a famous quote from *Julius Caesar*: "The fault is not in our stars, dear Brutus, but in ourselves." That's a clear message. We are responsible for ourselves. We are responsible for our own luck. What an empowering thought! If you see responsibility

as a bum deal, then you are not seeing it for what it really is—a great opportunity. . . . What will separate you from the complaining crowd will be how you choose to look at your situation. If you believe you are in control of it—and you are—you will know exactly who to look for when you need help: yourself.[45]

Lincoln's advice was to study a slice of history, while embracing the value of education as society's most important work for citizens to be engaged in. While running for public office for the first time, he wrote a letter in March 1832 that he sent to the residents of Sangamo County in Illinois:

I can only say that I view it as the most important subject which we as a people can be engaged in. That every man may receive at least a moderate education, and thereby be enabled to read the histories of his own and other countries, by which he may duly appreciate the value of our free institutions.[46]

Then there's this piece of brilliance he wrote to a certain William H. Grigsby after Lincoln's law partner, Herndon, had turned down Grigsby's application to join the firm: "If you wish to be a lawyer, attach no consequence to the *place* you are in, or the *person* you are with, but get books, sit down anywhere, and go to reading for yourself. That will make a lawyer of you quicker than any other way."[47]

Trump uses the words *tenacious* and *indomitable* to pinpoint his keys to success, which in his case has often meant facing a firewall of cynics and critics, such as when he moved his operations into Manhattan despite being told that this was a bad time to be investing in real estate in the Big Apple. "I overcame some great setbacks just by being obstinate. I refused to give in or give up. To me, that's an integrity of purpose that cannot be defeated or interfered with to any significant level. Being steadfast in your intentions can reap great results."[48]

But Donald Trump had his village too when it came to acquiring those high-rise properties he sought in Manhattan real estate. Aside from the boost he might have received initially from building with his father, he was a natural at drawing the people into his orbit that he needed to help him rise. He had a knack for enticing potential business partners with convincing hyperbole such as, "It's the greatest project," or he would tell bankers and city officials, "It's the most spectacular view you'll ever see." Call it chutzpah, call it energy, call it being "hot to trot" (according to Jordan Gruzen, an architect on one of Donald's early projects.)[49] Whatever you call it, Trump had it in spades. And he used it to bring attention, influence, and power into his corner of the ring.

Ned Eichler, Trump's real estate associate on the ambitious West Side Rail Yards development, was "taken by the sheer energy on the other end of the [phone] line" when he first spoke with the as-yet-unknown Manhattan developer (who at the time was still just a twenty-something dreamer).[50] Gwenda Blair writes in *The Trumps*, "That air of confidence" and "his overwhelming eagerness [were] engaging."[51] Also, it was an "intense drive . . . that made up for his lack of cash."[52] This same *chutzpah* (which, by the way, is Yiddish for *audacity, nerve, guts*, if you will) became The Donald's hallmark for drawing people to him—like bees to honey. If it wasn't deal-makers and takers, it was New York City elites, social movers, and shakers, and a constant buzz of obsessive press, including society-page reporters and tabloid gossip columnists. But later it became *The Apprentice* wannabes, celebrities of all makes and models, golf aficionados, and eventually an American public, swarming to his rallies to cheer and chant for a man they helped install in the White House.

A relentlessly positive mindset helps, too. Trump hit what might have been the lowest point in his business career around 1990, when he found himself about a billion dollars in debt with banks threatening foreclosure. This was just after Trump had indulged in a third casino, an airline, the world's second-largest yacht, and the Plaza Hotel. Painted into a corner with seemingly no way out, Trump engaged in weeks of around-the-clock negotiations, coming out of them relatively unscathed and still very much in business. In a 2009 interview with *Psychology Today*, he gave credit to Norman Vincent Peale's all-time bestselling book *The Power of Positive Thinking*, giving a shout-out to his father Fred's friendship with Peale while calling himself a "firm believer in the power of being positive." He added, "What helped is I refused to give in to the negative circumstances and never lost faith in myself. I didn't believe I was finished even when the newspapers were saying so."[53]

Even in those days, "fake news" wasn't going to stop Trump.

CHAPTER 8

MASTERS OF
COMMUNICATION

— ❧ —

I memorized the Gettysburg Address as a fifth grader (along with millions of other kids!). In Kentucky we were all glad to take part in the exercise. Our parents and teachers instilled in us a sense of pride in having shared a birthplace with the great American president. I can still remember the beginning and the end—lilting with biblical phraseology and historical significance—but the middle of the famous speech is a bit foggy after so many years.

I considered Abraham Lincoln a serious statesman then. But I discovered a whole new facet to his public-speaking image as I dug deeper. The descriptions "entertainer of the masses" and "impresario extraordinaire" came to seem more appropriate. These descriptions sound surprisingly like Donald Trump at one of his rallies. Could it be that genuine passion for the subject and the people link these two original showmen?

Without a doubt Lincoln and Trump proved masters of the political stage. Each built a unique crowd-pleasing public image and donned a style of speaking that clearly and simply roused crowds of eager fans. A head-on, in-your-face boldness guided these oh-so-similar, but oh-so-provocative virtuosos of the American soap box.

I realize that "Fourscore and seven years ago . . . " and "What the hell do you have to lose?" have nothing in common, but the sincerity of the message and its enthusiastic reception in the ears of its fans always (dare I say it) trumps eloquence.

❧

Abraham Lincoln and Donald Trump didn't just master the art of public speaking, they treated it as performance art. They did it in manners unique to their respective personas and yet with styles similar to one another, captivating their audiences with plain, impactful language that trumpeted authenticity, stirred emotions, and resonated with their followers—all rarely with the benefit of a teleprompter (never for Lincoln, obviously). Lincoln and Trump both were or are originals—*mavericks* might be a better word—speaking and writing with a style, clarity, power, and panache unlike any other major politician of their eras. When these two men addressed the masses, people didn't just listen (or read), they bought in 100 percent, hearing and seeing verbiage that rarely needed a dictionary to be understood. Master communicators: the best of the best.

In the case of Trump, it chafes the back sides of his detractors to no end that he can fill speaking venues with enthusiastic audiences that hang on his every word. More often than not, what Trump says reflects exactly what his followers are thinking, and he relays it with a certain dramatic flair—something he readily admits. "A great portion of life and business involved acting," Trump says in *Think Like a Champion*.

> Life *is* a performance art, no matter what field you are in. I've come to understand that fact over the years, and it's a helpful thing to realize. It includes people skills, negotiation skills, public relations, salesmanship, and the ability to read your audience, whether that audience is four people in your office or forty thousand at a speech. The same technique applies.[1]

It's helpful to note that *Think Like a Champion* was published in 2010, meaning Trump wrote those words about five years before he began campaigning for the 2016 presidential election. Political handlers didn't teach that stuff to Trump; more than likely he taught them about injecting panache into politics, something Lincoln had done well, too.

Trump developed the ability to entertain early in life by mastering bigger and better showmanship. He used savvy self-promotion to build his brand—in large part through his popular reality TV show *The Apprentice*. Lincoln veered in a different direction with a flair that was a bit less P. T. Barnum glitz and a bit more grounded, yet quirky. In terms of getting their messages across, their methods worked wonders once they became president.

Lincoln's shtick was his storytelling; he was full of stories, some of a ribald sort, some metaphors and real-life anecdotes. Often his stories taught moralistic lessons while they left listeners awash in laughter and cheers. Long before he ran for president, Lincoln had already established himself as one of the best storytellers in central Illinois. Starting in his early thirties, his offbeat yet affable countenance earned him prominent mention among the most renowned of jesters and jokesters in that part of the state. There was more to the young, up-and-coming Lincoln than his reputation as a backwoodsman and his knack for handling an axe as skillfully as a symphony conductor brandishing a baton.

William Herndon put Lincoln in the same class as fellow area performers William Engle and James Murray, each of whom were highly skilled at telling stories—an art much appreciated in a place where newspapers were few and the local town folk had to be content with other forms of entertainment. This is where Lincoln really developed his skills, not only in telling stories but also in the craft of mimicry, a talent that would serve him and his audiences well for years to come.

"From 1840 to 1853 this section [of Illinois] was not known for a very high standard of taste, the love for the beautiful or the good," Herndon wrote.

> We had not many newspapers; people in all of these counties would attend court at the respective county seats. Lincoln, Engle, and Murray would travel around from county to county with the court, and those who loved fun and sport, loved jokes, tales, stories, jests, would go with the court, too, from county to county. . . . In the evening, after the court business of the day was over and book and pen had been laid [down] by the lawyers, judges, jurymen, witnesses, etc., the people would generally meet at some barroom, "gentleman's parlor," and have a good time in storytelling, joking, jesting, etc., etc.
>
> The barroom, windows, halls, and all passageways would be filled to suffocation by the people, eager to see the "big ones" and to hear their stories told by them. Lincoln would tell his story in his very best style. The people, all present, including Lincoln, would burst out in a loud laugh and a hurrah at the story. The listeners, as soon as the laugh and the hurrah had passed and silence had come in for its turn, would cry out: "Now, Uncle Billy (William Engle), you must beat that or go home." Engle would clear his throat and say: "Boys, the story just told by Lincoln puts me in mind of a story that I heard when I was a boy." He would tell it and tell it well. The people would clap their hands, stamp their feet, hurrah, yell, shout get up, hold their aching sides. Things would soon calm down.[2]

The comedic influences that Engle, Murray, and others had who traveled the law circuit rubbed off on the future president, helping Lincoln expand his repertoire and enhance his success as a politician on the rise.

Although he was a somewhat moody, almost dour personality away from the madding crowd, Lincoln came to life when facing an audience, especially when he was competing against other skilled, quick-witted reporters. He had to be on his toes, and at times like this he shined brighter than a brand-new penny. *Lincoln on Leadership* author Donald T. Phillips writes,

> Over the years, Lincoln not only built up a good supply of tales but also perfected his skill at relating them. Lincoln's humor was a major component of his ability to persuade people. He knew the effect it had and used it to the utmost. It also aided him politically by becoming an obsession with the public. People became fascinated with his quick wit and hilarious stories; as a result, many of his humorous anecdotes found their way into print while he was still alive.[3]

A performer's craft is honed through ample preparation. When you are getting up on stage, getting behind a podium, or standing in front of a live camera and mic as a crowd presses in around you, that is not the time to start thinking about what you're going to say, how you're going to use your hands, or when and how you want to change your voice's inflection. Whatever entertainment value Lincoln brought or Trump brings to a public setting is built on years of practice and constant fine-tuning. They aren't just winging it up there.

Trump has said,

> I also thought about the people who would be in the audience instead of my own performance. That perspective frees you up from nervousness to allow you to focus on and know your audience. . . . You also have to have the goods to hold your audience, no matter what the size may be. Performers prepare for every performance. That's showmanship, and that's life. Prepare yourself every day. Learn, know, and show. It's a proven formula.[4]

Trump showcased his winning formula for performance success—and communication success—by keeping *The Apprentice* going strong for fourteen seasons, pulling in high ratings much of the time it was on the air. His preferred audience was the general public; his media philosophy is that there is no such thing as "bad" publicity, and through his shameless bravado and accompanying hype, he has always kept the public and the press—even those in the practice of cranking out "fake news"—wanting more. "I play to people's fantasies," Trump wrote in 1987, thirty years before he was sworn in as the nation's forty-fifth president.[5]

If we go back in time even farther, to 1976, we can see thirty-year-old Donald Trump featured in *The New York Times*, expounding on the millions he had already made in metropolitan real estate and showing off his penthouse apartment and Cadillac. As part of providing background for the high-profile story, Trump allowed the reporter to accompany him to job site visits and tag along for lunches at the "21" club before taking an evening flight to the West Coast for another round of deal making. Nothing shy about this guy.

"Young and ambitious, Trump worked just as hard at building the image as he did at expanding his real estate empire," Associated Press reporter Nancy Benac wrote in 2016. "Along the way, he honed the communications skills that would benefit him at the negotiating table, turn him into a reality TV star, and launch a presidential campaign."[6]

Trump inherited much of his drive from his businessman dad Fred—at least his penchant for shrewd promotion. At times their promotions pushed the line of good taste (of course, the definition of that line depends heavily on your perspective and perhaps even your faith). Fred Trump—and keep in mind this goes well back in terms of decades—spent a good chunk of his life constructing homes and apartments in Brooklyn and Queens, where he used various promotional gimmicks to push his products at would-be buyers. One of Fast Fred's gimmicks was filling a bulldozer bucket with beautiful, bikini-clad women. Other times, Fred released balloons stuffed with fifty-dollar coupons over a beach full of Coney Island sunbathers. Often, the lobbies of his apartment buildings included bird cages that had been positioned to catch the eyes (and ears) of passersby.

"[Donald is] a media natural," said Aaron Kall, director of the University of Michigan's Debate Institute and the school's debate team, comparing the younger Trump's ability to perform as being on the level of "a maestro. . . . He really understands audiences and tailors a message to what he thinks that they want to hear."[7]

What Trump's detractors and naysayers don't seem to grasp is that the scathing comments he makes in press conferences that seem off the cuff and reckless—or his highly opinionated tweets, sometimes several a day—are just part of his work as an experienced and modern-day, plugged-in communicator who knows how to market himself. He's been doing it going on fifty years, beginning right out of college.

Benac writes:

Long before NBC's *The Apprentice* turned Trump into a reality TV star in 2004 [more than fifteen years ago! Trump is no unwitting novice.], he was advancing his biz-whiz image in TV and movie cameos, chatting up Howard Stern on the radio and filming ads for Pizza Hut, McDonald's, and more. Then, over fourteen seasons of *The Apprentice* and *Celebrity Apprentice*, he sharpened his ability to work the camera, think on his feet, and promote the Trump brand.

As a presidential candidate, he's drawn on those same skills to keep himself in the news, dishing out provocations and insults sure to guarantee the public's attention.[8]

Many big shots, like those in the business world, grow obsessively protective of their millions or billions, striving to shun the press and keep out of the public eye. Not Donald Trump. As the subject of overwrought media coverage for well over half his life, he has willingly subjected himself to the constant attention. Along the way he has learned as much about how the media game is played as those in the news and entertainment business have learned about him. Trump can bathe as comfortably in the hot waters of intense media coverage as he can dish it back at those looking to pin him to the mat. A message to any newshound planning to go in for the kill? Wouldn't be prudent.

Trump can't stay out of the news, nor does he want to. Good news is okay by him; bad news is, too. Fake news gives him something to crow about; it feeds into his nonstop narrative of self above circumstances. No news means it's time for him to make something happen. Media attacks on him only make him stronger. When the story broke in 1990 that he was having an affair with Marla Maples, Trump spent eight straight days on the cover of the *New York Post*—New York's tabloid version of the *National Enquirer*. Such coverage—literally, on the cover—just didn't happen in those days. What would be a nightmare, even for a public-relations whiz and master of spin, was catnip to Trump. He craved the attention, and yet he was as much admired by the public as he was scorned in other quarters. This is a big part of how he communicates, and his staunchest following is the general public—average Joes and Janes.

Susan Mulcahy, a New York writer, editor, and consultant, and former tabloid writer, wrote a piece for politico.com in 2016 (before Trump had won the Republican presidential nomination) that painted a picture of how even the tabloids' best arrows just bounce off him:

> If you worked for a newspaper in New York in the 1980s, you had to write about Trump. As editor of the *New York Post*'s Page Six, and later as a columnist for *New York Newsday*, I needed to fill a lot of space, ideally with juicy stories of the rich and powerful, and Trump more than obliged.

I wrote about his real estate deals. I wrote about his wife, his yacht, his parties, his houses. At times, I would let several months go by without a single column mention of The Donald; this doubtless upset him, as he loves Page Six and used to have it brought to him the moment it arrived in his office. But eventually I returned to the subject, as did a legion of other writers. We didn't see it at the time, but item by inky item we were turning him into a New York icon.[9]

CB ℠

Lincoln didn't hone his skills by building Big Apple high-rise towers, by stuffing scantily clad women into construction machinery, or by tooling around the big city in a boat-sized fancy car. No mystery why. Rather, Lincoln first honed his communications skills at home. Though Thomas Lincoln could neither read nor write, he was adept at spinning yarns, even if his storytelling skills never made it to the spotlight of nineteenth-century Springfield, Illinois. What the elder Lincoln did have, and what he passed on to his son, was wit, the ability to mimic, and an amazing memory of great stories that he told well. He had an ear for them, exchanging anecdotal material with farmers, carpenters, and peddlers as they met and passed one another along the old Cumberland Trail. Young Abraham was privy to much of this, seated nearby as he raptly listened to these men sharing their stories. Abe tried to remember the gist of these stories so he could relate them to his friends, entertaining them as best he could.

"He thrived when holding forth on a tree stump or log captivating the appreciative nature of his young audience, and before long had built a repertoire of stories and great storytelling skills," author Doris Kearns Goodwin writes in *Leadership in Turbulent Times.*

> At the age of ten, a relative recalled, Abraham learned to mimic "the Style & tone" of the itinerant Baptist preachers who appeared regularly in the region. To the delight of his friends, he could reproduce the rip-roaring sermons almost word for word, complete with gestures of head and hand to emphasize emotion. Then, as he got older, he found additional material for his storytelling by walking fifteen miles to the nearest courthouse, where he soaked up the narratives of criminal trials, contract disputes, and contested wills, and then retold the cases in lurid detail.[10]

Those fifteen-mile excursions to the courthouse actually took Lincoln to Boonville, an Indiana town perched on a river as the county seat of Warrick County. One of the cases he listened in on was a murder trial that grabbed his attention, mostly because of a defense attorney by the name of Breckenridge. Lincoln was so impressed with Breckenridge's impeccable oratorical skills that he stuck around to introduce himself to Breckenridge and congratulate the attorney for his eloquence and success. It was a brief meeting between the two men before they went their separate ways, although they would meet again decades later, while Lincoln was in the White House. By then a resident of Texas, Breckenridge came to Washington, DC, to pay his respects to the president, who was nothing but accommodating to someone who had also been one of his three rivals in the 1860 presidential election. The conversation quickly moved to their days in Indiana, with Lincoln bringing up the subject of the murder trial at which he had met Breckenridge, saying, "If I could, as I then thought, have made as good a speech as that, my soul would have been satisfied, for it was up to that time the best speech I had ever heard."[11]

Lincoln was an original, one of a kind for his time, not only in appearance—there were few men as tall, for starters—but also in temperament, comportment, personality, and speech. He was a self-educated man, having never gone to college. Had he gone to college, Lincoln likely would have had his rough edges rounded off and his rough-hewn personality sanded down to a smooth finish that would have left him lost in a crowd of like-minded legal minds and politicians. As Herndon once put it:

> He would have been a rounded man in an artistic way, would have sunk into the classic beautiful. But it so happened, was so decreed, that his style, manner, method of utterance, expression, its strength, its simplicity, and rugged grandeur, were crystallized long before he became acquainted with the smooth, weak, and artistic style of today. Lincoln was Lincoln, and no one else; and he spoke and wrote in Lincolnisms.[12]

Measured in political years at the federal level, any elected official under the age of forty is considered remarkably young, perhaps even too inexperienced and short on seasoning to be trusted to make key speeches supporting presidential candidates. But in recognition of his profound powers of persuasion and propensity for communication, Lincoln was just thirty-nine—a pup by DC's standards—when in 1848 he spoke on the U.S. House of Representatives floor on behalf of the Whigs' presidential candidate. The candidate was war hero General Zachary Taylor, and Lincoln made a strong case for Taylor's fitness for the highest office in America.

During this speech, Lincoln didn't just stand in place, he walked up and down the aisle in a manner as entertaining as it was inspiring, dramatically gesturing and peering around the room, his facial expressions and voice inflection changing by the moment. His words flowed like a lazy river one moment and hard-charging rapids the next. So energized and animated was Lincoln's impassioned presentation that when a stunned spectator rhetorically asked the identity of the young man, a nearby colleague—his eyes never leaving Lincoln—simply replied, "Abe Lincoln, the best storyteller in the House." For his speech, Lincoln earned widespread kudos from his fellow Whigs and reporters alike, all of them impressed by the young man's ability to mix thoughtfulness with humor.[13]

Sometimes, usually in a more informal setting, Lincoln would bring out his skillful mimicry to further tickle the ears of those assembled, such as he did during nightly post-court gatherings of local lawyers. They would typically congregate at a local tavern, putting aside courtroom differences and battles to share tall tales and anecdotes with one another.

Often the festivities would begin with everyone seated at a long table to share supper, with Judge David Davis presiding at one end. After this the well-fed men would gather near a blazing fire to imbibe and smoke while engaging in conversation that would be taken up a notch from what was respectable at the dinner table. Lincoln didn't smoke or drink, but he was still a welcome part of the gathering. His unending stream of stories was much anticipated and appreciated by all, but his most loved talent came out when he would start in on his imitations of others.

"His power of mimicry and his manner of recital were, in many respects, unique if not remarkable," Herndon wrote. "His countenance and all his features seemed to take part in the performance. As he neared the pith or point of the joke or story, every vestige of seriousness disappeared from his face. His little gray eyes sparkled . . . [and] no one's laugh was heartier than his."[14]

Trump is an original, too. Anyone who has paid any attention to him over the years knows this to be true. Think about it. Name anyone in American political history—other than Abraham Lincoln, of course—who can compare to Trump. As his son Donald Jr. says, "There's no one else like him." Neither Lincoln (with his penchant for poking fun of others or lacing his anecdotes with off-color remarks) nor Trump believed or believes in the kind of political correctness "where every statement you make, you have to vet carefully through thousands of people." Donald Jr. continues: "If people really break down what he's trying to say, there's no malice in there. He's just cutting through the nonsense and getting to the point and not wasting time. . . . He's an amazing guy, and I wouldn't change a thing about him. He really is a unique individual."[15]

He's unique in other ways as well, such as his resilience. A cloak of Teflon always seems to adorn the Donald, protecting him from crises and controversies that would cripple the reputations and lofty political aspirations of other prominent people. Instead, these slide off Trump, like raindrops off a tin roof.

"The rules that govern others just don't apply to Trump," writes Jackie Calmes, at the time a *Los Angeles Times* reporter. Calmes noted that his willingness to carry hundreds of millions of dollars of debts on his books and file multiple bankruptcies for his company's casinos have failed to slow down the juggernaut that is Donald Trump, the Trump organization, and, now, his breadth of acquired political capital. "Even in 2004," Calmes writes, "as Trump's casino business was in bankruptcy again, *The New York Times* notes—in words that would ring true during his campaign years later—'His name has become such a byword for success that even the most humiliating reverses barely dent his reputation.' "[16]

Of course, this hasn't kept the press from trying. For instance, there was that time in January 2017 when a report filed by a *Time* magazine reporter went viral. The reporter claimed Trump had removed a bust of Dr. Martin Luther King Jr. from a White House office and replaced it with a bust of Winston Churchill, apparently suggesting on his first day in office that Trump was a "white, imperialistic, racist" president, and now America was stuck with him. This being Inauguration Day 2017, much of the national media swooped in and picked up the story in what would infamously become the first instance of "fake news" in the Trump presidency. The *Time* report was proven false before the day was out. The King bust had been there all along, hidden from the view of the reporter who had failed to be diligent in verifying the bust's location. "Keep in mind, all this reporting happened immediately after Trump had given an inaugural speech that was completely antidiscriminatory and reaffirmed Trump's position that to be racist is to be unpatriotic and unAmerican," former U.S. Speaker of the House Newt Gingrich writes in *Understanding Trump*.[17] A part of the segment of Trump's inaugural address that Gingrich cites in his book follows:

> It is time to remember that old wisdom our soldiers will never forget: that whether we are black or brown or white, we all bleed the same red blood of patriots, we all enjoy the same glorious freedoms, and we all salute the same great American flag.
>
> And whether a child is born in the urban sprawl of Detroit or the windswept plains of Nebraska, they look up at the same night sky, they fill their heart with the same dreams, and they are infused with the breath of life by the same almighty Creator.

Finally, Gingrich adds, "But these words—which came out of the president's mouth in front of the entire nation—did not fit the media's narrative of who this president is, so they ignored him."[18]

 C3 80

An argument could be made that Lincoln and Trump both were or are master public speakers. A better way of describing them—and now we get into semantics—is that they were or are masters of speaking *to the public*. Neither fits the mold of a classical public speaker with a perfectly trained lilt and carefully cultivated posture and bearing; their respective styles are a marked departure from other skilled orators of their eras. Yet their ability to be easily and thoroughly understood, and consistently embraced, by their rapt audiences is unquestioned. Both were or are rough around the edges, and that makes them unique in their own appealing manner. Neither is what you would call a smooth talker, but smooth might be better left for radio deejays as each man was or is certainly effective in his own way.

Lincoln became an overnight sensation as a speaker when he was twenty-eight years old. It was in 1837 when he delivered a carefully prepared address that at the time was described by one set of ears as a "Young men's Lyceum." His speech was entitled "Perpetuation of Our Free Institutions" and it has been included for posterity's sake in assorted publications that list many of Abe's public speeches. As described in *Herndon's Lincoln*,

> It was highly sophomoric in character and abounded in striking and lofty metaphor. In point of rhetorical effort, it excels anything he ever afterward attempted. Probably it was the thing people expect from a young man of twenty-eight. . . . As illustrative of his style of oratory, I beg to introduce the concluding paragraph of the address. Having characterized the surviving soldiers of the Revolution as "living histories," he closes with these thrilling flourishes:
>
> "They were a fortress of strength; . . . They were a forest of giant oaks; but the all-resistless hurricane has swept over them, and left only here and there a lonely trunk, despoiled of its verdure, shorn of its foliage, . . . to murmur in a few more gentle breezes, and to combat with its mutilated limbs a few more rude storms, then to sink and be no more. They were pillers [sic] of the temple of liberty, that . . . have crumbled away. . . . Passion has helped us, but can do so no more. It will in future be our enemy. Reason—cold, calculating, unimpassioned reason—must furnish all the materials for our further support and defense. Let these materials be moulded into general intelligence, sound morality, and, in particular, a

reverence for the Constitution and the laws. . . . Upon these let the proud fabric of freedom rest as the rock of its basis, and . . . 'The gates of hell shall not pervail [sic] against it.' "[19]

Flourish is a good word to describe parts of Lincoln's early speeches; so is *flowery* or even *overcooked* to use a more contemporary description. Take, for example, this piece of "purple prose" from another of Lincoln's more youthful offerings:

And what a noble ally this, to the cause of political freedom. With such an aid, its march cannot fail to be on and on, till every son of earth shall drink in rich fruition, the sorrow quenching draughts of perfect liberty. Happy day, when, all appetites controlled, all passions subdued, all matters subjected, *mind*, all conquering *mind*, shall live and move the monarch of the world. Glorious consummation! Hail fall of Fury! Reign of Reason, all hail![20]

Having heard the young Lincoln on many occasions—such as at those nightly gatherings around the tavern supper table—Judge David Davis showed his great admiration of Lincoln's profoundly descriptive elocution, declaring him "the best stump speaker in the state," while also revealing his "want of early education, but he has great powers as a speaker."[21] Even more to Lincoln's credit, he was able to adapt over time, toning down his use of colorful metaphors and flowered speech and maturing into a more eloquent speaker "with less gaudy ornamentation," as David Herbert Donald puts it. "[Lincoln] grew in oratorical power, dropping gradually the alliteration and rosy metaphor of youth, until he was able at last to deliver the grandest of all orations—the Gettysburg Address."[22]

Lincoln's expert communications skills covered much more than just giving speeches—he was also a maestro in the courtroom, where quick thinking and practical applications of the law were at a premium. Lincoln knew the law, including all its idiosyncrasies. He also knew all the facts and nuances of whatever client or cause he was representing. When Lincoln rose to speak, everyone in the courtroom listened. They knew they were in the presences one of the greatest legal minds in American history, or at least one of its greatest purveyors of the process and politics inside those four walls.

Lincoln on Leadership author Donald T. Phillips lays it out:

As a successful lawyer in Illinois, Lincoln was also well known for his extraordinary courtroom abilities. He pleaded more cases in front of the State Supreme Court than any lawyer had prior to him, or has since [presumably as of 1993, when Phillips's book was published]. His timing and intuitive sensing of the mood of a jury was unparalleled. Lincoln was also bright and had an alert and lucid mind that made him quick on his feet. He could recall facts and figures on a moment's notice and was also capable of using appropriate anecdotes and humorous stories.[23]

Lincoln was aware of the impact his oratorical skills could have not only on his audiences but on his career and political aspirations as well. He had a gift for gab that was well rooted and researched in his work as a lawyer and as a master entertainer (again, with a nod to the positive influence of his storytelling dad, Thomas). Public speaking aimed primarily at the common man—a speaking trait Donald Trump would exercise so adeptly 150 years later—hit home with Lincoln. It gave him comfort in public settings, with crowds numbering in the hundreds or thousands. His ability to communicate in such a delightful and yet informative manner served his purpose to become well known. It was a strategy that would eventually carry him to the White House.

In the six years leading up to the presidential election of 1860, Lincoln was a nineteenth-century version of an itinerant motivational speaker. He boosted his popularity immensely among the citizens of Illinois by making 175 speeches in various locales during that time, many of them extemporaneously,[24] his quick wit and mental acuity often served him better than scribbled notes or an outline on paper or parchment. That averaged out to more than two speeches a month on top of his already workaholic schedule. And his speeches, even the ones performed without the benefit of notes or outline, involved significant preparation.

"Often he would write out every word of his address and then read from the text during the preparation," Phillips writes.

> He spent hours, sometimes days and weeks, researching his subject and, as one contemporary observed, "he never considered anything he had written to be finished until published, or if a speech, until he delivered it." Lincoln's most famous speeches were exhaustively researched, analyzed, and practiced; frequently they were printed and handed out to reporters before he presented them. This was the case for Lincoln's renowned "House Divided" speech given at the Republican state convention at Springfield in 1858. Nicolay and Hay [John George Nicolay and John Hay, private secretaries to Lincoln in the White House] called it "the most carefully prepared speech of his whole life. Every word of it was written, every sentence had been tested."[25]

By now, Lincoln's mature voice had long displaced the more ornate flowery prose of his youth. His exuberance to prove himself worthy of public attention had given way to a more modest, quiet sense of responsibility. This tone was influenced in large part by Lincoln's role model Henry Clay, a prominent attorney and statesman and former U.S. House Speaker and Secretary of State, regarded by many as the "man for a crisis." Goodwin further illustrates that Lincoln's "spoken and written words were pared down, leaner, more measured, cautious, centered, more determined, displaying a rhetoric less hectic yet no less impassioned than the poetry he had delivered half a lifetime earlier at the Lyceum."[26]

All that Lincoln had processed, fine-tuned, and harnessed as a public speaker would come to bear in 1858, when he engaged political rival, Democrat Stephen Douglas, in a landmark series of debates that to this day remain unparalleled in terms of historical significance. It was a match between two of the greatest orators and debaters in American history. Two years later they would face off in the presidential election of 1860.

The Lincoln–Douglas debates consisted of seven face-to-face encounters that, per Goodwin, were witnessed in person by tens of thousands of people, with tens of millions more following along via transcripts published in leading newspapers nationwide.

> If it was Douglas, the leading Democratic candidate for president in 1860, who drew the public and national journalists to the debates, it was Lincoln, then barely known outside his state (Illinois), who made the lasting impression. "Who is this man that is replying to Douglas in your State?" an eastern political figure asked an Illinois journalist. "Do you realize that no greater speeches have been made on public questions in the history of our country; that his knowledge of the subject is profound, his logic unanswerable, his style inimitable?"[27]

The Lincoln–Douglas debates of 1858 were noteworthy in another respect—they were essentially Lincoln's last hurrah as a prodigious public speaker. Once he started campaigning for the presidency in 1859, he curtailed his public appearances (especially those of the extemporaneous variety). Instead he chose to err on the side of silence and thus improve his chances of winning by alienating fewer voters at a time when the opposing Democratic party had been weakened by a split of its Northern and Southern electorates. Confiding to others, Lincoln admitted a fear of being misquoted or misrepresented at a time when "fake news," or the nineteenth century version of it, could have disastrous effects for a nation engaged in an actual Civil War being fought on actual battlefields.

> "In my present position," Lincoln would say in 1862, more than a year into his first term as president, "it is hardly proper for me to make speeches.

Every word is so closely noted that it will not do to make trivial ones." . . .
In 1864 he stated: "Everything I say, you know, goes into print. If I make
a mistake it doesn't merely affect me nor you, but the country. I therefore
ought at least try not to make mistakes."[28]

By his keeping silent, save for the occasional speech made requisite by
events beyond his control—such as the Gettysburg Address—Lincoln was
keeping his "mistakes" as well as other thoughts, opinions, strategies, and
anecdotes better left to himself out of the press. This wasn't much of a problem, not by today's standards, because in the 1860s there was neither a 24-7
news cycle nor daily press briefings. By 2020 the presidential media circus
had become nothing more than a chance to spar with or placate a hungry
press looking for sound bites and fodder to feed their own narratives.

 G8 ഇ

In today's world of nonstop news and entertainment, with an emphasis
on the latter growing stronger by the day, there is no keeping news out of
the media. That's because whenever there is a lack of worthy news on a given
day, media members can fill the gaps themselves. This has been going on for
years, and it continues to ramp up. The news need not be supported by facts
or objective truths in a world where opinion, conjecture, bias, and political
correctness provide ample content. Often this content contains nothing but
a lot of noise, and it's where those who most ardently tout concepts such as
"diversity" and "inclusion" practice hate speech.

Contemporary media doesn't need statements issued by the White
House press office or given through press briefings to report on the presidency; they can say whatever they want when they want. They will constantly drum up their own stories to fit whatever tempo they choose. If the
president were to keep silent, as Lincoln did for much of his time in office,
or if the president spoke daily with the media, it would make no difference.
But with Trump the media can do very little to stop him from getting his
unfiltered message out to the people. His words are untainted by media and
other critics, and he accomplished this almost every day he was in office. His
main modus operandi in going to the people was through his frequent use
of Twitter and other social media, as well as his many public appearances
around the United States and throughout the world. He knows national
media can't resist chasing him and covering him. At times, he even shifted
the media narrative through his determined influence or by simply baiting
the press, calling them out for their own mistakes and biased reporting.

He could pin them down when they pushed a part of their narrative that he described as "fake news." The media dishes it at him relentlessly, and he dishes it right back.

Again, this tactic goes back to the Trump maxim that while good publicity is preferable to bad, and bad publicity—from a bottom-line perspective—is preferable to no publicity at all. Trump knows that controversy sells, period, He says whatever he wants to say, and taking that chutzpah into the political world has tipped a lot of cows along the way. Like Lincoln many decades preceding him, Trump is amazingly effective and comfortable when it comes to speaking extemporaneously. Time and again, such as when he was on the campaign trail in 2016 and again in 2020, Trump frequently spoke without notes or a teleprompter or, apparently, without much preparation at all. This approach would have horrified his walk-on-eggshells predecessor Barack Obama and his 2020 Democratic opponent Joe Biden. Actually, Biden has gone off script hundreds of cringe-worthy times during his half century in politics, straying into misspeaking purgatory and staying there long enough to remind the world that some very offensive things are truly better left unsaid.

It is the performance art aspect of public communication that Trump seems to enjoy the most, as he writes in *Think Like a Champion*:

> Most of us have been exposed to the work of Shakespeare, and he spends a great deal of time dwelling on the characteristics of human nature. Some of the examples are extreme, but they aren't so far-fetched as to be unbelievable, or Shakespeare wouldn't still be performed today. There's something about his work that is timeless, and the timeliness comes from his insight into human nature. . . .
>
> I think most people want to be the best they can be. That's probably one reason you're reading this right now—you've chosen the high road, the path to more knowledge and experience. It's one of the reasons I enjoy giving speeches and teaching.[29]

As much as Trump might enjoy public speaking, experts in the craft fault him for what they describe as his "juvenile" vocabulary, jumbled syntax, casualness when it comes to accuracy, his demeaning tone, his weakness on policy details, and a voice characterized as thin and nasally. Picky, picky. About that last part, the same thing could be said about Lincoln, whose high-pitched, nasally voice—topped off by a predominantly Kentucky accent—was often the one thing about Lincoln's delivery that stuck out for people who heard him speak for the first time.

Ruth Sherman, a public-speaking coach quoted by Benac in her "Road to Debate" piece referenced earlier, suggests that while Trump, in her expert opinion, has a poor speaking voice, much of the American public has heard him so much for so long (that's what fourteen seasons of *The Apprentice* on TV can do for you) that they are willing to give him "a pass" on his speaking voice. "He doesn't get criticized for the quality of his speaking voice, but he should," Sherman says. "It's a thin voice. It's not smooth. It's somewhat nasal."[30]

Phillips says that being present for one of Lincoln's speeches had to be "quite an experience" as much for his voice as for the content of his addresses:

> He had a high-pitched, treble voice that tended to become even more shrill when he became excited. At times, it was even unpleasant. But his voice was a great asset because it could be heard at the farthest reaches of the crowds that gathered outdoors to hear him speak. At times, he also used considerable body language when he spoke. To emphasize a point, for example, Lincoln would "bend his knees, crouch, and then spring up vehemently to his toes."[31]

೦ଃ ৪ා

Shrill voices and all, Lincoln and Trump shared an ability to draw large crowds wherever they went spoke, crowds of people who came on their own volition. They didn't need to be bused in by event organizers looking to manufacture a full house so there would be no—or at least just a few—empty seats in the direction the cameras were pointed.

With both Lincoln and Trump, their public speaking engagements take on the ambiance of tent revivals, without the religious trimmings, yet with a spirit of secular salvation that few politicians have ever been able to generate. The enthusiasm of their listeners isn't just palpable, it is genuine, with audience members willing to lend their hearts as well as their ears to the spoken message. And as mentioned previously, it's been done without teleprompters; in Lincoln's case, because the technology didn't yet exist; in Trump's case, because he doesn't need that crutch to find the words to speak from the heart and soul to tell people what they want, and need, to hear. In Trump's case, especially, his is the power of positive thinking, the entrepreneurial mindset. He focuses on what can be achieved with personal work ethic and responsibility. It's great news for the people and bad news for his political opponents.

"You know, I don't believe in teleprompters," Trump has said.

You read a speech, and you read it—and then you leave, and nobody goes crazy. I give it very much from the heart. You know, the greatest speaker I think I've ever witnessed was Dr. Norman Vincent Peale, and he would speak the power of positive thinking. He would speak so much— and he'd bring it into modern-day life. He talked about success stories and people that were successful and became alcoholics, and then they conquered it. . . . I grew up watching that. He wasn't reading. I've [heard] plenty of pastors and ministers that read. It's not the same thing. . . .

You go into Mobile with thirty-one thousand or Dallas with twenty thousand people—and you don't even have literally notes in front of you. It's a little bit nerve-wracking because you know, maybe who knows, right? But it's exciting, and the energy really does something to me that's incredible. You saw the crowds, you saw the response to standing ovations for five and ten minutes sometimes, so it's very exciting.[32]

It's no mistake or coincidence that Trump speeches generate the fervor of a religious revival. As mentioned in this book, Trump periodically sought out the counsel and eventual friendships of a number of Christian leaders, pastors, and evangelists, even before he ran for president. Some came to him. At first most were skeptical of Trump, questioning his sincerity and where he stood with the Christian faith. Eventually many opened up to Trump on the practice of reaching out to people and spreading the good word, even if, in his case, it wasn't often taken straight from Scripture.

One of those Trump converts was Dallas evangelist Lance Wallnau, a conservative Pentecostal Christian, who, in September 2015, found himself heading to New York to join other Christian leaders to meet with Trump at Trump Tower. Wallnau was replacing another evangelist, Kim Clement, who had fallen ill and couldn't make the trip. Wallnau enjoyed congregating with other like-minded Christian leaders and he was glad to have met the presidential candidate, but upon boarding the airplane for the flight back to Dallas, he knew he still wasn't sold on Trump. Then something happened.

"The Word of the Lord that was going to come to Kim about the presidential candidate—it came to me. This was new territory for me," Wallnau said, "but I came home, and when I was standing in my study in my office, I heard these words: 'Donald Trump is a wrecking ball to the spirit of political correctness.' . . . And that was the moment that I got behind Donald Trump. I was enthusiastic for him from that moment on."[33] At one point during Trump's meeting with the Christian leaders, some black as well as white, the conversation turned to what should happen during a worship service when the preacher is preaching a good sermon and someone in the audience feels inspired to storm the pulpit and attempt to grab the microphone away from the preacher. How would you deal with that?

"Nobody even stopped to say, 'Let's be careful how we answer this,'" Wallnau said,

> because in an African-American church, the very thought of you getting up and interrupting the man—no, they've got more respect for the man of God, like the Catholic respects the priest. In the African-American church, you'd better respect clergy. They told Trump, "We'd take the person out—and we may not even be pleasant on the way out the door. We wouldn't be worried about hurting your feelings if you're going to try to storm the pulpit when the preacher's preaching."

According to Wallnau, Trump waited until the other men in the room were finished speaking, then looked them in the eye and said, "That's all I'm saying. The rallies are like my church service. I'm the preacher, and I'm trying to deliver my sermon."[34]

Trump's campaign rallies in 2015 and 2016 were the stuff of legend. In a 2019 podcast, *Wall Street Journal* reporter Mike Bender described a Trump rally as a multi-day event for many Trump supporters. They would hear about the event a week or two in advance, and soon the line would start forming at the venue. Aspiring attendees arrived early to increase their chances of getting a seat before the fire marshal closed down further admittance into the venue.

According to Bender:

> There is an old-time tent revival aspect to these rallies. And a sort of ritual of it. And there's a certain validation to it, too. I mean, for a lot of Trump supporters, and especially the Front Row Joes, they were among the first people in America to recognize the resonance of Trump's political message. And they were right. They picked a horse early on, stuck by him, and they won.
>
> All of the people I talked to, the one thing they talk about is the energy they get from these rallies, and it's kind of psychic cleansing that comes from ninety minutes of participating in the same chants and cheering the same applause lines as twenty thousand other people, like-minded people, that a lot of them don't get out of their normal daily lives.[35]

Still, the attacks kept coming in Trump's direction. Though touted by media as legit journalism these are in fact a transparent veil for liberal thought and culture, and even strands of Marxist activists, to bring down Trump. Through it all, he absorbs the punches and keeps on ticking . . . and thriving.

"I don't mind being attacked," Trump says.

> I use the media the way the media uses me—to attract attention. Once I have that attention, it's up to me to use it to my advantage. I learned a long time ago that if you're not afraid to be outspoken, the media will write about you or beg you to come on their shows. . . . So sometimes I make outrageous comments and give them what they want—viewers and readers—in order to make a point. . . . But now I am using those talents, honed through years of tremendous success, to inspire people to think that our country can get better and be great again and that we can turn things around.[36]

Lincoln had plenty of that tent-revival DNA in him as well. He often spoke in a manner similar to a tent-revival preacher beseeching audience members to bust out of their shackles and step forward to accept Jesus Christ as their Savior. Except Lincoln wasn't a preacher in the religious sense; he was about manifesting his politically driven destiny and saving the Union. Again, Lincoln specialized in performance art, tinged with a high degree of personal sentiment and brash emotions. He connected with his listeners at the same time he was inspiring them and even humoring them, as depicted in the following excerpt about a speech he gave in Bloomington, Illinois. This was during the first Republican State Convention of Illinois in 1848. Lincoln was insisting to citizens that America should not be, and would never be, a Socialist nation (praise the Lord!):

> He began hesitatingly, with suppressed emotion, but grew vigorous and impassioned as he went on. As he moved slowly toward the front of the platform, eyes flashing, he seemed to the audience to grow taller and taller. . . . Here Lincoln spoke more of the Union than of slavery. He strove to warn rather than to convince. At the climax, apostrophizing invisible adversaries, Lincoln exclaimed, "We won't go out of the Union, and you sha'n't!" The fame of this speech soon spread throughout Illinois.[37]

Lincoln had a gift for robustly communicating his feelings and emotions with barely a hint of manufacture. Perhaps no speech of his was more impassioned than the one he made at eight in the morning on February 11, 1861, at the Great Western Depot in Springfield, Illinois. This was just as he was about to board his coach for the trip to Washington, DC, to assume the presidency. Actually it was more than just a speech; it was his farewell to the people who had gathered at the train station to see him off, many of whom he knew by name. They were more than a thousand in number, including loved ones, friends, neighbors, and colleagues. It was one of his shortest speeches, but certainly one of his most moving—extemporaneously delivered, of course.[38] Several variations of the minute-long speech exist; this one is taken from Abraham Lincoln Online, at abrahaml;incolnonline.org:

> My friends, no one, not in my situation, can appreciate my feeling of sadness at this parting. To this place, and the kindness of these people, I owe everything. Here I have lived a quarter of a century, and have passed from a young to an old man. Here my children have been born, and one is buried. I now leave, not knowing when, or whether ever, I may return, with a task before me greater than that which rested upon Washington. Without the assistance of the Divine Being who ever attended him, I cannot succeed. With that assistance I cannot fail. Trusting in Him who can go with me, and remain with you, and be everywhere for good, let us confidently hope that all will yet be well. To His care commending you, as I hope in your prayers you will commend me, I bid you an affectionate farewell.[39]

⊛⊛

Ronald Reagan has often been called "the Great Communicator," but historians are more likely to confer that honorary label to Lincoln. For one thing, Lincoln wrote his own speeches, while Reagan had plenty of help. Phillips writes that many of Lincoln's addresses merited description as "masterpieces of poetic and artistic expression," and when spoken—or perhaps a better word would be *performed*—by Lincoln, they took on a life of their own, capable of raising the emotions of his audiences. There's no question that Lincoln's extemporaneous performances were among the best ever offered, but his writings deserve special attention. "He penned the Emancipation Proclamation and wrote thousands of letters and notes to anyone with whom he felt he needed to communicate," Phillips adds. "The sheer volume of his collected works (which amounts to more words than are in the Bible) is testament to his commitment to effective communication."[40]

Lincoln's penchant for meticulously researching and writing his own speeches allowed him the time to carefully contemplate what he was going to say, essentially choosing words one by one, making sure each fit a particular purpose. In this way, Lincoln made absolutely sure that his message would be heard and interpreted exactly as planned, without room for mistakes that can creep into the narrative when speaking off the cuff or departing from the script in front of him. Having cut down on his public speaking once he started running for and then serving as president, Lincoln relied much more on the written word than the spoken word in getting his message out, and he was a terrific writer. Great communication comes in different forms.

"To approach Lincoln's presidency from the aspect of his writing is to come to grips with the degree to which his pen, to alter the proverb, became his sword, arguably the most powerful weapon of his presidency," Douglas L. Wilson writes in a piece entitled "Lincoln the Persuader" that appeared in *The American Scholar*.

> To explore Lincoln's presidential writing is to create, in effect, a window on his presidency and a key to his accomplishments.
>
> One of the dramas that this perspective brings into focus has already been referred to, the gradual realization by the public that its unprepossessing president was actually an accomplished writer. A parallel drama had to do with how the power of Lincoln's words gradually grew during the course of his presidency. While blessed with considerable self-confidence, Lincoln did not think of himself as a great writer. His private secretaries Nicolay and John Hay declared emphatically in their joint biography of Lincoln, "Nothing would have more amazed him while he lived than to hear himself called a man of letters." . . . His all-consuming purpose was, of course, not literary, but political—to find a way to reach a large and diverse American audience and to persuade them to support the government in its efforts to put down the rebellion.[41]

Wilson contends that Lincoln's writings were a vital part of his attempts to deal with the pressures of office exerted upon him by the never-ending "crossfire involving congressmen, governors, generals, office seekers, ordinary citizens—all dissatisfied and many sincerely convinced that his incompetence was leading the nation down the path to destruction."

Where have we heard that before? Answer: during Trump's presidency. Unlike Lincoln, though, Trump is not known as a literary virtuoso, a man of letters. He's more a man of characters, as in how many characters can you squeeze into one tweet and hope to get your message out to American citizens across the country? Throughout his presidency, Trump sent out untold thousands of tweets, many of them crossing the lines of political correctness, but all of them with a purpose in mind—to reveal to Americans what was on his mind without having those thoughts filtered by the press. Trump's use of social media, particularly Twitter, has pushed him over the top in terms of U.S. presidents making effective use of the personal communication tools at their disposal.

"President Trump has already proven to be an expert in using social media to bypass the elite news media and speak directly with the American people through Facebook, Twitter, YouTube, or other new social media platforms," Gingrich writes in *Trump's America*. "He could use these skills to connect directly with the American people—much like FDR did with his fireside chats, a series of radio broadcasts he made during his presidency."[42]

Trump has often been known to take control of the day's news cycle soon after he gets out of bed by tweeting out to millions of his supporters whatever happens to be on his mind. It might be a tweet about a possible executive order he has been contemplating, or a he might tweet out a critical comment about a political opponent such as Joe Biden, or he might take to task a Democratic mayor who was unwilling to curtail protest-related violence in their city.

"It was routine for Trump to get millions of dollars' worth of free media without spending a penny," Gingrich points out in *Understanding Trump*.[43]

Lincoln had his share of scoffers and needlers to deal with, in and out of the media, and he, too, found that his pen served him better than his vocal chords. There was the matter of the War Between the States to deal with, and one of Lincoln's biggest chores was either boosting or reshaping public opinion when necessary to counter the Confederacy's criticism and propaganda. At times like this, he needed to speak to the people on a grander scale than what was available through public speeches and rallies.

In order to be a proactive communicator, Lincoln first needed to enact a paradigm shift. For the first year or so in office, he had seen his role as president as one of administration. His was a passive philosophy, in which he would convey to Congress his planned actions and wishes and then sit back and see where things went. It soon became clear, though, that as events unfolded on the battlefield, Lincoln needed to take firmer control of the Army of the Potomac, and to do that he needed to steer public opinion in his favor. He became much more proactive, again, with a pen mightier than the sword.

Lincoln started taking up pen and paper more often, dashing off public letters aimed at specific issues with specific agitators. As a bonus benefit, these letters were published in newspapers for all the world to see and they helped shape public opinion in his favor, thanks to Lincoln's keen employ of the English language.

In one such letter, sent in August 1862 to Horace Greeley of the *New York Tribune*, Lincoln angrily took issue with an open letter Greeley had published in his newspaper. The original letter expressed disdain over Lincoln's delay in enforcing the "emancipating provisions" of the Second Confiscation Act, which had been passed several weeks earlier. Lincoln wrote back in a clear, succinct manner worthy of an attorney making his final argument before a jury. He told Greeley—and the world—that his paramount objective at the time was to save the Union, whether that was accompanied by not freeing any slaves, by freeing some slaves and not others, or by freeing all slaves.

> What I do about slavery, and the colored race, I do because it helps to save the Union; and what I forbear, I forbear because I do not believe it would help to save the Union. I shall do less whenever I shall believe what I am doing hurts the cause, and I shall do more whenever I shall believe doing more will help the cause. I shall try to correct errors when shown to be errors; and I shall adopt new views so fast as they shall appear to be true views.[44]

Case closed.

If all else fails, in today's world anyway, there's always Trump to dish it right. There's this exchange between Trump and pollster/pundit Frank Luntz during a televised one-on-one Q&A in which Luntz opens by tossing Trump a softball question about public education policy. Trump swings and connects:

> "Common Core has to be ended, It's a disaster," Trump said, earning applause by echoing every other GOP candidate's answer on the subject. But then he added Trumpian color: "It is a way of taking care of the people in Washington that frankly, I don't even think they give a damn about education, half of them. I am sure some maybe do."
>
> "Do you want to use that word in this forum?" Luntz asked with a smile. The audience leaned in.
>
> "I will, I will. Because people want to hear the truth, Frank," Trump said. "I watch you all the time; they want to hear the truth."
>
> Applause erupted.
>
> "I mean, exactly what Frank said is what is wrong with our country. We are so politically correct that we cannot move anymore."[45]

Donald Trump was notorious for ad-libbing and going off-script during his rally speeches. Audiences knew when he followed the teleprompter and when he added his own sideline quips, thoughts, and hyperbole that only Trump could pepper throughout an otherwise carefully written speech—and they loved it! In between memorized soundbites the inevitable colorful language, stream of consciousness comments, and personal Trumpisms fed the crowds during the 2016 campaign. No one knew what he was going to say next. Even as president, Trump maintained a mostly unfiltered pathway from mind to mouth. And that's not likely to change . . . ever.

At one August 2016 campaign rally in Michigan, he implored African Americans for their vote with "What have you got to lose?" He repeated the plea several times before finalizing it with an ad-lib expletive undoubtedly generated by thousands of excited rally-goers—"What the hell do you have to lose?!"

In his earlier years, Lincoln often went off-script as the mood of the crowd prompted him to add passionate and patriotic phrases. However, in his years as president, he learned to prepare speeches carefully, to condense the greatest, clearest meaning into much shorter speeches. The emotion of Lincoln the campaigner subsided in favor of the measured precision of a more polished politician. Lincoln's Gettysburg Address, famous only after his death, was delivered with a most notable ad-lib.

Beginning with "Fourscore and seven years ago . . ." Lincoln uttered this meticulously crafted speech, a mere 272 words, in just over two minutes. In it the president condensed American history, the Civil War, and his future national policy into so short an interval that the official photographer was caught flat-footed and missed the shot. Only a blurred image exists of Lincoln delivering his address to the 20,000 plus crowd.

Lincoln's ad-lib is best described by Historian Louis A. Warren in his *Little Known Facts About the Gettysburg Address*:

> Lincoln's preliminary draft of the Gettysburg Address makes no mention of Deity, and this has been made a great point by those who would prefer to have it so. Every stenographic report of what Lincoln actually said, however, includes the expression "under God" in the president's remarks. Back in Lincoln's childhood days, he had been greatly impressed by Weems's story of George Washington, and Lincoln was able to quote many passages from this inspirational biography. Weems had one expression which he frequently used in his book, a word couplet—"under God."
>
> President Lincoln, like Trump, may very well have considered the setting for this speech to be "his church," and from his pulpit he offered this benediction: " . . . this nation, under God, shall have a new birth of freedom; and that this government of the people, by the people, for the people shall not perish from the earth."[46]

Amen!

CHAPTER 9

BORN TO LEAD

———— ❧ ————

Undertaking to read everything about Abraham Lincoln might be an impossible task. Thousands upon thousands of volumes exist about our sixteenth president and the times in which he lived. Is there anything we don't know about him? Apparently, yes. Books continue to be published, even today, revealing new perspectives and unique nuances about this American icon. One gem I unearthed from his past was about his own short term of military service.

As commander in chief, Lincoln wielded great power over soldiers and sailors—but an enlisted man himself? Yes, and I found it to be a humorous episode, not intrinsically (though Abe himself used the brief stint as comic relief in some of his own speeches) but in connection to Donald Trump. No, the Donald never served in the military—bone spurs, super-high draft number, or some such—but I discovered a most unusual likeness.

Lincoln, while in his early twenties, joined other local young men in volunteering for the Illinois state militia in a regional skirmish with natives that was later called the Black Hawk War. He related the never-ending marching through marshes, and how they never, not once, even tussled with the enemy. But he joked that he had many bloody struggles with the mosquitoes. What stuck with him most was the great satisfaction he felt in being voted captain by his peers—a success he found profoundly satisfying.

Donald Trump was also elected captain by his peers—on his high school baseball team. I'm pretty sure the baseball team never saw combat either. Whether Trump valued the experience is not known, but depending on the intensity of the competition and how aggressively Donald slid into home or ducked pitchers' wild balls, his stint as captain may have drawn more blood than Lincoln's mosquitoes.

CB SO

The leadership debate continues and might never end: Are great leaders born or made; is it nature or is it nurture that imbues a young Abraham Lincoln or Donald Trump with the right ingredients to handle the reins of an entity as considerable and consequential as America? On closer look, it took both nature and nurture for both of them, even if neither ever included *nurture* in his vocabulary.

The seeds of presidential-style leadership are planted in childhood, when parental upbringing and influence can give (or deny) a child the foundation he or she needs to have sufficient firm footing to handle the reins, rigors, and risks of leadership as they grow into such roles. Studies of prominent, successful leaders have shown that many came from households in which parents were authoritative while also giving their child the slack to make their own choices.

Such parents also support their child and offer encouragement and compliments when earned, but without spoiling the child and giving them a sense of entitlement. They also let their children take chances and experience the consequences of them—even the ones resulting from bad choices. This allows the child to experience and understand risk and results without the parents rescuing them at the last minute.

Both Lincoln and Trump had happy childhoods—at least in their early years (Lincoln until age nine, when his mother passed away; Trump until age thirteen, when he was enrolled in a military school to smooth off the rough edges). But both went through growing pains in their teen years, with Lincoln learning a stout work ethic while grinding under his demanding father Thomas; Trump learned about discipline and accountability during his years at New York Military Academy. Lincoln grew up mostly in backwoods poverty while Trump was raised in wealth, although the two shared an acquired appreciation for sweat equity that would prepare them for leadership positions over time.

Leadership usually isn't a great career choice for wallflowers, shrinking violets, and anyone who is afraid to speak up and be counted. Leaders will speak up and make a stand—even if it means being perceived as rude at times. Believe it or not, Abraham Lincoln, as deliberate in demeanor and as humble in spirit as he was, could show flashes of rudeness at times, even when he was still in his youth, under the employ of his dad, Thomas. As quoted previously, his biographer and former law partner William Herndon points this out in *The Hidden Lincoln*:

> Abe was a good boy, an affectionate one, a boy who loved his father and mother dearly and well, always minding them well. Sometimes Abe was a little rude. When strangers would ride along and up to his father's fence, Abe always, through pride and to tease his father, would be sure to ask the stranger the first question, for which his father would sometimes knock him a rod. Abe was then a rude and forward boy.[1]

It was a good thing for Lincoln that his dad was a disciplinarian, putting great value in work ethic while demanding good manners—traits that would benefit Honest Abe in years to come. He came from a poor family, relatively speaking, but it was a stable, secure family environment, providing a big chunk of the foundation of leadership that Lincoln kept building on over the years, through triumph and failure.

For the first nine and a half years of his life, up to when his mother passed away, young Abe enjoyed a mostly happy childhood in Kentucky, although years later he would often avoid discussing those years. When he was running for president and being pressed to reveal details of his life to newsmen, it was reported that Lincoln seemed "painfully impressed with the extreme poverty of his early surroundings" as well as "the utter absence of all romantic and heroic elements." When pushed to reveal more about himself and the life he had lived, Lincoln characteristically called these attempts to elicit information a "great piece of folly" in trying to "make anything out of my early life [except] a single sentence . . . in Gray's Elegy: 'The short and simple annals of the poor.'"[2]

Perhaps Lincoln judged his early years a bit too harshly, or at least he hinted at it through his reticence to speak of those first nine-plus years of his life, a good portion of which he must have remembered, even if he acted at times like he didn't recall the positive aspects of it. Lincoln biographer William W. Freehling, writing in *Becoming Lincoln*, paints a loftier picture of the president's earliest years and the family that provided him and his sister Sarah with love and security, even after the tragic death of youngest child, Thomas Jr., who passed away just a few days after his birth. "The place briefly became a family haven," Freehling says, referring to the tract of land that Tom Lincoln at the time was leasing on the 228-acre Knob Creek Farm in Kentucky.

> True, the parents lost their third and last child, Thomas Jr., after only a few days of life. But the survivors—mother, father, son Abraham, and daughter Sarah—formed a model nuclear family surrounded by a model

extended family. A bevy of aunts, uncles, and cousins, all survivors of Grandfather Abraham Lincoln, resided within a day's travel from Knob Creek Farm.

Tom Lincoln farmed a few acres of limestone bluffs (knobs) above Knob Creek. While father worked, Abraham and Sarah swam in the creek's clear waters or played hide-and-seek among overhanging knobs. In this natural playground, with no necessity [at the time] for his son to labor, Tom Lincoln ranked in the top 15 percent of Hardin County property owners.[3]

As he grew into adulthood, eventually to become a lawyer, politician, and statesman, Lincoln, at least on the surface, had the bearing and persona of an uncomplicated man. Beneath that stoic, reserved exterior, though, resided a burning cauldron of ambition and confidence. Lincoln itched to be in charge of something truly significant, to be a leader. His personality in many ways was "a puzzle and a paradox," as it is described in *Lincoln: His Words and His World*. In 1838, the same year in which the then twenty-nine-year-old Lincoln won his third term to the Illinois House of Representatives, he asked the following rhetorical question: "Is it unreasonable then to expect that some man possessed of the loftiest genius, coupled with ambition sufficient to push it to its utmost stretch, will, at some time, spring up among us?"[4] It is generally assumed that Lincoln was talking about himself and his own aspirations and qualifications, a likelihood borne out years later when, as president, he told an acquaintance, "You know better than any man living that from my boyhood up my ambition was to be president."[5]

CB ED

Unlike Lincoln, who grew up in a zone somewhere between poverty and lower middle class (cutting his family some slack there), Trump grew up in wealth. But like Lincoln and many other renowned leaders, Trump also grew up in a stable family, one that offered love and security, and at least a modicum of nurture mixed with discipline. Profanity was forbidden in the Trump household, where there were curfews and plenty of other rules that set firm boundaries for the five children. With all the house rules came ample discipline. Mom (Mary) gave Dad (Fred) a daily report when he got back from work. The report provided details on who had acted up and who would be punished, which often came at the big end of a wooden spoon.

"My family is very important to me and always has been," a grown-up Trump declared decades later, referring not only to his own family but the one he grew up in back in Jamaica Estates, New York. "I'm happiest when I'm with them."[6]

Born in 1946, Donnie Trump was at the forefront of the baby boom generation, grouping together those born during the period 1946 through 1964, with that first wave arriving in the wake of the end of the Second World War. This generation had a dynamic all its own, one that undoubtedly shaped young Donald Trump for life, as author Gwenda Blair explains in her book *The Trumps*:

> Although this generation's primary identity would be as members of their own families, they would also develop a secondary role as members of the baby boom family. Together with their boomer sisters and brothers, they would grow up on television, rock and roll, and the cold war. But for those born, as Donald Trump was, at the beginning of the boom, there may have been something more. Because the war had interrupted normal patterns of marriage and childbearing, children born in the first few years of the baby boom included a higher-than-normal proportion of firstborns. In turn, instead of having the full range of personality attributes associated with children of a variety of birth orders, children in the first wave of the baby boom would tend to have a similar, firstborn character: assertive, ambitious, and, above all, successful. Further, because of this heavily firstborn environment, a kind of herd effect may have taken over, with playmates and classmates who were not firstborns acting as if they were. . . . Donald Trump was one of these faux firstborns. Although the fourth-born in his family, by all accounts he was self-assured, determined, and positive from the start.[7]

With the war over and the world again safe from the likes of Adolph Hitler, the Third Reich, and like-minded tyrants, America hit the ground running. Soldiers around the world were returning home, new cars were rolling off the assembly lines in Detroit, and the first models of television sets were being planted in almost every living room or den in the United States.

It was a time in America, one that would last into the early sixties, when few people worried about locking their doors. It was also a time when kids freely roamed from one friend's house to another in the neighborhood; this was a world in which everyone knew their neighbor. Even the well-monitored (if not always well-mannered) Trump kids were free to go next door or across the street to see and play with friends. There were always other possibilities beyond just the four walls of your own house.

For the Trump kids, their favorite go-to neighbor was Bernice Able MacIntosh and Bernice's daughter, Heather. Bernice could speak German and years earlier had been friends with Fred Trump's mother. "It seemed like every morning I would have two or three Trumps at the breakfast table with Heather," Bernice said many years later. "There were three cookie jars, and they were always open. So was the refrigerator. The Trumps didn't have that [freedom] at their house, so they came over to mine."[8]

The Trump kids were close to Bernice and Heather, enough so that Mrs. MacIntosh would buy gifts for the Trump kids. Donald's favorites were toy vehicles. "Every Christmas and for each birthday, I'd buy him the strongest truck I could find," Bernice said. "He'd always take it apart immediately. By the time my daughter got home from his birthday party, he'd have dismantled it. 'Oh, Mom, he's got it all in pieces,' she'd say."[9]

Trump also had the benefit of specialized schooling beginning with Carousel Preschool, which emphasized hands-on learning experiences, like\ building blocks, which became one of young Donald's greatest early influences and passions.[10]

Writing in his bestselling book *The Art of the Deal*, Trump saw himself as a natural leader from an early age, saying,

> I was always something of a leader in my neighborhood. Much the way it is today, people either liked me a lot, or they didn't like me at all. In my own crowd, I was very well-liked, and I tended to be the kid that others followed. As an adolescent, I was mostly interested in creating mischief, because for some reason I liked to stir things up, and I liked to test people.[11]

Lincoln never had the benefit of avant garde schools like little Donnie Trump did, but during the times he was in school—limited as it was during his younger years because of work duties mandated by his dad—young Abe showed himself to be a diligent student blessed with an extraordinarily good memory, one so impressive it soon put him in the forefront among his fellow students, who looked up to him. Lincoln had no problem drawing attention to himself: he was not only tall but also adept at performing for an audience, such as the retold sermons he memorized and then gave from a tree stump.

"Sharing his knowledge with his schoolmates at every turn, he soon became 'their guide and leader,'" historian/author Doris Kearns Goodwin writes.

> A friend recalled the "great" pains he took to her to explain "the movements of the heavenly bodies," patiently telling her that the moon was not really sinking as she originally thought; it was the earth that was moving, not the moon. "When he appeared in Company," another friend recalled, "the boys would gather & cluster around him to hear him talk."[12]

Herndon tells how one of Abe's acquaintances described Abe as possessing a distinctive ability to win friends and influence people:

"His mind and the ambition of the man soared above us. He naturally assumed the leadership of the boys. He read and thoroughly read his books whilst we played. Hence he rose above us and became our guide and leader, and in this position he never failed to be the leader. He was kind, jocular, witty, wise, honest, just human, full of integrity, energy, and activity. . . . He made fun and cracked his jokes, making all happy."[13]

Lincoln wasn't lacking confidence, either. He had a strong self-awareness of what he was good at (as well as his weak points) and wasn't reticent about taking on responsibility and the pressure that goes with it. He had just turned twenty-three a month earlier, when, in March 1832, he announced that he was running for the Illinois state legislature. It was a gesture sourced from a robust self-confidence, presumably rooted in the belief that he was superior to any man he had ever met. Even though he lost that first political contest, he returned two years later to run again, this time winning the first of what would be four consecutive terms in the state legislature. In the middle of his time in the state legislature (in 1837) he was admitted to the bar for practicing law.

Perhaps the most important key to Lincoln's confidence—and therefore his well-cultivated penchant for leadership—was his ability to think quickly on his feet and deflect verbal jabs from opponents. One such opponent was a political rival by the name of George Forquer, a well-to-do lawyer who had just switched to the Democratic Party. At a political rally in Springfield, Illinois, Forquer jabbed away at Lincoln in a speech dripping with sarcasm. Forquer's base message was that Lincoln was a brazen, young (Lincoln was twenty-five at the time), up-and-comer who was in over his head. Lincoln calmly bided his time as he listened, knowing he would soon get his chance to fire back. As Lincoln was about to take his turn, it dawned on him how Forquer had recently installed a lightning rod—a rarity in those days, and something Lincoln had never before seen—atop his house.

Once Forquer was finished, Lincoln stepped to the podium and immediately launched his counterattack. Speaking of his competitor, he said,

The gentleman commenced . . . by saying that this young man [Lincoln himself] will have to be taken down.. . . . I am not so young in years as I am in the trick and trades of a politician; but . . . I would rather die now than, like the gentleman [Forquer], change my politics and simultaneous with the change receive an office worth three thousand dollars per year, and then have to erect a lightning rod over my house to protect a guilty conscience from an offended God.[14]

◌3 ౭◌

Lincoln and Trump were their respective era's poster boys for the power of positive thinking, a key ingredient for becoming and being a strong leader. A leader must have an optimistic approach to life and an upbeat spirit in order to inspire and motivate others, as well as fend off or at least bounce back quickly from verbal attacks. Both Lincoln and Trump were on the receiving end of plenty of those.

Note that when Lincoln was running for office for the first time, in 1832, he had been described just a year earlier as a "friendless, uneducated, penniless boy, working on a flatboat—at ten dollars per month,"[15] and those were his words, not an opponent's. One skill Lincoln had mastered was the art of using self-deprecation to his advantage, if for nothing else than to loosen up an audience and charm potential supporters with his candor and humor.

Lincoln eagerly did whatever he had a mind to do at times like this. He wasn't likely to get discouraged in such situations because he had a mind bent toward resilience. He would just forge ahead, like a skilled golfer who might flub a shot and then erase it from his immediate consciousness in time to hit his next shot flush with renewed confidence.

If Trump ever has pause or remorse for anything he has ever said or done, he rarely, if ever, shows or speaks it. His outsized personality is about staying bold and pushing ahead, leading from the front, such as he did in October 2020, when he joined millions of other Americans who had contracted the COVID-19 virus. The infection knocked Trump down for a few days, sending him to the hospital for personalized around-the-clock care. Thanks to his strength of will and body as well as the expert care and medications provided by a team of physicians, he was on his feet and back in the White House within three days. Soon after he was back out on the presidential campaign trail, as vigorous and outspoken as ever.

"I don't mind being called *brash* because to me it's being bold, it's having energy, it's getting things done," Trump said some years earlier, recalling a *Newsweek* magazine ad from the eighties that included a photograph of him with the caption, "Few things in life are as brash as *Newsweek*." Added Trump, he of the thick skin: "But the constraints are to be considered, and my momentum is carefully monitored. I'm not exactly brash in that sense, but I know you can't get things done if you're too timid. My persona will never be one of the wallflower—I'd rather build walls than cling to them."[16] Trump has also said, "You can't be scared. You do your thing, you hold your ground, you stand up tall, and whatever happens, happens."[17]

Like him or detest him, anyone who has seen or heard Trump speak—whether in front of huge crowds at campaign rallies or one-on-one with an inquiring reporter—can't dispute his unbridled confidence. He aims high and believes strongly in the acquisition of practical knowledge. In his case that has often meant being a leader who uses his hands and doesn't mind getting them dirty, either literally or proverbially. Those things also apply to Lincoln, without need for elaboration.

"[Trump] believes in aiming high and accomplishing what others say is impossible," political ally Newt Gingrich writes in *Understanding Trump*.

> "Trump values people who have gained practical knowledge—knowledge that must be learned by doing rather than by hearing a lecture or reading a book. Trump himself learned the bulk of the real estate trade by working with his father—not while he was attending the University of Pennsylvania's Wharton School."[18]

෴

A capable, competent leader has a strong moral core and code, and both Trump and Lincoln can and could boil down theirs to a simple question: Is this the right thing to do; is it just? Herndon put it this way in describing Lincoln:

> If the thing was just, [Lincoln] approved of it, and if the man was a sham, he said: "Begone." He was a man of great moral and physical courage and had the valor and bravery of his convictions and dared cautiously to do what he thought was right and just; he was cautious and conservative in his nature, was prudent and wise in his acts, and I have often thought over-cautious, sometimes bordering on the timid [This part of the description does not apply to Trump; that much we know for certain.]. . . . Come, was not Mr. Lincoln built and organized for the occasion? Was he not the right man in the right time, in the right place? Would you have made him different? How would you have grouped the atoms?[19]

When Herndon talked about Lincoln being "built . . . for the occasion," he might not just have been talking about Lincoln's fortitude of character and morality. He could also have been referring to the president's exceptional physical strength, acquired and honed by the years of intense physical labor he performed under the watchful eye of his father, Thomas Lincoln.

It was Abe's physical prowess, as much as his oratorical agility, that made Lincoln stand out among other men, earning him a great deal of admiration on its own. Historians and school students alike know the stories of Lincoln's ability to handle an axe like a monkey handles coconuts, but what Lincoln was able to do with it—such as splitting logs with an ease uncommon in his era—often surpassed belief. At least that's how Herndon describes it. Among his fellow leaders, Lincoln earned many of his stripes without having to open his mouth.

"One witness declares he was equal to three men, having on a recent occasion carried a load of six hundred pounds," Herndon writes.

> At another time he walked away with a pair of logs which three robust men were skeptical of their ability to carry. "He could strike with a maul [a tool similar to a sledgehammer] a heavier blow—could sink an axe deeper into wood than any man I ever saw," is the testimony of another witness.[20]

Herndon continues:

> Mr. Lincoln was six feet four inches high [note that Trump stands six feet, three inches at twenty years older], and when he left the city of his home for Washington was fifty-one years old, having good health and no gray hairs, or but few, on his head. He was thin, wiry, sinewy, raw-boned; thin through the breast to the back, and narrow across the shoulders; standing he leaned forward—was what may be called stoop-shouldered, including to the consumptive by build. His usual weight was one hundred and eighty pounds [Trump outweighs him by about sixty pounds, give or take]. . . . The whole man, body and mind, worked slowly, as if it needed oiling. . . . His mind was like his body, and worked slowly but strongly. Hence there was very little bodily or mental wear and tear in him. This peculiarity in his construction gave him great advantage over other men in public life. No man in America—scarcely a man in the world—could have stood what Lincoln did in Washington and survived through more than one term of the presidency.[21]

Trump can identify with that—surviving four years of the constant haranguing he has been subjected to as president. However it's doubtful Trump has ever been able to lift six hundred pounds.

Physical, mental, emotional, and spiritual endurance are a leadership requirement. In Lincoln's case, his size and strength enhanced his authority with peers. Putting it in layman's terms, it was not a good idea to mess with Lincoln. From an early age, he could outperform other boys in terms of athletic skill—outrunning, outjumping, or outwrestling anyone willing to take him on. Abe was always a willing foe, whether for fun or when the stakes were more serious.

"Relatives recalled that he was never sick," Kearns Goodwin writes.

Lincoln's physical dominance proved a double-edged sword, however, for he was expected, from the age of eight to the age of twenty-one, to accompany his father into the fields, wielding an axe, felling trees, digging up stumps, splitting rails, plowing, and planting. His father considered that bones and muscles were "sufficient to make a man" and that time in school was doubly wasted.[22]

Lincoln was certainly fit for the office of the presidency, demonstrating his great stamina in nonphysical endeavors as well, such as during the aforementioned Lincoln–Douglas debates. There were seven debates total, held between August 21 and October 15 of 1858, in each of the seven of Illinois's nine Congressional Districts in which Douglas had not yet spoken. There was an average of about eight days between each debate. The two men alternated going first in a format whereby the first speaker got an hour, after which the other had an hour and a half, followed, finally, by a thirty-minute rebuttal from the first candidate. Douglas got to go first four of the seven times.

Even though Douglas went on to win the contested Illinois Senate seat that year, Lincoln had a much-bigger prize awaiting him two years later. The consensus was that Lincoln had not only outdone his rival over the course of the seven debates, but he had also come out of them much more hale and hearty than the tuckered-out Douglas. Here's how Herndon assessed each candidate by the time they crossed the finish line of Election Day that fall:

Lincoln came out of the great Douglas race in 1858, after speaking probably fifty of sixty times, a new man, vigorous, healthy, fresh as a young man, better-colored, more elastic, more cheerful, less sad, stronger, and improved every way. Douglas was worn out, voice gone, broken down, a wreck, as it were. Saw both men during and just before and just after the race and state what I saw and know. Lincoln's voice was less husky, broken, wheezy; it improved all the time.[23]

About two and a half years later, Lincoln's stamina and resilience would once again be on display, beginning in the early morning hours of April 12, 1861, when Confederate guns around Charleston Harbor opened fire on Fort Sumter in South Carolina. That moment essentially marked the beginning of the Civil War and the start of the most tragic and tumultuous—and deadly—four years in American history. This was just over a month after

Lincoln had been inaugurated for his first term. Herndon describes that time as follows:

> In the weeks after the firing on Fort Sumter, the demands on the president's time were incessant and exhausting, but now that he could clearly see what had to be done, he bore up well under the strain. When the writer Bayard Taylor visited Washington, he was delighted to discover, contrary to rumor, that Lincoln was not exhausted or sick but instead appeared "very fresh and vigorous . . . thoroughly calm and collected." Even (Secretary of State William H.) Seward was impressed. "Executive skill and vigor are rare qualities," he wrote his wife in June. "The president is the best of us; but he needs constant and assiduous cooperation."[24]

A cursory check of Donald Trump's fascinating past doesn't reveal any great physical feats with an axe or a maul, but tales of what has been described as his "Olympic vigor" became more common following his election in November 2016. For a full four years after his election, Trump was continually under assault by devious political opponents and an outrageously biased media, apparently working in tandem to overturn the 2016 election. Their conspiracies ranged from the ultimately false charges of Russian collusion and election interference to a three-ring impeachment circus that succeeded in further disparaging the president while failing to remove him from office.

Not only did Trump prove himself a fighter worthy of the U.S. presidency but also a highly skilled politician (even though he refused to call himself one). "His work ethic is actually hard to describe," said Mike Pence, Trump's vice president.

> His energy level is actually hard to describe. I heard once that President Teddy Roosevelt was described by a contemporary as pure energy, and I've often said that must come around every hundred years at the White House, because the president and I will generally talk early, we'll talk late, we talk throughout the day. It's amazing. . . . He has an indefatigable capacity. Every day is a new day; we're back working on what we came here to do. I ultimately believe that springs from his faith and his upbringing, and a lifetime of building and overcoming. When you're president, there is a need to balance two important concepts: law and grace.[25]

While Trump's indefatigability and world-class fighting spirit has come as a shock to his liberal opponents, it doesn't surprise him at all. Trump has long fancied himself an elite athlete, although it's hard to tell if he is being facetious at times, such as when he once declared he was definitely "the best baseball player in New York." He claimed he might have turned pro had the pay been better. Although Trump may have exaggerated his athletic skills and potential for major league baseball success, he certainly has few peers when it comes to his ability to win—whether on the field, in a negotiation, or in his romantic life. He managed to place a diamond ring on three beautiful, accomplished women, making Trump, in some ways, both the most admired and most envied man in America. "This focus on his athletic achievement is as much about establishing the man's interest in competition as it is about a desire to communicate some verifiable record," author Michael D'Antonio writes in *Never Enough*.

> Trump wants people to know that he always had the heart and the ability of a winner, and these claims come with certain proof. Trump can prove, too, that he has always been especially interested in attractive women. At (New York Military Academy), where hand-holding was forbidden, the cadets nevertheless identified him as the official "ladies' man" of his class in the academy yearbook, appropriately titled *Shrapnel*.[26]

⊂⊃

Ask a dozen people who have been in leadership positions for five years or more what they believe to be the three or four most important qualities in a good leader, and you will hear at least a couple dozen different answers. Most likely, all of them would be good answers, worth taking to heart if you are a leader wannabe or even in a managerial position for a company or other organization looking to get bumped up in that next promotion. Let's take a look at several of those leadership qualities to examine more closely how well Lincoln and Trump fare in those areas.

TEAMWORK

Legendary football coach Vince Lombardi, who coached the Green Bay Packers to victory in the first two Super Bowls, was the source of many great, memorable sayings, one of which was, "Individual commitment to a group effort—that is what makes a team work."[27] Put those last two words together and you get *teamwork*.

Neither Lincoln nor Trump ever accomplished much of anything without the assistance and input of others, and a good leader is expected to make that team work together in a collaborative manner, even if it means sometimes replacing or moving players. Trump was criticized for his relatively frequent changes of staffers or cabinet members, but he is far from alone in that regard. Bill Belichick, winner of six Super Bowls with the New

185

England Patriots, is notorious for trading away or releasing several players almost every year in order to keep his team in peak competitive form. At the college level, there are many head coaches (such as the University of Alabama's Nick Saban) who replace assistant coaches almost at will in order to have the best minds and motivators on his staff. This same sort of replacement dynamic is a regular practice of coaches and managers across many sports as well as among businesses and other hierarchal organizations.

The goal is to have the best available personnel on your team, regardless at what level you are with any team, business, or organization; the most important aspect of this is having everyone working in a truly collaborative, cooperative manner. Sometimes changes have to be made, and good leaders act boldly when circumstances call for a change. It also means supporting your team members when they are in your stead, and inspiring them toward a sense of camaraderie, loyalty, fellowship, and pride.

"I don't like firing anyone," Trump said, when asked about his longtime reality television show *The Apprentice*, where someone got fired at the end of each episode. His stated outlook is also reflective of his leadership style in the real world of business and government. He continued,

> Sometimes, it's necessary, but I'd rather keep people around me for a long time. I have employees who have been with me for over thirty years. The best working environment is when everyone has the same work ethic and focus and does their best. That's the case with most of my employees, but not always, and, if not, then a change has to be made.[28]

Trump also adds,

> If you can get a core group around you that you like and who understands your needs, you will be heading in the right direction. Sometimes I think it's divine intervention when the right people show up. . . . You have to give people a chance to prove themselves. But in the interim, it helps a lot if you like having them around to begin with. . . . Every person has unique talents that may or may not be in their job description or listed on their resume. . . . Although I may be demanding, I am also fair. My door is always open, and they feel confident that when they have something to say, I'll be listening.[29]

Plugging the right people into the right spots in your organization is crucial to maintaining an optimal team, but it can be hit and miss. Things don't always work out. Trump has told the story of how he hired what he described as a "dynamic, very well-qualified, very well-educated young man." Trump was expecting great things of his new hire, but it didn't take him long to figure out he had made a bad decision. The young man couldn't explain things in a few words, and his long-windedness was ill-suited for Trump's fast-paced management style and work environment, so the young man eventually left the organization. He wasn't a bad guy, just a bad fit.

On the other hand, Trump years ago hired a project manager whose job description included collecting rent from tenants. In time, Trump realized that the man was intensely politically incorrect and also insulting around others—a con man, no less—but he was able to work quickly, effectively, and got things accomplished. He had a knack for collecting rent from reluctant tenants, a job requirement that screams for a certain kind of art form. And this guy nailed it. "He got Swifton Village [one of Trump's development properties] running well enough so that I didn't have to be in Cincinnati very often," Trump said. "I knew he was probably ripping me off, but he kept the place well and people actually paid their rent. The project was a resounding success."[30]

Sure, Trump sometimes does accommodate team members who are less than perfect in terms of team play and even ethics, but Lincoln cut the same sort of slack with Ulysses S. Grant, who served as Lincoln's top commanding general during the Civil War and who later became president himself. The word among insiders was that Grant was allegedly a drunk, with a particular hankering for whiskey. The following account comes from the September 18, 1863, edition of the *New York Herald*:

> After the failure of the first experimental explorations around Vicksburg, a committee of abolition war managers waited upon the president and demanded the General's removal, on the false charge that he was a whiskey drinker, and little better than a common drunkard.
>
> "Ah!" exclaimed Honest Old Abe, "you surprise me, gentlemen. But can you tell me where he gets his whiskey?"
>
> "We cannot, Mr. President. But why do you desire to know?"
>
> "Because, if I can only find out, I will send a barrel of this wonderful whiskey to every general in the army."[31]

In terms of what really happened under Lincoln's leadership, it's worth noting how he pieced together his administration's cabinet after winning the 1860 election. It was a hodgepodge of political loyalties, parties, and party factions; in other words, it included some members who had been his political opponents and who, frankly, were surprised they were even asked to join his team. It was, fair to say, the most unusual presidential cabinet in American history. It included a compelling mix of conservatives, moderates, and radicals, as well as hard-liners and conciliators. "'I began at once to feel that I needed support,' he later noted, 'others with me to share the burden.' "[32]

A common maxim among leaders is that those who are most secure in their position won't hesitate to hire team members who are smarter than they are and more proficient in areas specific to what they do. Lincoln admitted such himself, saying he wanted independent, strong-minded men who were more experienced in public life, better educated, and more celebrated than him. In fact, for his three most important positions—the heads of the State Department, the Treasury, and the Justice Department—he inserted his three main political rivals (William Seward, Salmon Chase, and Edwards Bates, respectively), each of whom believed he should have been president in place of Abe. "When asked why he was doing this, Lincoln's answer was simple: The country was in peril. These were the strongest and most able men in the country. He needed them at his side."[33]

One-time Lincoln naysayer Edwin Stanton was another political enemy—he had once called Lincoln a "giraffe" and stated that Abe had "no token of any intelligent understanding." Yet Lincoln at one point appointed him Secretary of War because he believed Stanton to be the best man for the job. Stanton enthusiastically accepted, immersing himself into the role and working tirelessly to help the Union win the Civil War. "Lincoln, Stanton began to think, was not the buffoon he originally believed him to be. Lincoln, in turn, came to respect, admire, and understand Stanton. He realized that under a somewhat surly exterior existed an honest, devoted, and thoroughly capable administrator," historian Donald T. Phillips writes.[34]

One conclusion to be made about leadership is that a leader is only as effective and successful insofar as his or her subordinates embrace the mission and their respective roles. A good leader is also one who inspires loyalty and respect from his or her people. Adds Phillips: "Those subordinates who will take risks, act without waiting for direction, and ask for responsibility rather than reject it, should be treated as your most prized possessions. Such individuals are exceedingly rare and worth their weight in gold."[35]

VISION OR INSPIRATION

A leader with vision encompasses more than just good eyesight and, in modern times, the ability to see the traffic light in front of you at the intersection. Having vision means being able to see the big picture where small snapshots are more readily apparent. A leader needs to see beyond today, not just to tomorrow, but to the days, weeks, months and even years ahead. As a leader, you must have a notion of how what you do today will affect your team, business, or organization in the long run.

Mike Huckabee, the former governor of Arkansas and twice a presidential candidate, says this: "A leader is the one who can outline the broad vision and the direction, and says here's where we are going to go, here's why we need to go there, and here's how we are going to get there."[36] Jack Welch, a former CEO at of General Electric (GE) added this: "Good business leaders create a vision, articulate the vision, passionately own the vision, and relentlessly drive it to completion."[37]

At Abraham Lincoln's first inauguration, in March 1861, a new iron dome was under construction atop the Capitol building but it was only half completed, its naked ribs stretching skyward. This was not a glorious look for a structure that supposedly represented the ideals of a nation—a nation now about to go to war against itself. Debate raged over whether the building effort should continue. The cost was exorbitant and the men who had been tasked to work on it were now becoming a part of the Union Army. Undeterred, Lincoln ordered the construction to continue, saying it was important, symbolically, that the task was completed. "If people see the Capitol going on, it is a sign we intend the Union shall go on," he said.[38]

That edict to continue rebuilding the Capitol dome illustrated Lincoln's transformational leadership. He was someone who could inspire others by having them identify with something larger than themselves, even an abstract representation of the nation's ideals. As Kearns Goodwin puts it, "Such leaders call for sacrifice in the pursuit of moral principles and higher goals, validating such altruism by looking beyond the present moment to frame a future worth striving for."[39]

It's almost impossible to determine when Lincoln became such a visionary. Perhaps even more of a mystery was how he became one at all, considering his political history. Even though Lincoln's political career had begun by nearly twenty-five years earlier, he never really climbed very far up the ladder—until he won the presidency. Before winning the 1860 election, he had never held an elective office higher than state legislator, except for a forgettable two-year stint as a U.S. Congressman from Illinois that had ended twelve years earlier. Then again, maybe those many political defeats sprinkled in over the years had given him time to pause and envision what kind of leader he would be once he had achieved his secret ambition of filling the seat of U.S. president. Maybe he became a better politician from his losses at the ballot box, as it is often said a person learns more from getting knocked down than from consistently winning.

Although undeniably a great orator who had been practicing and perfecting his craft from the time he was a youth, Lincoln lacked administrative skills, which became painfully evident when he reached the White House. As pointed out in *Lincoln: His Words and His World*,

> In his first few weeks as President, Lincoln seemed to fulfill the worst
> fears of the nation. But, after several weeks of vacillation and muddling,
> he finally decided that Fort Sumter should not be surrendered and, with
> that decision, Lincoln began his development toward becoming a great
> president. He never became much of an administrator, but he was an
> expert politician, a clear-headed thinker and a wise and courageous leader
> who knew when to be immovably firm and when to loosen the reins.[40]

Lincoln broke the mold forged by the three unimpressive yet self-promoting presidents who had immediately preceded him—Millard Fillmore, Franklin Pierce, and James Buchanan; Trump broke the mold, period. He's the ultimate outlier in Washington, DC, a forward-looking president who announced as he was taking office that his intent was to make America great again and "drain the swamp" of lifetime politicians who had an unspoken code and a long-entrenched manner of conducting business that didn't sit well with him.

Trump came to the White House stepping on toes and proclaiming an ambitious agenda, all geared toward improving the lives and restoring the patriotism of his followers. Washington got turned upside down, and Trump shook down the thunder. He saw a vision for America that was about building it up, not tearing it down. He would never apologize for America being America to the rest of the world, as his predecessor had done.

"The Left and much of the media are horrified, because the age-old power structures on which they rely are specifically the ones President Trump is seeking to demolish and rebuild," Gingrich writes.

> Some in the establishment are confused, because Trump's campaign—
> and his first months in office—are totally opposite from business as usual
> in Washington. His success calls into question their [the mainstream
> media's, especially] presumed expertise and collective worldview. But
> many Americans are happy. To them President Trump represents a force
> of change in Washington, the likes of which we've rarely seen in American
> history.[41]

Trump takes it up a notch from there, explaining his vision and purpose for America:

Leadership is leaders inducing followers to act for certain goals that represent *the values* and the motivations—the wants and needs, the aspirations and expectations—of both leaders and followers. And the genius of leadership lies in the manner in which leaders see and act on their own and their *followers' values* and motivations.[42]

In other words, make America great again!

Tammy Berberick, CEO of Crestcom International writes, "The ability to lead through influence, rather than authority, is the most important quality of a great leader. Influence requires strong coaching, emotional intelligence, effective communication, negotiation, and consensus building skills."[43]

Having a great vision and being able to explain it to followers in a way that is understandable and grabs their attention is one thing. Getting those followers to act on it, though, is another matter. That's where motivation and inspiration come to the front of the line, and few politicians of the last hundred years have been better at doing that than Trump. His ability to rally the masses in huge events is every bit as impressive as that of the fire and brimstone preachers America has seen and heard from over the last centuries. Donald Trump Jr. says it well in describing how his dad can discern the best in people and push them to excel: "He has recognized the talent and the drive that all Americans have. He's promoted people based on their character, their street smarts, and their work ethic, not simply paper or credentials." Ivanka adds, "He showed us how to be resilient, how to deal with challenges, and how to strive for excellence in all that we do. He taught us that there's nothing that we cannot accomplish, if we marry vision and passion with an enduring work ethic."[44]

Lincoln's influence as an inspirational leader reached well into the ranks of the Union soldiers. Consider this: in running for a second term in 1864—with the Civil War still at its bloody worst—Lincoln won about 70 percent of the votes from soldiers; they supported him, even knowing that by casting a vote on his behalf, they were casting a vote that would likely extend the war. In truth, the war did go on for nearly another six months into Lincoln's second term. But with that kind of support from his troops, Lincoln rolled to a 212–21 victory in the electoral college. Kearns Goodwin writes,

In casting their ballots for Lincoln, the soldiers . . . were voting against their self-interest for the greater collective interest that Lincoln had powerfully expressed in his talks with them. "This contest is not merely for to-day, but for all time to come," Lincoln had reiterated in numerous ways, . . . "in order that each of you may have through this free government which we have enjoyed, an open field and a fair chance for your industry, enterprise, and intelligence; that you all have equal privileges in the race of life, with all its desirable human aspirations. It is for this the struggle should be maintained."[45]

It's worth noting, too, that by casting a vote that extended the war (Lincoln's Republican motto was "No Peace Without Victory."), soldiers showed they were determined to prove that the lives of their departed buddies had not been lost in vain.

DECISIVENESS

Lincoln had a reserved, stoic personality. Today we might even say he was a chill person. Chances are, if he were alive today he would not be seeking or accepting offers for a reality TV show. But when it came to being assertive and decisive, history reveals few peers among the forty-plus other men who have held the office of the presidency—certainly not Trump's predecessor. Barack Obama spent more time building consensus, obsessing over polls, and waiting on focus groups to tell him what to do—or waiting for whatever he was supposed to say to get loaded into the teleprompter.

This doesn't mean Lincoln stayed in his ivory tower before making and communicating decisions autonomously. He often sought counsel and suggestions from his cabinet members and other advisers in important matters. But when it was time to pull the trigger on major decisions, many of them relative to the Civil War, it was Lincoln's finger that was on the trigger. Writing in *Lincoln on Leadership*, author Donald T. Phillips says,

> It is clear that Lincoln made most crucial decisions during his term in office. He alone bore the responsibility and would answer to the American people for his actions. . . . It is also clear that Lincoln skillfully steered the ship of state through the perilous waters of the Civil War. It was Lincoln who led the way while at times giving the impression that he was, rather, following the lead of his subordinates. And here, in essence, is one of the marks of his true leadership genius.[46]

Another aspect of Lincoln's leadership savvy was his open-door office policy, in which visitors—including members of Congress and advisers, of course—could enter almost at will. He would also often make himself available to others by strolling to their offices for a chat. Sometimes he would sit in on Senate working sessions, so he could be privy to the legislative process. This had to make a positive impression on his political friends and foes alike, considering that it had been more than twenty-five years since a sitting president had made such an appearance. It was, in fact, a practice that was understandably necessary in that time, with a nation at war.

"He knew he needed the help of congressmen and senators to win the war effort, and what better way to begin to gain their support than to be visible? So he established contact with them—human contact," Phillips says.

> And throughout his presidency, Lincoln continued to visit Congress periodically. Lincoln would work with Congress if they supported his efforts. He would not, however, tolerate delay or inaction. He was the commander-in-chief and would direct and lead the armed forces and the government. Congress would not deter his quest to preserve the Union.[47]

Lincoln wasn't only dealing with cabinet members, the House, and the Senate in contemplating the movement of soldier pieces on the chess board, he also had to interact with his military generals in maneuvering troops. For some of those generals, their challenges on the battlefield paled in comparison to their confrontations with authorities in Washington—namely Lincoln.

One of Lincoln's many tactical tussles was with Union General George B. McClellan, a Democrat to Lincoln's Republican. When McClellan found Confederates entrenched at Yorktown, he told bosses in Washington that he needed more troops, overstating the size of the opposing force. Mindful that McClellan had 100,000 troops at his command, Lincoln told the general, "I think you better break the enemies' line . . . at once." That infuriated McClellan. He wrote his wife that he was tempted to tell Lincoln to come down to Yorktown and do it himself. Impatient with McClellan's reticence to attack the Confederate force, Lincoln told a confidante that he was "dissatisfied with McClellan's sluggishness of action," after which he gave McClellan reassurance that he would do what he could to sustain troop levels as needed, accompanied by the stern warning, *"But you must act."*[48] Lincoln was not shy about demanding the same level of decisiveness from his subordinates that he expected of himself. Eventually, McClellan was relieved of his battlefield command in 1862. From then on, the festering distrust between the two men took on a more permanent status, especially in 1864 when McClellan was selected as the Democratic nominee for president, only to get handily defeated by Lincoln in the general election.

As it was with Lincoln, avid decision-making has been a Trump hallmark, unlike the waiting and waffling exhibited by his immediate White House predecessor. "There is always the possibility of failure," Trump said, "but there is a greater chance of success if you actually try to do something versus doing nothing."[49]

While traditional mainstream media has often called them reckless and even dangerous, the decisions Trump has made from the White House could just as easily be termed decisive, bold, and—to borrow a pet phrase from Democrats—*progressive*. Putting America first and making America great again can be considered progress, right? It's just a simple matter of perspective. Millions of liberal Americans and left-leaning media would disparage Trump, even if he were to engineer the eradication of cancer and reduce unemployment to zero percent. His sin and the source of the scorn is his winning a 2016 presidential election that most media said he would, and should, lose.

The list of Trump's significant bold and decisive actions as president is a long one that includes the following: greenlighting construction of the controversial Keystone XL Pipeline; establishing a sixth branch of the U.S. Armed Services, the Space Force; revising the U.S. tax code; issuing an executive order to promote excellence and innovation at historically black colleges and universities; ordering a cruise missile attack on a Syrian base; killing terrorist leaders Abu Bakr al-Baghdadi and Qassem Soleimani; and firing FBI Director James Comey.

It's all part of the unique leadership formula that forms the constitution of who Donald Trump is and what he is capable of doing—driving himself to one finish line after another and challenging others to keep up, even if it means following in his wake.

It also means giving back. "What I admire most are people who put themselves directly on the line," Trump said back in his pre-political days as a businessman, and perhaps describing himself in the process.

> I've never been terribly interested in why people give, because their motivation is rarely what it seems to be, and it's almost never pure altruism. To me, what matters is the doing, and giving time is far more valuable than just giving money.
>
> In my life, there are two things I've found I'm very good at: overcoming obstacles and motivating good people to do their best work. One of the challenges ahead is how to use those skills as successfully in the service of others as I've done, up to now, on my own behalf. Don't get me wrong. I also plan to keep making deals, big deals, and right around the clock.[50]

There you have it, yet another dimension of leadership—Donald Trump: servant-leader.

CHAPTER 10

SIGNS OF THE TIMES

I never knew how hated Abraham Lincoln was until I stood him next to Donald Trump. I must have received the sanitized and softened historical accounts in all of my schooling. Perhaps because Lincoln was assassinated, his more ignominious realities fell to the wayside after his death.

It just might be a toss-up which one is the most slandered and despised president in our history. I discovered that Lincoln burned the mountain of hate mail he received during his administration before it could accumulate. He was called every name in the 1860s book and threatened with hanging, shooting, burning, and caning—and he was hung and burned in effigy in more than one Confederate town square.

In twenty-first century politics I'm probably not going out on a limb in awarding Kathy Griffin's bloody, severed head of Trump top billing for presidential bashing. And ricin-laced mail delivered to the White House certainly moved the level of malicious intent up a notch.

The rising hostilities apparent in the months leading up to both the 2016 and 2020 elections generated calls for the death of the president. In October 2020 (after Donald Trump contracted the COVID-19 virus) a former Hillary Clinton spokeswoman just couldn't help herself when she tweeted: "I hope he *dies!*" Similarly in August 1864 the *La Crosse Democrat* in Wisconsin printed an editorial calling for "some bold hand [to] pierce [Lincoln's] heart with dagger point for the public good!" The thought of four more years in both cases was just too much for some to consider!

In a divided America with little room left for compromise, the political game has morphed into something less benign than just political mudslinging. The signs of the times mark an ever-widening gap. Lincoln saw it coming when he spoke of "A house divided against itself." In 1860 the two sides declared all-out war. And in 2020 it's not just tempers flaring on the streets of American cities. Hate is a uniquely human trait that tends to feed on itself and just might run rampant unless beaten back by what Lincoln called "the better angels of our nature."

CB ƏO

It was a presidency filled with partisan strife: a not-so-subtle political bias emanating from much of the media, acts of violence in the streets, constant chatter about plans and conspiracies to remove the president from office, bickering among members of both houses of Congress that teetered on the brink of the outrageous, and all this in a country with a citizenry arguably more divisive than it had been at any time in American history.

Much of this was revved up even before he had been inaugurated, and it reached a fever pitch within hours of his election that would carry on throughout his first term in office, like a runaway locomotive. It was remarkable that Abraham Lincoln was able to get anything accomplished as the White House's chief resident. That's the way it was in 1861, and history has recently repeated itself, this time with Donald Trump wearing the target on his back.

If the description in the previous paragraph sounded strikingly familiar to anyone—there's good reason for it. Trump has had to endure the same junk Lincoln weathered more than 150 years ago. The names, technology, and exact circumstances have changed, but all the rest? Instant replay. Like Lincoln, Trump had been subjected to an ongoing assault for months before he took office in January 2017. The incessant, derogatory attacks against Trump's politics, his character, his family, his past business dealings, his tax records, his fitness for office, his embrace of political incorrectness, his reliance on and ample use of social media to get his message out to the people—you name it, the hits just kept on coming. The animosity hit a fever pitch in the early morning hours of November 10, 2016. This was after it became clear that he had surpassed the electoral vote threshold needed to beat Democratic nominee Hillary Clinton, whose shock at losing was as profound for her as it was for her supporters. The rampant bitterness of the Democrats showed itself in many ways, not to exclude Clinton's inability to concede publicly until well into the next day. Donald Trump was president, and he has been paying for it ever since.

This is where the common paths between the Lincoln and Trump presidencies and the parallels between the men themselves are most evident. Each man took office against the backdrop of politically chaotic environments. Each won elections with less than 50 percent of the popular vote.

It was Trump who quickly coined the phrase "fake news" to describe the un-journalistic practices of a slothful, slanted, sloppy mainstream media that clearly demonstrated its primary mission was not just to hammer away at "Orange Man" from every angle conceivable, but to make his life and presidency miserable. The end game was to push him out of office, with U.S. House Speaker Nancy Pelosi leading the Democratic charge.

Lincoln had to deal with the same sort of sham media back in the nineteenth century. During this time the press played politics with an expertise even beyond twenty-first century news outlets. Democratic newspapers spouted Democratic ideology and solely supported their causes and candidates while castigating and condemning Republicans (and Lincoln.) Likewise, Republican papers embraced their own causes with the same targeted focus. Fair and balanced? Not in Lincoln's America! Within about a week after winning his first term, the following political "analysis" appeared in the November 13, 1860, edition of the *Memphis Daily Appeal*. Notice how the attacks are aimed not just at Lincoln, with open hostility dripping from the newspaper pages, but also at the Republican Party as a whole—with Lincoln being held responsible for that as well. Sound familiar? Just like Trump in 2016.

> Within 90 days from the time Lincoln is inaugurated (in March 1861), the Republican Party will be utterly ruined and destroyed. His path is environed with so many difficulties, that even if he had the ability of Jefferson and the energy of Jackson, he would fail, but he is a weak and inexperienced man, and his administration will be doomed from the commencement. If he takes that radical section of the Republican Party, the conservative wing of it will cut loose and repudiate him. If, on the other hand, he courts the conservatives and pursues a moderate conciliatory policy, the radicals will make open war upon his administration.[1]

Media hostility is nothing new for U.S. presidents, but the intensity that Trump had to deal with has little precedent in U.S. history, as former U.S. Speaker of the House and current political pundit Newt Gingrich describes:

> The intensity of the media's hostility to President Trump resembles the media reaction to Presidents Andrew Jackson, Abraham Lincoln, and Franklin Delano Roosevelt. When a president comes along who

challenges existing orthodoxies and power structures, he or she has to be ready for vicious, intense condemnation from those currently in power.[2]

There were also public protests, some taking place simply because of a hate for Lincoln, and others with more of a policy bend to them—namely, Lincoln's stated desire to abolish slavery, a stance that didn't sit well with southerners, more specifically southern Democrats. The Democratic Party of the nineteenth century (and well into the twentieth century) was the pro-slavery party, just as it would be the anti–civil rights party of the 1950s and 1960s—a fact that present-day liberal Dems will either deny or rationalize.

Following are two more newspaper clippings from that era, both presented by Newt Gingrich in *Understanding Trump*. They both talk about the protests and other indications of the political and public tensions of the time. Again, keep in mind, these are about Lincoln and the 1860s, even though they could easily be applied to Trump in the twenty-first century:

This is from the *Lancaster Ledger* (a South Carolina paper), and it was published in November 1860: "There is intense excitement here. Large crowds have gathered in the streets. The pervading spirit among the masses is resistance to Lincoln's administration [which was still four months away!], and everywhere that determination is manifest."[3]

Then there's this excerpt from the *New York Herald*, written by their Charleston-based correspondent:

> "Thursday night the streets were filled with excited crowds. Till nearly midnight, the streets presented the most animated appearance. The crowd illuminated their passage by rockets and other fireworks, and made the air resound with their deafening cries. No one talks of anything but the necessity for prompt action. It is believed that separate and immediate action on the part of this state will be followed by action on the part of several other southern states forthwith. It is hardly prudent for any man to express his opinion adverse to immediate secession. So heated are the public passions, so intolerant of restraint is the popular will."[4]

In presenting these newspaper clippings from nineteenth-century media coverage of Lincoln, Gingrich draws a parallel between Charlestonians pushing for secession in defense of slavery and twenty-first century liberal Democrat activists protesting Trump's bold plan for making America great again. There was no real purpose to protesting Trump, no specific issue to zero in on, other than the fact that he was still breathing and the protestors hated him. Trump's biggest sins were his general endorsement of conservatism and having the gall to beat an entitled Hillary Clinton in the 2016 presidential election.

Lincoln did not take the Democrat protests lightly, but neither was he about to back off in his war against slavery. What concerned him most about the protests and politics of his day was the "hyperemotionalism" running through all things political. It was a subject he had been addressing for nearly a quarter of a century, starting in January 1838. In his speech titled, "The Perpetuation of Our Political Institutions," given to the Young Men's Lyceum, he issued a warning that the nation's "proud fabric of freedom" was being threatened by the unbridled passion of the citizenry, specifically "the jealousy, envy, and avarice, incident to our nature." Such civil disorder, fueled by a cresting emotionalism, disturbed Lincoln greatly—just as it did Trump and much of America through his presidential term, and not just in the months following May 2020. That was when George Floyd and others were killed at the hands of policemen, sparking a new wave of racial unrest, protests, and violence linked to Antifa and the Black Lives Matter (BLM) movement that raged across much of the nation for the rest of 2020.

The mob violence that accompanied Lincoln's presidency wasn't just a southern phenomenon. He described it as pervading the entire country "from New England to Louisiana." It wasn't just about slavery, either. David Herbert Donald, author of *Lincoln*, mentions two incidents that Lincoln referred to as samples of particular concern—a spate of vigilante violence in Mississippi in which gamblers were killed, some left hanging from trees along roadsides; and the St. Louis burning of a biracial man, who had been accused of murdering a prominent area resident. David Herbert Donald quotes Lincoln: "If 'persons and property, are held by no better tenure than the caprice of a mob,'" "if the laws be continually despised,'" Lincoln warned, "citizens' affection for their government must inevitably be alienated."[5]

Among historians and students of history, Lincoln's tenure as U.S. president is most closely associated with slavery and the Civil War. But the heightened emotionalism he talked about was also an outgrowth of major demographic and industrial shifts that were radically changing America, pulling the national consciousness in different, sometimes divisive directions. "Lincoln was troubled by what he perceived as the rapid change in American life," Donald writes.

> Canals and railroads were bringing about a transportation revolution; the population was swiftly spreading across the continent; immigration was beginning to seem a threat to American social cohesion; sectionalism was becoming ever more divisive as the controversy over slavery mounted; (and) the political battles of the Jackson era had destroyed the national political consensus.[6]

The Trump years had similarly potent forces pulling U.S. citizens apart, leaving us with a citizenry where tempers are short, distrust is high, and, in so many ways, we are surrounded by endless piles of dry kindling. A single spark can set off a firestorm that always seems to end up at the feet of Donald Trump. In place of canals and railroads and a massive westward migration of the populace, the world before and under Trump was best illuminated by the explosion of digital technology and social media. The results were major breakdowns in human interaction and communication; major economic shifts, centered around a diminishing middle class; identity politics whose flames were lit and abetted by America's first black president; a growing secularization of a nation that was founded on the principles of a Judeo-Christian faith now being gradually replaced by a humanism that has no room for God and the Ten Commandments. We also saw a shifting awareness in which Americans increasingly lost touch with traditional values and morals. These values are now being rooted out of our fabric and gradually replaced by the normalization of socialistic mores in a way that just several decades ago would have been considered reprehensible.

All this explains why half of America sees Trump as the savior and restorer of what once made America great while the other half sees him as the ultimate enemy of the state. That's how twisted our nation has become, as wrong now assumes the role of right. Along with that, the Deep State has now made Trump out to be an Enemy of the State. Those powerful forces were aligned against Trump throughout his presidency, trying to bring him down.

In this respect, it's worth going back to Lincoln and reading what else he had to say during that 1838 Lyceum speech. He could just as well have been giving that speech in 2020 when Americans went to the polls to decide whether to give Trump a second term. In his last debate with Democratic nominee Joe Biden two weeks out from the November 2020 election, Trump even made passing reference to "Honest Abe," touting his own efforts toward benefitting the black community as second only to Abraham Lincoln's. This was a perfectly valid and timely remark to make, even if it did get ridiculed by his Democratic detractors.

"I know I am over wary," Lincoln said in that Lyceum speech,

> but if I am not, there is even now, something of ill-omen amongst us. I mean the increasing disregard for law which pervades the country; the growing disposition to substitute the wild and furious passions, in lieu of the sober judgment of courts. . . . Accounts of outrages committed by mobs form the everyday news of the times. . . . [But] men who love

tranquility, who desire to abide by the laws, and enjoy their benefits, who would gladly spill their blood in the defense of their country; seeing their property destroyed, their families insulted; and their lives endangered; their persons injured; and seeing nothing in prospect that forebodes a change for the better; become tired of, and disgusted with, a Government that offers them no protection; and we are not much averse to a change in which they imagine they have nothing to lose.[7]

Another thing that is not well known about Lincoln, but that makes his ties to Trump even stronger—he was disliked, even disdained by many of his political contemporaries, including members of his own political party. "Liberal Republicans thought he was too calculating, too quick to weigh public opinion. Democrats thought he was a tyrant, a rube, and was destroying the Constitution [in today's world that would truly be the pot calling the kettle black]," says Edward Achorn, author of *Every Drop of Blood: The Momentous Second Inauguration of Abraham Lincoln*.

> I think a lot of this was airbrushed out of history after he was assassinated, when he became a martyr. But when you go back to that day and look at what people were saying, you get a stunning sense of what Lincoln was up against. There's a lot of hostility from all sides. I'm not sure how he withstood it.[8]

Here's another angle to the Lincoln-Trump connection, as it relates to violence in the streets, mob behavior, and so forth. Even though in both eras the violence was initiated and carried out by groups politically opposed to the sitting president, and publicly supported by politicians on the opposite side of the aisle, it is the president who gets blamed. It's a head scratcher.

In the spring and summer of 2020, BLM-led protests turned into riots and rampant destruction (buildings and businesses burned, bystanders and homeowners attacked, police assaulted—the usual tactics of tolerant "progressives"). These protests occurred most notably in cities such as Minneapolis, Chicago, Atlanta, Seattle, and Portland—all with Democratic mayors who essentially allowed the violence to continue by taking a hands-off approach in law enforcement and refusing to condemn the attacks. They also adamantly opposed any intervention by federal officials to quell the riots. On top of all that, it was reported that at least thirteen members of Biden's 2020 campaign team made donations to the Minnesota Freedom Fund,[9] which used contributions to bail out protesters or rioters who had been arrested in the wake of George Floyd's death. Wrong was right, and, still, the blame went against Trump, the Republican president.

Lincoln knew what it was like to be tagged with blame for protests and riots that were against him. At times it was the media itself that did the blaming. Case in point: the New York City draft riots in July 1863 featured violent disturbances in lower Manhattan in the wake of new laws passed by the U.S. Congress that greenlighted the drafting of men to fight in the Civil War. The press called Lincoln a "tyrant" and a "dictator." When they don't know what to speak and which words to use to properly express their beliefs, that's all that angry contrarians can manage to say.

> The *New York World*, like all the city's newspapers, had much to say about the riots. Who was at fault? While deploring the violence, its editor, Manton Marble, pinned most of the blame on Lincoln. "Will the insensate men in Washington now at length listen to our voice? Will they now give ear to our warnings and adjurations? Will they now believe that Defiance of the Law to rulers breeds Defiance of Law in the people?" And what did the defiant people want? They wanted a war for "the Union and the constitution"—not one for abolition. Two years earlier, they had thronged Union Square in support of the war. And what did Lincoln do? He ignored them. Yes, these "are the very men whom his imbecility, his wanton exercise of arbitrary power, his stretches of engrafted authority have transformed into a mob."[10]

CS SO

Two years before Lincoln was elected to the presidency, he ran for one of Illinois's two U.S. Senate seats. He lost to Democrat Stephen Douglas, even after effectively beating Douglas in a series of seven debates that comprised one of the great political oratorical battles in American history. But it was earlier that summer that Lincoln gave one of his most memorable speeches—second perhaps in notoriety only to his Gettysburg Address of 1863—in which he said, "A house divided against itself cannot stand." Although criticized at the time, the speech remains noteworthy 150-plus years later for its prophetic accuracy in predicting what would become of the United States three years later with the breakout of the Civil War. "A House Divided" took on almost mythical status for its applicability to a divided nation, and it gets added credence today because of how it applies to where America stood headed into the 2020 elections. Not since the days of Lincoln and slavery had America been so angrily at odds along politically partisan lines, with little, if any, middle ground for compromise and conciliation to take place.

This twenty-first century divisiveness didn't start with Trump's election in 2016. This latest edition of extreme partisanship dates back at least to the controversial presidential election of 2000. That's when George W. Bush was edged out in the national popular vote by Democratic rival Al Gore Jr., but won a narrow Electoral College victory that wasn't decided until weeks later. The U.S. Supreme Court finally ruled the vote recount in Florida over, its razor-thin advantage for Bush giving him the last slice of electoral votes he needed to squeak past Gore in an election that left Democrats bitter and claiming they had been robbed.

It was a similar deal sixteen years later, when Hillary Clinton won the national popular vote, only for Trump to narrowly win several key battleground states, allowing him to upset Clinton. However Trump finished with a comparatively comfortable margin in the Electoral College count. It was a bitter loss for Clinton and Democrats, and they didn't bother hiding their shock and utter contempt for Trump the president as well as Trump the man. Conservatives and others who supported Trump had no pity for the defeated Clinton and Democrats—they had had to put up with eight years of Barack Obama's two-term reign as America's Liberal in Chief. Obama made identity politics a cornerstone of his administration and set America on a course toward socialism. Obama fanned the partisan flames by saying it was time for America to redistribute the wealth, by following an economic model that is the basis for communism, and by showing a hands-off approach toward Islamic extremism and terrorism, as evidenced through his consistent reluctance to even mention those terms.

America's electoral election of Trump was an act of defiance against the political correctness movement that had flourished under the Obama/Biden administration. Trump wasted no time declaring his "Make America Great Again" (MAGA) commitment after announcing his run for the presidency. It's worth noting that a century and a half earlier, Lincoln had used his own take on an "America Great" mission statement, one in which he proposed to "motivate and mobilize followers by persuading them to take ownership of their roles in a more grand mission that is shared by all members of the organization," as Donald T. Phillips wrote in his book *Lincoln on Leadership*. Phillips elaborates further, writing,

> Lincoln's grand mission, his "common purpose," was essentially the American experiment and the ideals expressed in the Declaration of Independence. He aimed at the "elevation of men," opposed anything that tended to degrade them, and especially lashed out at the institution of slavery. . . . He lifted people out of their everyday selves and into a

higher level of performance, achievement, and awareness. He obtained extraordinary results from ordinary people by instilling purpose in their endeavors.[11]

While running for office, Trump quickly showed he wasn't expecting mainstream media to help him to get his message out to the public. Instead he defied the established media elite by launching his own media apparatus through countless TV appearances. Any of Trump's televised appearances at one of his rallies was catnip to networks and stations subservient to ratings. Even more conspicuously, he ambitiously and creatively used social media, particularly Twitter, to get his messages out with full impact and without filter.

The prize fight was on: Donald Trump in his corner, his many detractors in another. Here's how Gingrich, writing in 2018, around the midpoint of Trump's first term, described the dynamic between Trump and whatever parts of the country opposed him:

> For decades, this conflict has been fought quietly in city halls, classrooms, school boards, courtrooms, town squares, and state houses across the country. However, the election of President Trump has clarified the battle lines in this struggle and elevated these individual fights into a united national conflict.
>
> On one side of this conflict is a factional anti-Trump coalition—a strange amalgam of radicals, liberals, globalists, establishment elites from both parties, and blatantly anti-American groups loosely held together by their hostility and disdain for the president. On the other side is Trump's America—the millions of hardworking people who are united by respect for our foundational freedoms, traditional values, and history of limited commonsense governance.[12]

The anti-Trumpsters didn't waste any time mounting their charges against the new president, insisting with zero evidence that he was a tyrant-in-waiting set to destroy America, when in fact Trump was here to clean up a mess that had festered under eight years of an Obama Administration. Nationwide, liberals had praised the Obama presidency, some even ranking him the greatest U.S. president of all time, but for what? Certainly not for making America better. Americans who'd had their eyes open for those eight years had watched in anger, and horror, as the federal government took and then squandered tax dollars, ruining America's businesses, and making it much harder to earn a decent living. Still, in the eyes of liberals, Trump had "stolen" the election. For good measure, they hatched a Russian collusion story, giving Democrats hope that the election could soon be over-turned—if only their ludicrous charges had any truth to them.

Inauguration Day in January 2017 brought out the dichotomy in twenty-first century America as both sides showed up to witness Trump being sworn in as forty-fifth president of the United States. On one side of the spectrum were diehard Republicans and Trump supporters, many conspicuously wearing their bright red MAGA hats, streaming out of their hotels in Washington, DC, to make their way to the U.S. Capitol grounds and see Trump sworn in by Supreme Court Chief Justice John Roberts.

"Then the other America showed up—the one that blocked people from entering checkpoints to the Capitol grounds, harassed Trump supporters, set cars on fire, smashed storefronts, and hurled rocks at police," Gingrich says.

> CNN reported the following day that six police officers were injured and 217 protestors arrested after "ugly street clashes in downtown Washington." On Saturday, the less-violent side of that America came. It was made up mostly of people enraged that the Trump-supporting side of America was getting any attention at all.
> Much of the news media covered the weekend with nothing short of vindictiveness. Instead of pointing out how gracefully the supporters at the Capitol handled being confronted with virulent hate and vulgarity from the Left (no Trump supporters were arrested), the media decided to focus on how big the crowd was compared with past inaugurations.[13]

Deflection, filled with untruths.

It wasn't just in DC that this anti-Trump-motivated civil unrest—to put a diplomatic spin on it—was taking place. During the weekend of the inauguration, other locales in which police arrested violent left-wing protesters included New York, Dallas, Chicago, Portland, and Seattle. Gingrich adds,

> In Oregon, the protestors were armed with clubs, setting fire to American flags, and throwing rocks, bottles, and flares at police, according to local news reports. Protestors at the University of Washington campus threw bricks at officers. But according to the Left, it's the Trump supporters who are hateful, closed-minded, and dangerous. . . . But as a very senior former prosecutor said to me recently, "This has now become a blood sport. The goal is not justice or truth, the goal is destruction of conservatives."[14]

At the time of Trump's election in 2016 and then his inauguration, the biggest issue dividing America was Trump himself. His supporters embraced him because he was a Beltway outsider willing to make positive changes in America, while Trump haters hated him, well, just because he was there. To support their discrediting of Trump, they fabricated and twisted narratives about him, loading them with inaccurate generalities and other falsehoods that, when parroted by a compliant media, gained momentum in the avenues of public discourse, growing into misleading talking points that were continually tweaked and augmented over the next four years.

As we all know so well now, Lincoln also had two opposite Americas to deal with. In his time it was slavery—and not so much Lincoln himself—that divided America. It all came down to something Lincoln once said, summing up where things stood with these words: "Slavery: You believe it right, and we believe it wrong."

Voter turnout on Election Day 1860 was a record for its time, at 81.2 percent. With four candidates on the ballot splitting the numbers—including Lincoln's 1858 senatorial rival Stephen Douglas—Lincoln won 39.8 percent of the popular vote (Douglas finished with 29.5 percent). Although Lincoln wasn't on any of the ballots in the South, he enjoyed an overwhelming win in terms of electoral votes, winning 180 electoral votes while running the table among northern states. The other three candidates totaled just 123 electoral votes between them.

Reaction to Lincoln's victory, even with a plurality of the votes, was just as you might have expected: exuberance in the North and anger and contempt in the South. South Carolina quickly started talking about seceding from the Union, which was no surprise, even going so far as to issue a secession declaration that described what had happened as "the election of a man to that high office of president of the United States whose opinions and purposes are hostile to slavery." Likewise, Mississippi declared, "Our position is thoroughly identified with the institution of slavery—the greatest material interest of the world." Even before the election, many Southerners had already been openly contemplating secession in the event of a Lincoln triumph. Framing their secession around the election made it, at least in their eyes, the fault of the North. Lincoln became someone they could blame. Hearing of this sort of scuttlebutt, Lincoln said, "That is cool. A highwayman holds a pistol to my ear and mutters through his teeth, 'Stand and deliver or I shall kill you, and then you will be a murderer!' "[15]

The similarities between Lincoln's first inauguration speech in 1860 and Trump's speech in 2016 are worth noting, both for their shared tone of forceful clarity and for the common topics of their respective messages. "Both were clear statements of nonnegotiable principles to bitter opposition, both had survived some of the most divisive campaigns in American history, and both appealed to patriotism," Gingrich writes.[16] Gingrich, however, wanted a second opinion regarding his assessment of the two men and their opening presentations as presidents. So he wrote Dr. Allen Guelzo, at the time the Henry R. Luce Professor of the Civil War Era and the director of Civil War Studies Program at Gettysburg College. Following is part of what Guelzo wrote back:

> "Your points are entirely on the mark. I have done a quick comparative outline of both inaugural addresses, and while the existential situation of the two are different . . . there is this common thread, the sovereignty of the people. Lincoln used that principle to deny that one part of the nation, the seven seceding states, could break up the union, without the consent of the American people, as well as denying that one branch of the government, the Supreme Court, could overrule the American people's will. . . . Trump invoked that principle. [Both men denied] that a federal bureaucracy can enrich and empower itself at the expense of the people, as well as denying that identity enclaves can overrule the fundamental unity of the American people. . . . America is deeply divided along a political-cultural fault line. One side wants to see America return to prosperity, strength, and its traditional values. The other wants to fundamentally change America into a different nation that rejects many of its founding principles."[17]

What we now have, like we did in 1860, is an ideological divide that was widened by Trump's election. Trump was not personally responsible for that, but his election and later his presidency touched off a liberal outrage that was poised and predictable, fueled by the likes of Clinton. During her presidential campaign, she had fed into Democrats' biases by describing half of Trump's supporters as "deplorables," who were "racist, sexist, homophobic, xenophobic, Islamophobic—you name it," adding on that all that made them "irredeemable."[18] The intensity of the national divide has continued to climb ever since, along the lines of what Dennis Prager wrote in a *National Review* op-ed that ran in January 2017. In it, he declared that we were in an American Civil War, not one fought on soil or the water or in the air (at least not yet), but one on political and ideological grounds.[19]

Again, we turn to Gingrich for a description of the angry liberal outrage that has been a thorn in Trump's side longer than the four years he was in office:

> The Left was dealt a strong blow by the 2016 election. It was stunned for a moment but has recovered, ready to continue its ideological war. . . . The hyper-Left wants to create an America that's unacceptable to the vast majority of Americans. . . . They focus on insidiously divisive identity

politics, branding all Republicans as racist, and keeping Americans dependent on the government. . . . Yet the hard Left can't solve anything. The Left has no solutions for Chicago's violence, West Virginia's poverty, or disastrous schools in Baltimore. All they can do is yell "racism!" and "sexism!" and hope that holds their coalition together.[20]

CぐƐめ

One hundred fifty years ago, the pro-slavery Democrats embraced the plantation mentality. That's how they kept the reins on their black servants, holding them as slaves and mostly treating them as less than human. The existence and well-being of slaves was almost wholly dependent on the will, attention, and generosity of their white owners. Now, twenty-plus years deep into the twenty-first century, nothing much has changed except that today the Dems' plantations have moved from the agrarian South to the urban jungles of cities across America. And now tax-obsessed Democrats keep many unwitting voters dependent on them for welfare and other government entitlements and handouts. In return, the Dems—through political cunning and patronization—are paid back through overwhelming ballot-box loyalty from these modern-day slaves, who come in an assortment of ethnicities. Chalk one up for today's socialist state, administered by the all-powerful Liberal elites. This is progressivism hard at work, right? Well, here's what's really at work: the more things change, the more they remain the same.

Lincoln served as president in a world where the plantation mentality was a potent political force, and so it was in our day with Donald Trump in office. Again, we see the ties that bind together two presidents a century and a half apart. At stake was and is America's future existence, which goes well beyond just which political party happens to be in charge at any given time. In his Lyceum Address in 1838, Lincoln suggested that if America ever ceased to exist, it would perish through internal ruin, not from an attack by a foreign power. "Shall we expect some transatlantic military giant to step the Ocean, and crush us at a blow? Never! . . . If destruction be our lot, we must ourselves be its author and finisher. As a nation of freemen, we must live through all time, or die by suicide."[21]

Here's one way the twenty-first century works as it did on the plantations. If you step out of line and try to expose—or even succeed in exposing—the true workings, agendas, and goals of the Liberal state, also known as socialism, you will incur the wrath of the Democratic Deep State. That's what happened to best-selling author, political commentator, and film-maker Dinesh D'Souza. Here's part of his story, in his own words:

> A few years ago, I witnessed a determined, ruthless effort to kill my American dream. Shortly after I released a highly successful film criticizing Barack Obama, the FBI came banging on my door. Soon I discovered that Preet Bharara, the prosecuting attorney for the Southern District of New York, had charged me with violating campaign finance laws. My heinous offense was to give $20,000 of my own money to a longtime college friend of mine running a quixotic campaign for U.S. Senate in New York.[22]

He was charged with a felony. The judge could have thrown the book at D'Souza, but he didn't. The verdict, though: guilty. D'Souza was sentenced to eight months of overnight confinement at a halfway house, where his dormitory confinement kept him a bunk bed in proximity to sixty hardened federal felons. He also had to pay a fine, perform community service, and serve out five years of probation. From D'Souza's perspective, he was a nonwhite immigrant born the same year as Obama (1961), but he saw an America different from the one that Obama viewed. D'Souza believed the forty-fourth president wanted to remake America into a socialist state, one that killed the American dream for a well-educated immigrant such as himself. D'Souza was seeing the impending loss of "the America that I love and represent."[23]

He continues, tying in his dream to the visions of Abraham Lincoln:

> Such a death would involve not only the collapse of America's founding principles but also the extinction of its characteristic mores and values and what Lincoln termed its "mystic chords of memory." In effect, we'd still have the American people, but they would no longer bear the recognizable American stamp. They—we—would no longer dream American dreams. The America that I and so many of my fellow Americans have come to love would no longer exist.[24]

In the early part of the nineteenth century, there were an abundance of antislavery forces in the South, numbering more than a hundred organizations intent on ending slavery. They included in their ranks planters who regarded such bondage as immoral, and they were joined by church leaders. But public sentiment, mostly among Democrats in the South and in some parts of the North, began to shift. By the 1830s, according to historian Stanley Elkins, "the hostility to slavery that had been common in Jeffersonian times . . . all but disappeared." According to John Blasingame, writing in a publication called *The Slave Community,* "By the 1840s, the propagandists had largely succeeded in silencing the [abolition-endorsing] churches." Not only that, but clergy were being persistently pressured into becoming advocates of slavery, and many caved.[25]

As D'Souza points out, planters initiated a mostly successful campaign to prevent antislavery literature from being distributed via mail. Besides that, every southern state other than Maryland and Kentucky passed laws prohibiting the teaching of reading and writing to slaves. Just like today's PC culture trumpeted by Democrats, a "cancel culture" was in place before Lincoln moved into the White House. By the 1850s there was even talk of reopening the African slave trade. All things considered, the time and circumstances were ripe for the Democratic Party to step in and enthusiastically align themselves with the slave proponents. Democrats were eager to represent slavery's interests and press its claims, as D'Souza puts it, at the local level as well as at the national level. This became a cultural and political match made in political correctness heaven, with the Democrats, such as Douglas, now manipulating the puppet strings. At this point, Douglas introduced and championed the doctrine of "popular sovereignty," whereby northern Democrats would do their part to protect and grow slavery. This doctrine was "one equally imbued with racism and one that identified the cause of slavery with the cause of democracy itself."[26]

Adds D'Souza:

Today's democratic plantation is grimly visible in the urban black ghettos, the Latino barrios, the Native American reservations. . . . Obama presided over the Democrats' move toward a multicultural plantation, complete with a sustaining ideology of identity politics that reconciles each ethnic group to its political captivity, seeking to create the modern equivalent of the contented slave. Of course, today's enslaved, while free in principle to leave the plantation, in practice rarely do so.[27]

When Trump rails against things such as the "deep state," "draining the swamp," and even "fake news," this is the sort of the thing he is talking about. More specifically, "The past has not disappeared from the present," D'Souza writes.

As we will see, there is a continuity between the Democrats of the mid-nineteenth century and the Democrats now, and a system of enforced dependency is the precise way in which Democrats today maintain their ethnic plantations. . . . There is an important difference between the old Democratic plantation and the new one. The old one was based on forced black labor; the new one is based on the dependent black, Latino, or Native American voter. The voter ideally does not work but rather lives off welfare and government provision, which becomes, of course, his motive to sustain the providing party in power. Democrats use coalitions of dependent ethnic minorities in order to generate an electoral majority, thus placing progressive Democrats in charge of the Big House. From there they loot the national treasury in the shameless fashion that the old Tammany bosses looted city hall [in long-ago New York City].[28]

⊗⊗

Just as Democrats would try to overturn Trump's 2016 election, starting with an attempt to change the Electoral College vote by convincing electors to go against their state's mandates, followed by the Russian collusion fiasco, and the failed attempt to impeach and then remove Trump from office, Lincoln faced a similar threat from Democrats after he won the 1860 election. One of their first ploys was to introduce legislation in Congress, known as the Crittenden Compromise. It was aimed at preserving the Union, whereby states threatening to secede would not do so under the Compromise. But there was a quid pro quo: slavery would be made a permanent part of the U.S. Constitution, while also barring future Congresses from ending slavery. The choice, which ultimately landed at Lincoln's feet when the bill made it to him for his signature, was between preserving the Union or abolishing slavery and risking an almost inevitable civil war. Lincoln had won a free election, but suddenly his presidency was at stake. Lincoln eventually rejected the Crittenden Comprise, effectively putting the North and South on the road to what became the Civil War, even though he knew the conflict would be a severe one with substantial loss of life on both sides. But Lincoln would not surrender his commitment to abolish slavery, even at such a high price.

In a special message to Congress on July 4, 1861, Lincoln explained himself, saying,

> Our popular government has often been called an experiment. Two points in it our people have already settled—the successful establishing and the successful administering of it. One still remains—its successful maintenance against a formidable attempt to overthrow it. We must settle this question now, whether in a free government the minority have the right to break up the government whenever they choose, [because] if we fail, it will go far to prove the incapability of the people to govern themselves.[29]

211

Part of Lincoln's legacy to his successors—and that would eventually include Trump—was a staunch determination to take on the Democratic plantation, as D'Souza puts it. The fact that Trump was a political outsider, just as Lincoln had been, made them the right men for the job. It's also interesting to note that Lincoln and Trump shared a dislike of Democrats and disrespect for the Left, with Lincoln expressing his scorn for them by calling them names such as "Locofocos" and "Mobocrats," while Trump preferred just to outright describe them as "stone cold crazy."

Other descriptions Lincoln assigned to pro-slavery Democrats indirectly referred to them as "skunks" and "evil." In 1859, he gave more than a dozen talks across the Midwest in which he focused his attacks on slavery, hoping to stimulate open discussion about it across the country. "Slavery is doomed, and that within a few years," he said to an audience in Columbus, Ohio. "Evil can't stand discussion. . . . What kills the skunk is the publicity it gives itself. What a skunk wants to do is keep snug under the barn—in the daytime, when men are around with shotguns."[30]

It's no wonder that Trump went into the 2020 presidential election voicing his concerns about the legitimacy of the election process. He was mindful of the dirty tricks and apparent election rigging Democrats had allegedly been engaged in for decades, if not for hundreds of years. In his chapter entitled "Urban Plantation" from his book *Death of a Nation*, D'Souza talks about bygone days (at least we hope they were only in the past) in which Democratic bosses "controlled political appointments and the dispensing of patronage; they also controlled the voting process. In several cities, including New York, the bosses didn't rely on immigrants to vote correctly. Rather, they supplied the immigrants with filled-in ballots."[31]

This is how it worked: when immigrants showed up at polling places to cast their votes, they would be handed a blank ballot and then, when the voting monitor wasn't looking, the filled-in ballot would be substituted for the blank ballot and cast, assuring favorable outcomes for the Democratic bosses.

"As the machines grew established, they also grew bolder, now going beyond filled-in votes to also deliver dead people's votes in favor of Democratic machine candidates," D'Souza writes. "The ethnic exploitation of vulnerable people and the callous use of their votes to rip off the general population are somehow presented as triumphs of democratic inclusion."[32]

Aside from voting "irregularities," to put it nicely, there has long been a Democratic Party practice of creating false narratives about the likes of

Lincoln (yes, even back then) as well as Trump. It's an old story. Truth has no room in the Progressive playbook.

"Lincoln was portrayed by the Democrats and their allies, just as Trump is now, as being a grave threat to their fundamental liberties," D'Souza says.

> Yet we may ask about Trump the same question that Lincoln asked about himself. Has Trump actually violated any of the basic constitutional rights of his opponent? Has he deprived them of their free speech or the right to assemble or vote? No, he has not. And yet they persist in trying to drive him from office for the same reason their Democratic forbears sought to bring Lincoln to his knees, because they cannot abide the result of a free election.[33]

NOTES

—————————— ~∘⟲⟳∘~ ——————————

CHAPTER 1: IT'S IN THE GENES

1. Thomas B. McGregor, "Some New Facts about Abraham Lincoln's Parents," The National Republican, October 16, 1921, 213-218, https://www.google.com/books/edition/The_Register_of_the_Kentucky_State_Histo/uXw7AQAAMAAJ?hl=en&gbpv=1&dq=Saturday,+June+8,+1816,+the+Baptist+Church+of+Jesus+Christ&pg=PA214&printsec=frontcover, viewed April 24, 2019.

2. Abraham Lincoln, "Lincoln's Milwaukee Speech," September 30, 1859, https://www.nal.usda.gov/topics/lincolns-milwaukee-speech, viewed October 29, 2020.

3. William W. Freehling, *Becoming Lincoln* (Charlottesville, VA: University of Virginia Press, 2018), 7.

4. Freehling, *Becoming Lincoln*, 7.

5. Gwenda Blair, *The Trumps: Three Generations That Built an Empire* (New York: Simon and Schuster, 2000), 25.

6. Blair, *The Trumps*, 90–93.

7. Blair, 116.

8. Blair, 116–17.

9. David Herbert Donald, *Lincoln* (New York, New York: Simon and Schuster, 1996), 21.

10. Freehling, 5.

11. Donald, *Lincoln*, 19.

12. Donald Trump, *The Art of the Deal* (New York: Ballantine Books, 1987), 33.

13. Donald J. Trump, *Great Again: How to Fix Our Crippled America* (New York: Threshold Editions, 2015), 128.

14. William H. Herndon, *Herndon's Lincoln: The True Story of a Great Life,* paperback (CreateSpace Independent Publishing Platform, 2014), 1:2.

15. Herndon, *Herndon's Lincoln,* 1:2.

16. Michael D'Antonio, *Never Enough: Donald Trump and the Pursuit of Success* (New York: Thomas Dunne Books, 2015), 52.

17. Donald, 32.

18. Dinesh D'Souza, *Death of a Nation: Plantation Politics and the Making of the Democratic Party* (New York: All Points Books, 2018), 71.

19. D'Antonio, *Never Enough,* 23.

20. Herndon, *Herndon's Lincoln,* 2:4.

21. Herndon, *Herndon's Lincoln,* 2:4.

22. Donald, 32.

23. David Brody and Scott Lamb, *The Faith of Donald J. Trump: A Spiritual Biography.* (New York: Broadside Books, 2018), 14–15.

24. Newt Gingrich, *Understanding Trump* (New York: Center Street, 2017), 133.

25. Thomas B. McGregor, "Some New Facts out Abraham Lincoln's Parents."

26. Blair, 218.

27. Donald J. Trump, *Great Again: How to Fix Our Crippled America* (New York: Threshold Editions, 2015), 128.

28. Blair, 228–29.

29. Freehling, 24.

30. McGregor, "Some New Facts out Abraham Lincoln's Parents."

31. Donald, 28.

32. D'Antonio, 36.

Chapter 2: Man of Faith

1. David Brody and Scott Lamb, *The Faith of Donald J. Trump: A Spiritual Biography* (New York: Broadside Books, 2018), 73.

2. Brody and Lamb, *The Faith of Donald J. Trump,* 73.

3. Emma Green, "Trump's Sunday School," *The Atlantic,* July 24, 2016.

4. Green, "Trump's Sunday School."

5. Brody and Lamb, 76–77.

6. Dalia Fahmy, "Most Americans Don't See Trump as Religious; Fewer Than Half Say They Think He's Christian," Pew Research Center, March 25, 2020.

7. Pew Research Center, "Our History," https://www.pewresearch.org/about/our-history/, viewed April 23, 2020.

8. Fahmy, "Most Americans Don't See Trump as Religious; Fewer Than Half Say They Think He's Christian."

9. Donald T. Phillips, *Lincoln on Leadership for Today: Abraham Lincoln's Approach to Twenty-First Century Issues* (Boston, MA: Mariner Books, 2017), 272.

10. Thomas B. McGregor, "Some New Facts about Abraham Lincoln's Parents," *The National Republican*, October 15, 1921, republished by the *Register of the Kentucky State Historical Society*, "Some New Facts about Abraham Lincoln's Parents," 1921, pp. 213–18, https://www.google.com/books/edition/The_Register_of_the_Kentucky_State_Histo/uXw7AQAAMAAJ?hl=en&gbpv=1&dq=Saturday,+June+8,+1816,+the+Baptist+Church+of+Jesus+Christ&pg=PA214&printsec=frontcover, viewed April 24, 2019.

11. Thomas B. McGregor, "Some New Facts about Abraham Lincoln's Parents."

12. McGregor.

13. McGregor.

14. McGregor.

15. McGregor.

16. Abraham Lincoln and Roy P. Basler, ed. *The Collected Works of Abraham Lincoln*, 9th edition (New Brunswick, NJ: Rutgers University Press, 1953), Volume 1, 382.

17. Bob Blaisdell, ed., *The Wit and Wisdom of Abraham Lincoln: A Book of Quotations* (Mineola, NY: Dover Publications, 2005), 53.

18. William H. Herndon, *The Hidden Lincoln: From the Letters and Papers of William H. Herndon* (London: Forgotten Books, 2018), 77.

19. Gwenda Blair, *The Trumps: Three Generations That Built an Empire* (New York: Simon and Schuster, 2000), 301.

20. Brody and Lamb, 290.

21. Brody and Lamb, 251.

22. Benjamin Fearnow, "Trump's Spiritual Advisor Paula White Appeals to Christians to Give to the Church Before Paying Mortgages, Electric Bills," *Newsweek*, February 18, 2020.

23. Brody and Lamb, 138.

24. Brody and Lamb, 406.

25. William H. Herndon, *Herndon's Lincoln: The True Story of a Great Life,* paperback (CreateSpace Independent Publishing Platform, 2014), 6:4.

26. Herndon, *Herndon's Lincoln*, 6:4.

27. Herndon, *Herndon's Lincoln*, 6:4.

28. Herndon, *Herndon's Lincoln*, 6:5.

29. Herndon, *Herndon's Lincoln*, 14:6.

30. Herndon, *Herndon's Lincoln*, 14:6.

31. Herndon, *The Hidden Lincoln*, 48.

32. *Abraham Lincoln, His Words and His World* (New York: Country Beautiful Foundation for Hawthorn Books, 1965), 31.

33. *Collected Works*, Volume 7, 543.

34. Emil Ludwig, *Abraham Lincoln: And the Times that Tried His Soul* (New York: Fawcett Publications, 1956), 259.

35. *Collected Works*, Volume 1, 289.

36. Blaisdell, *The Wit and Wisdom of Abraham Lincoln,* 54.

37. David Herbert Donald, *Lincoln* (New York, New York: Simon and Schuster, 1996), 204.

38. Allen C. Guelzo, "Abraham Lincoln and the Doctrine of Necessity," *Journal of the Abraham Lincoln Association*, Winter 1997.

39. Herndon, *The Hidden Lincoln*, 209.

40. Michael Medved, *God's Hand on America: Divine Providence in the Modern Era.* (New York: Crown Forum, 2019), 310.

41. Brody and Lamb, 286.

42. Brody and Lamb, 209.

43. Brody and Lamb, 192.

44. Brody and Lamb, 203.

45. Brody and Lamb, 236.

46. Brody and Lamb, 235.

47. Brody and Lamb, 185.

48. Brody and Lamb, 266.

49. Newt Gingrich, *Trump's America.* (New York: Center Street, 2018, 56.

50. Brody and Lamb, 259.

51. Brody and Lamb, 301.

Chapter 3: Born to Fight

1. Gregg Re, "Trump, at Fox News Town Hall, Suggests Biden Isn't Competent: 'There's Something Going On There,'" Fox News, March 5, 2020, https://www.foxnews.com/politics/trump-fox-news-town-hall, viewed March 5, 2020.

2. Daniel Kurt, "Donald Trump's Success Story," Investopedia, July 7, 2019, https://www.investopedia.com/updates/donald-trump-success-story/, viewed March 6, 2020.

3. Bill O'Reilly, *The United States of Trump: How the President Really Sees America* (New York: Henry Holt and Company, 2019), xi.

4. O'Reilly, *The United States of Trump*, 16–17.

5. Glenn Plaskin, "The Playboy Interview with Donald Trump," *Playboy*, March 1990, https://www.playboy.com/read/playboy-interview-donald-trump-1990, viewed March 3, 2020.

6. Gwenda Blair, *The Trumps: Three Generations That Built an Empire* (New York: Simon & Schuster, 2000), 238.

7. Michael D'Antonio, *Never Enough: Donald Trump and the Pursuit of Success* (New York: Thomas Dunne Books, 2015), 59.

8. Blair, *The Trumps,* 270–71.

9. Blair, 272.

10. Blair, 275–77.

11. Blair, 277.

12. Blair, 278.

13. Daniel Kurt, Investopedia. "Donald Trump's Success Story."

14. David Brody and Scott Lamb, *The Faith of Donald J. Trump* (New York: Broadside Books, 2018), 120.

15. Blair, The Trumps, 266.

16. Donald J. Trump with Meredith McIver, *Trump: Never Give Up: How I Turned My Biggest Challenges into Success* (Hoboken, NJ: Wiley, 2008), 126.

17. O'Reilly, 144.

18. O'Reilly, 145.

19. Adam Edelman. "Trump Says NFL Players Who Kneel During National Anthem 'Maybe Shouldn't Be in the Country,'" nbcnews.com, May 24, 2018, https://www.nbcnews.com/politics/donald-trump/trump-says-nfl-players-who-kneel-during-national-anthem-maybe-n876996, viewed March 8, 2020.

20. John Fritze and David Jackson, "Donald Trump Reacts to Robert Mueller's First Public Statement: 'Case is Closed!'" USA Today, May 29, 2019, https://www.usatoday.com/story/news/politics/2019/05/29/donald-trump-reacts-robert-muellers-statement-case-closed/1269744001/, viewed March 8, 2020.

21. Dan Mangan, "Trump Says Democrats 'Not Nice!' for Holding Impeachment Hearings While He's Overseas—but GOP Did Same to Clinton," cnbc.com, December 2, 2019, https://www.cnbc.com/2019/12/02/trump-criticizes-democrats-for-impeachment-timing.html, viewed March 8, 2020.

22. Trump, *Trump: Never Give Up*, 132.

23. David Herbert Donald, *Lincoln* (New York: Simon and Schuster, 1996), 81.

24. Doris Kearns Goodwin, *Leadership in Turbulent Times* (New York: Simon and Schuster, 2018), 102.

25. Donald, *Lincoln*, 81.

26. Donald T. Phillips, *Lincoln on Leadership: Executive Strategies for Tough Times* (New York: Warner Books, 1993), 109.

27. Goodwin, *Leadership in Turbulent Times*, 101.

28. Abraham Lincoln and Roy P. Basler, ed. *The Collected Works of Abraham Lincoln*, 9th edition (New Brunswick, NJ: Rutgers University Press, 1953), Volume 2, 383.

29. Bob Blaisdell, ed., *The Wit and Wisdom of Abraham Lincoln: A Book of Quotations* (Mineola, NY: Dover Publications, 2005), 11.

30. William H. Herndon, *The Hidden Lincoln: From the Letters and Papers of William H. Herndon* (London: Forgotten Books, 2018), 278.

31. Robert L. Polley, ed., *Lincoln: His Words and His World* (Waukesha, WI: Country Beautiful Foundation, 1965), 76.

32. Goodwin, 16–17.

33. Herndon, *The Hidden Lincoln*, 191.

34. Dan Abrams and David Fisher, *Lincoln's Last Trial: The Murder Case That Propelled Him to the Presidency.* (New York: Hanover Square Press, 2018), excerpt at https://www.history.com/news/abraham-lincoln-last-trial-murder-case, viewed March 9, 2020.

35. Herndon, 107–08.

36. https://www.findagrave.com/memorial/80546181/peachy-quinn-harrison, viewed March 9, 2020.

37. Donald, 446–47.

38. Donald, 447.

39. Donald, 447.

40. James McPherson, *Tried by War: Abraham Lincoln as Commander in Chief.* (New York: Penguin Books, 2009), 261–62.

Chapter 4: Common Man

1. Dinesh D'Souza, *Death of a Nation: Plantation Politics and the Making of the Democratic Party* (New York: All Points Books, 2018), 258.

2. Gene Ho, *Trumpography: How Biblical Principles Paved the Way to the American Presidency.* (iUniverse, 2018), 146.

3. Ho, *Trumpography*, 146.

4. Donald T. Phillips, *Lincoln on Leadership: Executive Strategies for Tough Times* (New York: Warner Books, 1993), 156.

5. Emil Ludwig, *Abraham Lincoln and the Times that Tried His Soul* (New York: Fawcett Publications, 1956), 261.

6. Phillips, *Lincoln on Leadership*, 16.

7. Phillips, *Lincoln on Leadership*, 16.

8. Donald J. Trump, *Great Again: How to Fix Our Crippled America* (New York: Threshold Editions, 2015), 29.

9. Donald J. Trump. *Think Like a Champion: An Informal Education in Business and Life* (New York: RP Minis, 2010), 63.

10. Trump, *Think Like a Champion*, 63.

11. David Brody and Scott Lamb, *The Faith of Donald J. Trump: A Spiritual Biography* (New York: Broadside Books, 2018), 125.

12. Brody and Lamb, *The Faith of Donald J. Trump*, 169.

13. Brody and Lamb, 233.

14. Doris Kearns Goodwin, *Leadership in Turbulent Times* (New York: Simon and Schuster, 2018), 236–37.

15. David Herbert Donald, *Lincoln* (New York: Simon and Schuster, 1996), 513.

16. Donald T. Phillips, *Lincoln on Leadership for Today: Abraham Lincoln's Approach to Twenty-First Century Issues* (Boston, MA: Mariner Books, 2017), 211.

17. William W. Freehling, *Becoming Lincoln* (Charlottesville, VA: University of Virginia Press, 2018), 35.

18. Freehling, *Becoming Lincoln*, 35.

19. Kevin Peraino, *Lincoln in the World: The Making of a Statesman and the Dawn of American Power* (New York: Broadway Books, 2014), 279.

20. Brody and Scott, 172.

21. Joanna Weiss, "Trump Pokes Fun at Himself. Why Do Only Some People See It?" *Politico Magazine*, November 9, 2019.

22. Newt Gingrich, *Trump's America* (New York: Center Street, 2018), 91.

23. Newt Gingrich, *Understanding Trump* (New York: Center Street, 2017), 43.

24. Andrew Restuccia and Ben Schreckinger, "In MAGA World, Trump's Jokes Always Land," www.politico.com, October 19, 2018.

25. Ho, 102.

26. Donald J. Trump with Meredith McIver, *Never Give Up: How I Turned My Biggest Challenges into Success* (New York: Wiley, 2008), 90.

27. Phillips, *Lincoln on Leadership*, 72.
28. Phillips, *Lincoln on Leadership*, 159.
29. Phillips, *Lincoln on Leadership*, 158.

CHAPTER 5: FAMILY MAN

1. William W. Freehling, *Becoming Lincoln* (Charlottesville, VA: University of Virginia Press, 2018), 82.
2. David Herbert Donald, *Lincoln* (New York: Simon and Schuster, 1996), 55.
3. Donald, *Lincoln*, 55.
4. William H. Herndon, *Herndon's Lincoln: The True Story of a Great Life,* paperback (CreateSpace Independent Publishing Platform, 2014), 5:9.
5. Herndon, *Herndon's Lincoln*, 5:9.
6. William H. Herndon, *The Hidden Lincoln: From the Letters and Papers of William H. Herndon* (London: Forgotten Books, 2018), 259.
7. Herndon, *The Hidden Lincoln*, 259.
8. Herndon, *The Hidden Lincoln*, 233.
9. David Brody and Scott Lamb, *The Faith of Donald J. Trump.* (New York: Broadside Books, 2018), 122.
10. Herndon, *Herndon's Lincoln*, 6:1.
11. Herndon, *Herndon's Lincoln*, 6:2.
12. Herndon, *Herndon's Lincoln*, 6:2.
13. Herndon, *Herndon's Lincoln*, 7:1.
14. Robert L. Polley, ed., *Lincoln: His Words and His World* (Waukesha, WI: Country Beautiful Foundation, 1965), 14.
15. Herndon, *Herndon's Lincoln*, 7:7–8.
16. Gwenda Blair, *The Trumps: Three Generations That Built an Empire* (New York: Simon and Schuster, 2000), 298.
17. Blair, *The Trumps*, 299.
18. Ivana Trump, *Raising Trump* (New York: Gallery Books, 2017), 5.
19. Bill O'Reilly, *The United States of Trump: How the President Really Sees America* (New York: Henry Holt and Company, 2019), 68.
20. O'Reilly, *The United States of Trump*, 68–69.
21. Donald J. Trump, *Great Again: How to Fix Our Crippled America* (New York: Threshold Editions, 2015), 129.
22. Ivana Trump, *Raising Trump*, 2–3.
23. Blair, 399.
24. Blair, 399.

25. Donald, *Lincoln*, 84.

26. Donald, 85.

27. Freehling, *Becoming Lincoln*, 82.

28. Donald, 36.

29. Donald, 37.

30. Donald, 37.

31. Herndon, *Herndon's Lincoln*, 9:4.

32. Herndon, *Herndon's Lincoln*, 9:5.

33. Donald, 90.

34. Donald, 93.

35. Donald, 107.

36. Donald, 107.

37. Donald, 157.

38. Herndon, *The Hidden Lincoln*, 401.

39. Donald, 158.

40. Herndon, *Herndon's Lincoln*, 16:6.

41. Herndon, *The Hidden Lincoln*, 105.

42. Donald, 428.

43. Donald, 311.

44. Donald, 324.

45. Donald, 324.

46. Donald, 338.

47. Donald, 160.

48. O'Reilly, 242.

49. Bethania Palma, "Is Melania Trump Fluent in Five Languages?", Snopes, December 30, 2019, https://www.snopes.com/fact-check/melania-trump-multiple-languages/, viewed July 3, 2020.

50. Gabriella Paiella, "Melanie Trump's Daily Mail Lawsuit Settled for $2.9 Million," *The Cut*, April 12, 2017, https://www.thecut.com/2017/04/melania-trumps-daily-mail-lawsuit-settled-usd2-9-million.html, viewed July 3, 2020.

51. Isabel Vincent, "Melania Trump's Girl-on-Girl Photos from Racy Shoot Revealed," *New York Post*, August 1, 2016, https://nypost.com/2016/08/01/melania-trumps-girl-on-girl-photos-from-racy-shoot-revealed/, viewed July 4, 2020.

52. Isabel Vincent, "Melania Trump Like You've Never Seen Her Before," *New York Post*, July 30, 2016, viewed July 4, 2020.

53. David Smith, "Melania Trump in New Plagiarism Row over Online Safety Pamphlet," *The Guardian*, May 8, 2018. https://www.theguardian.

com/us-news/2018/may/07/melania-trump-plagiarism-row-be-best-campaign, viewed July 4, 2020.

54. Kate Anderson Brower, "Melania Shows She's a Trump Through and Through," CNN, December 15, 2018. https://www.cnn.com/2018/12/13/opinions/melania-trump-interview-poll-brower/index.html, viewed July 3, 2020.

CHAPTER 6: KEEPING IT REAL

1. Marc Thiessen, "Trump Could Be the Most Honest President in Modern History," Washington Post, October 11, 2018, https://www.washingtonpost.com/opinions/trump-could-be-the-most-honest-president-in-modern-history/2018/10/11/67aefc5a-cd76-11e8-a3e6-44daa3d35ede_story.html, viewed July 26, 2020.

2. Donald Trump, *The Art of the Deal* (New York: Ballantine Books, 1987), 58.

3. Donald J. Trump, *Great Again: How to Fix Our Crippled America* (New York: Threshold Editions, 2016), 8–9.

4. Thiessen.

5. Thiessen.

6. Thiessen.

7. Trump, *Great Again*, 7.

8. Thiessen.

9. Trump, *Great Again*, 137.

10. Tammy Bruce, *Varney*, Fox Business Channel, January 31, 2020.

11. Donald Trump, "President Trump Goes One-on-One with Chris Wallace," Fox News, July 19, 2020, https://www.youtube.com/watch?v=W6XdpDOH1JA, viewed July 20, 2020.

12. Gene Ho, *Trumpography: How Biblical Principles Paved the Way to the American Presidency* (iUniverse, 2018), 159.

13. Newt Gingrich, *Understanding Trump* (New York: Center Street, 2017), 11.

14. Trump, *The Art of the Deal*, 58.

15. Donald T. Phillips, *Lincoln on Leadership: Executive Strategies for Tough Times* (New York: Warner Books, 1993), 56.

16. Donald J. Trump, *Think Like a Champion: An Informal Education in Business and Life* (New York: RP Minis, 2010), 32.

17. William H. Herndon, *The Hidden Lincoln: From the Letters and Papers of William H. Herndon* (London: Forgotten Books, 2018), 144.

18. Abraham Lincoln and Roy P. Basler, ed. *The Collected Works of Abraham Lincoln*, 9th edition (New Brunswick, NJ: Rutgers University Press, 1953), Volume 2, 502.

19. *Collected Works*, Volume 2, 502.

20. David Herbert Donald, *Lincoln* (New York: Simon and Schuster, 1996), 275.

21. Phillips, *Lincoln on Leadership: Executive Strategies for Tough Times*, 78.

22. Donald, 259.

23. Donald, 259.

24. Phillips, *Lincoln on Leadership*, 56–57.

25. Phillips, *Lincoln on Leadership*, 148.

26. Phillips, *Lincoln on Leadership*, 148.

27. Doris Kearns Goodwin, *Leadership in Turbulent Times* (New York: Simon and Schuster, 2018), 115.

28. Goodwin, *Leadership in Turbulent Times*, 115.

29. Herndon, *The Hidden Lincoln*, 323.

30. *Collected Works*, Volume 8, 248.

31. David Herbert Donald, *Lincoln*. (New York: Simon and Schuster, 1996), 566.

32. *Herndon's Lincoln*, 14:7.

33. Herndon, *The Hidden Lincoln*, 45.

34. Herndon, *The Hidden Lincoln*, 325.

35. William H. Herndon, *Herndon's Lincoln: The True Story of a Great Life,* paperback (CreateSpace Independent Publishing Platform, 2014),, 18:1.

36. Gingrich, *Understanding Trump*, 11.

37. Trump, *Think Like a Champion*, xi.

38. Herndon, *The Hidden Lincoln*, 45.

39. David Brody and Scott Lamb, *The Faith of Donald J. Trump* (New York: Broadside Books, 2018), 260.

40. Brody and Lamb, *The Faith of Donald J. Trump*, 260.

41. Trump, *Great Again: How to Fix Our Crippled America*, 132.

Chapter 7: Self-Made Man

1. Newt Gingrich, *Understanding Trump* (New York: Center Street, 2017), 4.

2. Gwenda Blair, *The Trumps: Three Generations That Built an Empire* (New York: Simon and Schuster, 2000), 250.

3. Donald J. Trump, *Great Again: How to Fix Our Crippled America* (New York: Threshold Editions, 2015), 99.

4. Blair, *The Trumps*, 251.

5. Gene Ho, *Trumpography: How Biblical Principles Paved the Way to the American Presidency* (iUniverse, 2018), 127.

6. Doris Kearns Goodwin, *Leadership in Turbulent Times* (New York: Simon and Schuster, 2018), 9.

7. Goodwin, *Leadership in Turbulent Times*, 5.

8. Goodwin, 106.

9. William H. Herndon, *Herndon's Lincoln: The True Story of a Great Life,* paperback (CreateSpace Independent Publishing Platform, 2014), 2:7.

10. David Herbert Donald, *Lincoln* (New York: Simon and Schuster, 1996), 29.

11. Donald, *Lincoln*, 29.

12. Goodwin, 5.

13. Donald, *Lincoln*, 31.

14. Herndon, *Herndon's Lincoln*, 2:10.

15. Donald, *Lincoln*, 31.

16. Goodwin, 8.

17. Blair, 231.

18. Blair, 232.

19. Blair, 232–33.

20. Blair, 236.

21. Blair, 237.

22. Blair, 239.

23. Blair, 240.

24. Blair, 242.

25. Blair, 242.

26. Herndon, *Herndon's Lincoln*, 3:7.

27. Donald, 67.

28. Donald, 67.

29. Donald, 67.

30. Goodwin, 6.

31. Goodwin, 8.

32. Goodwin, 8.

33. Goodwin, 8.

34. James M. McPherson, *Tried by War: Abraham Lincoln as Commander in Chief* (New York: Penguin Books, 2009), 3.

35. Gingrich, *Understanding Trump*, 12.

36. Gingrich, 53.

37. Gingrich, 8.

38. Donald, 29.

39. Herndon, *The Hidden Lincoln*, 134.

40. Herndon, *Herndon's Lincoln,* 5:12.

41. William W. Freehling, *Becoming Lincoln* (Charlottesville, VA: University of Virginia Press, 2018), 69.

42. Blair, 239.

43. Donald J. Trump, *Think Like a Champion: An Informal Education in Business and Life* (New York: RP Minis, 2010), 49.

44. Trump, *Think Like a Champion*, 49.

45. Donald J. Trump with Meredith McIver, *Trump Never Give Up: How I Turned My Biggest Challenges into Success* (Hoboken, New Jersey: Wiley, 2008), 46.

46. Bob Blaisdell, ed., *The Wit and Wisdom of Abraham Lincoln: A Book of Quotations* (Mineola, NY: Dover Publications, 2005), 5.

47. Abraham Lincoln and Roy P. Basler, ed. *The Collected Works of Abraham Lincoln*, 9th edition (New Brunswick, NJ: Rutgers University Press, 1953), Volume 2, 535.

48. Trump, *Think Like a Champion*, 187.

49. Blair, 271.

50. Blair, 228.

51. Blair, 271.

52. Blair, 260.

53. David Brody and Scott Lamb, *The Faith of Donald J. Trump* (New York: Broadside Books, 2018), 94.

Chapter 8: Masters of Communication

1. Donald J. Trump, *Think Like a Champion: An Informal Education in Business and Life* (New York: RP Minis, 2010), 157.

2. William H. Herndon, *The Hidden Lincoln: From the Letters and Papers of William H. Herndon* (London: Forgotten Books, 2018), 100–01.

3. Donald T. Phillips, *Lincoln on Leadership: Executive Strategies for Tough Times* (New York: Warner Books, 1993), 157.

4. Trump, *Think Like a Champion*, 159.

5. Donald Trump, *The Art of the Deal* (New York: Ballantine Books, 1987), 32.

6. Nancy Benac, "Road to Debate: Trump Built Image as He Built Business," Associated Press, September 26, 2016, https://www.pbs.org/newshour/politics/road-debate-trump-built-image-built-business, viewed August 18, 2020.

7. Benac, "Road to Debate."

8. Benac, "Road to Debate."

9. Susan Mulcahy, "Confessions of a Trump Tabloid Scribe," politico.com, May/June 2016, https://www.politico.com/magazine/story/2016/04/2016-donald-trump-tabloids-new-york-post-daily-news-media-213842, viewed August 20, 2020.

10. Doris Kearns Goodwin, *Leadership in Turbulent Times*. (New York: Simon and Schuster, 2018), 6–7.

11. William H. Herndon, *Herndon's Lincoln: The True Story of a Great Life,* paperback (CreateSpace Independent Publishing Platform, 2014), 3:6.

12. Herndon, *The Hidden Lincoln*, 125.

13. Goodwin, *Leadership in Turbulent Times*, 103.

14. Goodwin, 108.

15. The Hollywood Reporter Staff, "Donald Trump's Wife, Children Open Up on '20/20 about GOP Candidate: 'There's No One Else Like Him,'" hollywoodreporter.com, November 21, 2015, https://www.hollywoodreporter.com/news/donald-trumps-wife-children-open-842637, viewed August 20, 2020.

16. Jackie Calmes, "Donald Trump: Life Before the Presidency," millercenter.org, date unknown, https://millercenter.org/president/trump/life-presidency, viewed August 21, 2020

17. Newt Gingrich, *Understanding Trump* (New York: Center Street, 2017), 87.

18. Gingrich, *Understanding Trump*, 87.

19. Herndon, *Herndon's Lincoln*, 8:11.

20. Abraham Lincoln and Roy P. Basler, ed. *The Collected Works of Abraham Lincoln*, 9th edition (New Brunswick, NJ: Rutgers University Press, 1953), Volume 1, 279.

21. David Herbert Donald, *Lincoln* (New York: Simon and Schuster, 1996), 113.

22. Herndon, *Herndon's Lincoln*, 8:11.

23. Phillips, *Lincoln on Leadership*, 147.

24. Phillips, 146.

25. Phillips, *Lincoln on Leadership*, 147.

26. Goodwin, *Leadership in Turbulent Times*, 123.

27. Goodwin, 118.

28. Phillips, *Lincoln on Leadership*, 151.

29. Trump, *Think Like a Champion*, 107.

30. Benac.

31. Phillips, *Lincoln on Leadership*, 146.

32. David Brody and Scott Lamb, *The Faith of Donald J. Trump* (New York: Broadside Books, 2018), 82.

33. Brody and Lamb, *The Faith of Donald J. Trump*, 185.

34. Brody and Lamb, 175.

35. Lauren Katz, "Trump Rallies Aren't a Sideshow—They're His Entire Campaign," vox.com, November 6, 2019, https://www.vox.com/policy-and-politics/2019/11/6/20950388/donald-trump-rally-2020-presidential-election-today-explained, viewed August 22, 2020.

36. Donald J. Trump, *Great Again: How to Fix Our Crippled America* (New York: Threshold Editions, 2015), 10–11.

37. Emil Ludwig, *Abraham Lincoln: And the Times that Tried His Soul* (New York: Fawcett Publications, 1956), 111.

38. Phillips, *Lincoln on Leadership*, 149.

39. Abraham Lincoln Online, http://www.abrahamlincolnonline.org/lincoln/speeches/farewell.htm#:~:text=Here%20my%20children%20have%20been,attended%20him%2C%20I%20cannot%20succeed, viewed August 22, 2020.

40. Phillips, *Lincoln on Leadership*, 145.

41. Douglas L. Wilson, "Lincoln the Persuader," theamericanscholar.org, September 1, 2006, https://theamericanscholar.org/lincoln-the-persuader/#.X0GrEshKiM-, viewed August 22, 2020.

42. Newt Gingrich, *Trump's America* (New York: Center Street, 2018), 192.

43. Gingrich, *Understanding Trump*, 18.

44. Public letter, Abraham Lincoln to Horace Greeley, August 22, 1862. (10-5-5)

45. Brody and Lamb, 147.

46. Louis A. Warren, *Little Known Facts about the Gettysburg Address* (Fort Wayne, IN: Lincoln National, 1938).

CHAPTER 9: BORN TO LEAD

1. William H. Herndon, *The Hidden Lincoln: From the Letters and Papers of William H. Herndon* (London: Forgotten Books, 2018), 278.

2. William W. Freehling, *Becoming Lincoln* (Charlottesville, VA: University of Virginia Press, 2018), 10.

3. Freehling, *Becoming Lincoln*, 10.

4. Robert L. Polley, ed., *Lincoln: His Words and His World* (Waukesha, WI: Country Beautiful Foundation, 1965), 7.

5. Polley, *Lincoln*, 7.

6. Donald J. Trump with Meredith McIver, *Trump Never Give Up: How I Turned My Biggest Challenges into Success* (Hoboken, NJ: Wiley, 2008), 19.

7. Gwenda Blair, *The Trumps: Three Generations That Built an Empire* (New York: Simon and Schuster, 2000), 224.

8. Blair, *The Trumps*, 230.

9. Blair, 230.

10. Blair, 230.

11. Donald Trump, *The Art of the Deal* (New York: Ballantine Books, 1987), 72.

12. Doris Kearns Goodwin, *Leadership in Turbulent Times* (New York: Simon and Schuster, 2018), 3.

13. William H. Herndon, *The Hidden Lincoln: From the Letters and Papers of William H. Herndon* (London: Forgotten Books, 2018), 357.

14. David Herbert Donald, *Lincoln* (New York: Simon and Schuster, 1996), 60.

15. Donald, *Lincoln*, 42.

16. Donald J. Trump, *Think Like a Champion: An Informal Education in Business and Life* (New York: RP Minis, 2010), 70.

17. Donald Trump, *The Art of the Deal* (New York: Ballantine Books, 1987), 89.

18. Newt Gingrich, *Understanding Trump* (New York: Center Street, 2017), 73.

19. Herndon, *The Hidden Lincoln*, 121.

20. Herndon, *Herndon's Lincoln*, 3:7.

21. Herndon, *Herndon's Lincoln*, 20:4.

22. Goodwin, *Leadership in Turbulent Times*, 8.

23. Herndon, *The Hidden Lincoln*, 240.

24. Donald, *Lincoln*, 301.

25. David Brody and Scott Lamb, *The Faith of Donald J. Trump* (New York: Broadside Books, 2018), 286.

26. Michael D'Antonio, *Never Enough: Donald Trump and the Pursuit of Success* (New York, New York: Thomas Dunne Books, 2015), 47.

27. Trump, *Think Like a Champion*, 181.

28. Trump, *Think Like a Champion*, 25.

29. Trump, *Think Like a Champion*, 182.

30. Trump, *The Art of the Deal*, 140.

31. https://quoteinvestigator.com/2013/02/18/barrel-of-whiskey/, viewed October 16, 2020.

32. Goodwin, 212.

33. Goodwin, 212.

34. Donald T. Phillips, *Lincoln on Leadership: Executive Strategies for Tough Times* (New York: Warner Books, 1993), 30.

35. Phillips, *Lincoln on Leadership: Executive Strategies for Tough Times*, 135.

36. https://transparency.kununu.com/compelling-qualities-of-great-leaders/, viewed October 16, 2020.

37. https://transparency.kununu.com/compelling-qualities-of-great-leaders/.

38. Edward Achorn, *Every Drop of Blood: The Momentous Second Inauguration of Abraham Lincoln* (New York: Atlantic Monthly Press, 2020), first page of chapter 3 (page number unknown).

39. Goodwin, 235.

40. Robert L. Polley, ed., *Lincoln: His Words and His World*. (Waukesha, WI: Country Beautiful Foundation, 1965), 50.

41. Newt Gingrich, *Understanding Trump* (New York: Center Street, 2017), xvi.

42. Donald J. Trump, *Great Again: How to Fix Our Crippled America*. New York: Threshold Editions, 2015, 3.

43. https://transparency.kununu.com/compelling-qualities-of-great-leaders/, viewed October 17, 2020.

44. Gingrich, *Understanding Trump*, 15.

45. Goodwin, 240.

46. Phillips, *Lincoln on Leadership*, 99.

47. Phillips, *Lincoln on Leadership*, 20.

48. David Herbert Donald, *Lincoln* (New York: Simon and Schuster, 1996), 350.

49. Donald, *Think Like a Champion: An Informal Education in Business and Life*, 29.

50. Donald, *The Art of the Deal*, 140.

CHAPTER 10: SIGNS OF THE TIMES

1. Newt Gingrich, *Understanding Trump* (New York: Center Street, 2017), 164.

2. Newt Gingrich, *Trump's America* (New York: Center Street, 2018), 187.

3. Gingrich, *Understanding Trump*, 164.

4. Gingrich, *Understanding Trump*, 165.

5. David Herbert Donald, *Lincoln* (New York: Simon and Schuster, 1996), 80.

6. Donald, *Lincoln*, 80.

7. Robert L. Polley, ed., *Lincoln: His Words and His World* (Waukesha, WI: Country Beautiful Foundation, 1965), 14.

8. Edward Achorn, "24 Tense Hours in Abraham Lincoln's Life," New York Times, February 23, 2020, https://zukus.net/2020/02/24-tense-hours-in-abraham-lincolns-life/#, viewed October 28, 2020.

9. Jason Lange and Trevor Hunnicutt, "Biden staff donate to group that pays bail in riot-torn Minneapolis," Reuters, May 30, 2020, https://www.reuters.com/article/us-minneapolis-police-biden-bail-idUSKBN2360SZ, viewed October 24, 2020.

10. Leonard L. Richards, *Who Freed the Slaves?: The Fight over the Thirteenth Amendment* (Chicago and London: The University of Chicago Press, 2015), 170.

11. Donald T. Phillips, *Lincoln on Leadership: Executive Strategies for Tough Times* (New York: Warner Books, 1993), 173.

12. Gingrich, *Trump's America*, 3.

13. Gingrich, *Understanding Trump*, 150.

14. Gingrich, *Understanding Trump*, 150–51, 160.

15. Donald T. Phillips, *Lincoln on Leadership for Today: Abraham Lincoln's Approach to Twenty-First Century Issues* (Boston, MA: Mariner Books, 2017), 98-99.

16. Gingrich, *Understanding Trump*, 141.

17. Gingrich, *Understanding Trump*, 141–42.

18. Gingrich, *Understanding Trump*, 99.

19. Gingrich, *Understanding Trump*, 146.

20. Gingrich, *Understanding Trump*, 151.

21. Dinesh D'Souza, *Death of a Nation: Plantation Politics and the Making of the Democratic Party* (New York: All Points Books, 2018), xiii.

22. D'Souza, *Death of a Nation*, xiii.

23. D'Souza, xv.
24. D'Souza, xvi.
25. D'Souza, 53.
26. D'Souza, 53, 55.
27. D'Souza, 25.
28. D'Souza, 25.
29. D'Souza, 276.
30. Phillips, *Lincoln on Leadership for Today*, 82.
31. D'Souza, 91.
32. D'Souza, 91.
33. D'Souza, 277.

BIBLIOGRAPHY

Abraham Lincoln, His Words and His World. New York: Country Beautiful Foundation for Hawthorn Books, 1965.

Abrams, Dan, and David Fisher. *Lincoln's Last Trial: The Murder Case That Propelled Him to the Presidency*. New York: Hanover Square Press, 2018.

Achorn, Edward. *Every Drop of Blood: The Momentous Second Inauguration of Abraham Lincoln*. New York: Atlantic Monthly Press, 2020.

Blair, Gwenda. *The Trumps: Three Generations That Built an Empire*. New York: Simon & Schuster, 2000.

Blaisdell, Bob ed. *The Wit and Wisdom of Abraham Lincoln: A Book of Quotations*. Mineola, NY: Dover Publications, 2005.

Brody, David and Scott Lamb. *The Faith of Donald J. Trump*. New York: Broadside Books, 2018.

D'Antonio, Michael. *Never Enough: Donald Trump and the Pursuit of Success*. New York: Thomas Dunne Books, 2015.

Donald, David Herbert. *Lincoln*. New York: Simon and Schuster, 1996.

D'Souza, Dinesh. *Death of a Nation: Plantation Politics and the Making of the Democratic Party*. New York: All Points Books, 2018.

Freehling, William W. *Becoming Lincoln*. Charlottesville, VA: University of Virginia Press, 2018.

Gingrich, Newt. *Trump's America*. New York: Center Street, 2018.

Gingrich, Newt. *Understanding Trump*. New York: Center Street, 2017.

Goodwin, Doris Kearns. *Team of Rivals: The Political Genius of Abraham Lincoln*. New York: Simon & Schuster paperbacks, 2005.

Herndon, William H., *Herndon's Lincoln: The True Story of a Great Life*, paperback. CreateSpace Independent Publishing Platform, 2014.

Herndon, William H. *The Hidden Lincoln: From the Letters and Papers of William H. Herndon*. London: Forgotten Books, 2018.

Ho, Gene. *Trumpography: How Biblical Principles Paved the Way to the American Presidency*. iUniverse, 2018.

Kouwenhoven, John A. *Adventures of America: 1857–1900: A Pictorial Record from Harper's Weekly*. New York and London: Harper & Brothers Publishers, 1938.

Lincoln, Abraham, and Roy P. Basler, ed. *The Collected Works of Abraham Lincoln*, 9th edition. The Abraham Lincoln Association, Springfield, IL. New Brunswick, NJ: Rutgers University Press, 1953.

Ludwig, Emil. *Abraham Lincoln and the Times that Tried His Soul*. New York: Fawcett Publications, 1956.

McPherson, James. *Tried by War: Abraham Lincoln as Commander in Chief*. New York: Penguin Books, 2009.

Medved, Michael. *God's Hand on America: Divine Providence in the Modern Era*. New York: Crown Forum, 2019.

National Geographic Society. *We Americans*. Washington, D.C: National Geographic Society, 1988.

O'Reilly, Bill. *The United States of Trump: How the President Really Sees America*. New York: Henry Holt and Company, 2019.

Peraino, Kevin. *Lincoln in the World: The Making of a Statesman and the Dawn of American Power*. New York: Broadway Books, 2014.

Phillips, Donald T. *Lincoln on Leadership: Executive Strategies for Tough Times*. New York: Warner Books, 1993.

Phillips, Donald T. *Lincoln on Leadership for Today: Abraham Lincoln's Approach to Twenty-First Century Issues*. Boston, MA: Mariner Books, 2017.

Polley, Robert L., ed. *Lincoln: His Words and His World*. Waukesha, WI: Country Beautiful Foundation, 1965.

Richards, Leonard L. *Who Freed the Slaves?: The Fight over the Thirteenth Amendment*. Chicago and London: The University of Chicago Press, 2015.

Trump, Donald. *The Art of the Deal*. New York: Ballantine Books, 1987.

BIBLIOGRAPHY

Trump, Donald J. *Great Again: How to Fix Our Crippled America.* New York: Threshold Editions, 2015.

Trump, Donald J., with Meredith McIver. *Trump: Never Give Up: How I Turned My Biggest Challenges into Success.* Hoboken, NJ: Wiley, 2008.

Trump, Ivana. *Raising Trump.* New York: Gallery Books, 2017.

ABOUT THE AUTHOR

Farmer, rancher, entrepreneur, and teacher by day, historian and author by night, Gretchen Wollert dares to present her first comparative biography on two seemingly polar opposite American icons: Lincoln and Trump. Her degrees in English and history, and her professional expertise in education, compliment her extended, in-depth study in the school of hard work.

Extremely active in life and always one to try new things, she is a forever fan of freedom and the benefits of knowing American history.

Gretchen lives and works with husband Mike in their recently empty nest just off the beaten path in southeast Wyoming.